# Mission Road

## A Journalist's Life from Kansas to Kandahar

by

Theodore Iliff

Dorrance Publishing Co
585 Alpha Drive
Suite 103
Pittsburgh, PA 15238
Visit our website at *www.dorrancebookstore.com*

ISBN: 978-1-6386-7079-7
eISBN: 978-1-6386-7899-1

*To all my fellow journalists.*
*Rest assured that history will validate your noble work*
*and vilify your oppressors.*

Among the many people who deserve thanks
for their help and encouragement in this effort are
my wife Julia, Frank Cook, Z.J. Czupor, Virginia Brackett,
Kat Miller, Rebekah Iliff, Scott Herron, Emily Musgrave,
Sandra Kruse, Timothy Dougherty,
Dr. Cindy Emmans, Dr. William Byxbee,
and everyone who ever said to me,
"You ought to write a book."

# Table of Contents

## *Table of Contents continued*

# Introduction

In the leafy, affluent southwest suburbs of Kansas City, Mission Road carves a straight 10-mile north-south path through several cookie-cutter suburbs with homogenous homes, businesses, and residents. It's a pleasant, unremarkable drive.

The foundation for all that I did—my life's mission—was laid along that road. Everything that happened on or near Mission Road pointed me toward journalism, global exploration, and personal introspection. My mission was to tell stories, and later to help others to do the same, all the while learning who I was and what I could do in venues as mundane as Topeka or as exotic as Afghanistan.

Within a half mile on either side of Mission Road are the two houses of my childhood, my church, all my schools, the two shopping center hangouts, the city swimming pool and tennis courts, fields where I stunk at football and baseball, my two paper routes, and many more touchstones of my youth.

Three concepts guided my life: Explore, Inform, and Instruct. After my first summer in Germany at age six, I ached to see the world. Inspirational teachers expanded my horizons beyond travel and tourist sites; they awoke in me a curiosity about other cultures and how they compared or contrasted with mine as framed by mid-20th century Kansas.

My early interest in teaching as a life's calling gave way to journalism, a less noble but more exciting podium for informing and influencing people, and a more likely portal to global adventures. After decades of active service journalism, an unwarranted termination propelled me into international consulting and teaching on four continents. I learned as much as I taught while occasionally wandering into harm's way.

The pivotal time of my career and, in hindsight, American broadcast journalism, came during my 13 years at CNN. I started in 1989, when straight news was still a "thing," and TV news strived for accuracy and balance to preserve credibility and therefore audiences. At the halfway point in the mid-90s, conservative talk radio had planted its flag in the broadcast landscape, and Fox News and MSNBC were challenging CNN's virtual monopoly on 24-hour news. When I left in 2003, the metamorphosis of TV news was nearly complete, with Fox the cable news rating leader, MSNBC finding its niche on the other end of the political scale, and CNN fading in ratings and stature.

As this evolution accelerated with the rise of the Internet and later social media, I entered my consulting/education phase as a media consultant and teacher in the Balkans, Armenia, and the Mideast. Language barriers forced me to concentrate less on writing and more on apolitical principles of production, technology, and administration. Nevertheless, I preached old-style ethical practices in newsrooms and classrooms to professionals and students who had grown up exposed to opinion-laced news from government-run media or their privately owned partisan successors—an ironic match to what was happening to U.S. broadcast news. To their credit, my students and mentees understood how the methods I espoused, while appealing to their professional idealism, could also shape a profitable alternative to the media status quo in their markets. I won't live long enough to know whether those young practitioners rose to newsroom positions of influence to implement my suggestions. I hope those best practices don't just atrophy from disuse and fade away.

With apologies to Dr. Martin Luther King Jr., I have seen the mountaintop of journalism, where responsible idealists practice a profession that the public trusts and respects. Nobody has reached that utopia, but journalists should keep trying. I yearn for a time when I read, hear, or see news without having to decode it by figuring out the political agenda of its source.

As for my life's mission, I'm satisfied with how it turned out. I had a glorious time along the way, even with the inevitable setbacks, missteps, and close calls. I'm writing this memoir as a celebration and a thank-you. All told, I wouldn't trade my life with anyone.

# CHAPTER 1
# Beginnings

*"Don't worry, dear, he'll turn out all right."*

I remember standing there, mesmerized. I was a chubby six-year-old in lederhosen, spending a warm, breezy summer afternoon picnicking in Germany's Black Forest. It was 1956. My mother and little sister were there, but the main attraction was my grandfather, wearing my Kansas City A's hat to keep the sun off his bald head and grinning like a fool. He certainly was no fool; he was a retired school rector who felt silly wearing an American baseball cap.

I revered my Opa, but at that moment I was gawking at the scene around us. Lush green grass carpeted the expanse between a small stream and the forest's edge. A streetcar would periodically rattle along the tracks paralleling a highway leading to the idyllic spa town of Bad Herren Alb a few miles up the road.

Standing on our powder blue picnic blanket, I told myself that this is where I wanted to be when I grew up. I don't remember telling myself that, but I know I did. That tranquil patch of my mother's homeland would keep its hold on me forever. I had yet to learn what path and what conveyances would take me through life, but Germany would pull me along the way.

Of course, that little boy picnicking in the Black Forest had no inkling of the adventures, misadventures, achievements, and disappointments ahead of him over the next half-century. But that's where it all started. It is not, however, where he started.

I think I didn't want to be born. I was in a good place—warm, dark, and mostly quiet. I was never hungry or thirsty, and if I got bored I could have fun kicking the walls. So I took my time. A week beyond my due date, I'm told. Then, for reasons beyond my control, I made my grand entrance into the world at 7:30 a.m. on Friday, September 2, 1949 at Kansas City's St. Joseph's Hospital. It did not begin well. I came out with a grotesque blood blister on my forehead that distorted my face into a disturbing copy of a medieval gargoyle. Before Mom could see me, an aunt walked into the room and cooed, "Don't worry, dear, he'll turn out all right."

Whether I did is for others to say, but at least the blood blister healed quickly. I was christened Theodore Alfred Iliff; if they had asked me, I would have vetoed Alfred. Maybe it was revenge for coming out of my five-foot-two mother at nearly 11 pounds. I would always be big boned, or put another way, short for my weight.

*1948: Parents Ruth and Ted Iliff honeymooning in Germany.*

My parents were Theodore and Ruth Iliff, two people thrown together in the aftermath of World War II. My dad, the oldest son of a dour, Edwardian couple in Topeka, Kansas, had served in World War II as a military government specialist thanks to the German language the Army had taught him. After the war he left the Army but stayed as a civilian administrator for the occupation office in Karlsruhe, a pleasant Rhine River city at the north end of the Black Forest 90 miles south of Frankfurt. My mom, the former Ruth Nagel, had grown up in the Nazi era and was a 19-year-old conscripted Labor Service worker when the war ended. She found work back home as a multilingual telephone operator in the occupation headquarters. She temporarily transferred to my future father's office, hated the work, and hurried back to the switchboard. But he was smitten by the petite strawberry blond and asked her out twice before she said yes. That led to courtship, marriage, relocation to Kansas City, and a year later, me.

I grew up in a stereotypical mid-20th century American suburb, Prairie Village, Kansas, teeming with Greatest Generation white couples and their baby boom kids. The safe, friendly neighborhoods gave me early opportunities to satisfy my wanderlust before I was in school. A frantic neighbor called Mom to warn her that I was standing in the middle of a busy Mission Road intersection a mile away—trying to direct traffic. One Sunday my father caught me walking north on Mission Road carrying a football and wearing a helmet; I was off to Chicago to play football for the Bears. At age 10, after arguing with my mother, I ran away from home. I covered five miles in five hours before a thunderstorm chased me to a friend's house for a call to my frantic parents.

In my pre-school years, my father traveled during the week for Ford's Lincoln-Mercury division, so I didn't see him much. On weekends, we'd spend most of our time together watching TV—particularly sports and World War II documentaries. Those evenings installed an array of curiosity buttons that would be pushed often in my life—military history, planes and aviation and motorsports, among others—all with professional applications down the road.

I didn't have many pets, and the few I had were gone quickly. When I was a toddler, friends gave my parents a Doberman named Debbie. Her stay ended the day my mother found Debbie standing over me, drooling. Gold fishes Willie and Tillie only lasted a couple of days. I remember catching my mom flushing their carcasses down the toilet. I think I'm still carrying emotional scars from that.

When I was four, I lost my familial monopoly with the arrival of my sister, Helen. That forced us to move to a bigger house a few miles south, the place I consider my childhood home. The neighborhood was middle class, conservative, white-collar dads and stay-at-home moms, two to four kids, Christian (except for one Jewish family), and exclusively white.

Imagine life in a bad episode of *Leave It to Beaver*, with rare exceptions. At least twice, we had a slight brush with bigotry in the form of anti-German slogans scrawled in red ink on the east side of the house. A couple of swastikas and stupid slogans were nothing compared to burning crosses on lawns or "Juden raus!" on storefronts, but it taught me how to empathize with victims of intolerance.

My elementary education was at St. Ann, our parish church and school on Mission Road. My years at St. Ann were not easy, but I don't think they were supposed to be. Mass every day, uniforms for boys and girls, a strict, old-school succession of nuns and lay teachers. I got a good education, and I learned that I was a good student.

Summers were repetitive to the point of monotony, the glowing exception coming in 1956. That summer, my mom took my sister and me to Germany, where I was immersed in a new language and culture while getting to know her side of the family. The top floor of the beige stucco house where she grew up was occupied by my grandparents, Max and Hedwig Nagel, Opa and Oma to me. Crowded into the main floor were Aunt Hildegard and Uncle Fred and their two daughters, Karin and Anita, both a little older than me. The day we arrived, they corralled me in the foyer and taught me my first German word—*spielen* (play) —as they brought out a German version of the board game Aggravation.

Everything was magical or mysterious or both. The strangeness, rather than intimidating, was exciting. I soon found playmates in the neighborhood, and they taught me German, the finer points of pilfering pears from trees, poking beehives (dumb), and other kids' stuff. My growing fascination with all things military was spurred as we explored abandoned bunkers and drove through the main business district still scarred by bombed-out gaps in the rows of buildings.

I saw Heidelberg, Frankfurt, Freiburg, and numerous little Black Forest towns, plus Lausanne and Basel in Switzerland. I grew unshakably attached to my extended family, including the esoteric and captivating Uncle Max, with his prosthetic arm and wooden leg, the work of a Soviet artillery shell in Ukraine. Even in my second language, I was transfixed by the sarcastic worldview and pungent eloquence of this pre-war journalist and musician.

Before I turned seven, I had learned to speak accent-free German, drink coffee, devour Black Forest cherry torte, harvest asparagus in the family garden, and survive without television. This was my promised land; the afterglow would never die.

When I was 10, I had what could be considered my first brush with my future vocation—delivering newspapers. I lugged a canvas bag full of weeklies (I never learned to ride a bike), placing each copy at the front door of every house on my route. I made a little pocket change to finance my chief hobby of building plastic models. Sometimes on delivery day I got home late because I had been reading when I should have been delivering; everything was so interesting. After two years, I quit when one paper-hating sociopath threatened me with a shotgun and an unleashed terrier took a bloody chunk out of my right shin—both on the same day.

I got a reminder of the Germany magic in late 1960 when Oma visited just after the birth of my brother Paul. She was with us the December day Dad slipped on black ice in the driveway and broke his leg. Our family doctor, Ben Good, lived across the street. He ran over to tend to dad and ordered me to fetch some blankets. As I waddled toward Dad with blankets piled in my arms, Ben yelled, "Don't step where he did!" I stepped where he did. My feet kicked out in front of me, and my right shoe with its reinforced toe caught my dad flush in the back of his head, knocking him out cold. Ben just shook his head and said, "Well, it's probably better for him this way." I think my dad's feelings toward me changed that day.

Another major influence on my life was one Sister Jean Therese. She was a young, short woman with a round, ruddy face. You didn't think about nuns in these terms, but I suspect that under her habit was a fit and wiry body. One day while writing on the blackboard she heard Sal Dasta talking in class. That was guaranteed to pull one of her many hair triggers. But instead of yelling at him, she silently spun around and side-armed her piece of yellow chalk, hitting poor Sal right between the horns. He was so stunned he couldn't even cry. It was an arm for the ages. A year later she was farmed out to Montana; I never learned why.

Sister Jean Therese was more than a chalk chucker. She pried open areas of learning that I had never explored at St. Ann. She didn't just teach geography by showing us maps; she talked about societies and cultures using films and slideshows. History came alive when she taught it. She taught us to sing in harmony. She even tried to make science interesting and relevant, eschewing the school's dogma-tainted textbook. No matter the subject or theme, she stoked my maturing curiosity about the world, past and present. She was my first inspirational teacher.

She was also my last teacher at St. Ann. My dad didn't like the political indoctrination I was bringing home from school, so he moved my sister and me to public schools. For me, that meant switching to Meadowbrook Junior High School for the seventh grade. In so many ways, it was a portal to a new life. I started to realize who I was, what I liked to do, what I was good at, how to talk to girls, and how to act when some were nice enough to talk back.

Music teacher Marilyn Curt taught me that I could sing, creating the basis for the most enduring pastime of my life. The most transformative teacher at Meadowbrook, however, was David Wolf, who taught a ninth-grade course called General Studies. It was humanities and social sciences packaged as he saw fit, and he was brilliant. Building on the work of Sister Jean Therese, he made the world come alive by blending literature, history, and geography.

My parents insisted on summer school as a pragmatic alternative to swimming, tennis, bowling, and other fun stuff. One summer was lost to eight weeks of typing class. I was good, fast, and too young to know how well that skill would serve me.

If Meadowbrook was transformational, Shawnee Mission East High School confirmed my talents and skills while giving me ample opportunities to enjoy those teenage years. My grades were good. My group of friends migrated with me from Meadowbrook and then expanded mostly due to vocal music as my primary extracurricular activity. I sang with a few award-winning groups, but I also offered early evidence of technical incompetence. The choir director, Jess Rose, gave me the simple task of rewinding an important tape of music on an old reel-to-reel machine. In the middle of rewinding, I hit a button I should have never touched. The tape broke, and all I could do was hide the break in the rewound spool. I never confessed my blunder, and Rose never mentioned it.

Oddly enough, journalism played no role in my high school years. I had visited a journalist for a school project—suburban newspaper publisher Stan Rose. Neither of us knew that we would meet again. I was more interested in geology, astronomy, and teaching for career choices.

That vague ambition I had formed in the Black Forest in 1956 condensed into an unshakable fixation in the summer of 1965—my second immersion in Germany. The house on Rosemarinstrasse had not changed and was still the nexus of the family, and the cast of characters from the first summer was still there. My passable German allowed me to converse more seriously than before with family and friends, most importantly Opa. He told of his service in World War I, his abhorrence of war, and the importance of education. He also explained the rules for safely consuming alcohol. He taught me about German wines and beers, and he tutored me on what and how to eat to avoid their painful side effects.

As I attended high school and university classes with my cousins and their friends, I started daydreaming about attending Heidelberg University. (I never tried.) And we travelled—Munich, Cologne, Bonn, the Rhineland, Frankfurt, Stuttgart, countless smaller towns and villages, and, at the end of the summer, Paris and London. I kept track of events at home through Armed Forces Radio and the international editions of the *New York Times* and *Herald-Tribune*. Sometimes I mused about what it would be like to work for them.

After that summer, the rest of my high school career was anticlimactic. Academics and singing consumed most of my time and energy. The highlight of my junior year had nothing to do with school but taught me a powerful lesson in human relations. As a rabid Kansas City Chiefs fan, I got it in my head that I might talk my way into some kind of on-field activity during a game. I wrote Coach Hank Stram a syrupy letter regretting that my family could not afford season tickets but offering my services if I could help the team some other way. Lo and behold, I got a letter back from Stram accepting my offer, and trainer Bobby Yarborough called me in to work the Oct. 8, 1966, game against Denver.

Ten tough hours started badly with an order to clean "stickum" off the helmet of tight end Fred Arbanas. Pass receivers in those days loaded their hands with stickum to better catch a ball, but it got on everything. I started rubbing the helmet, and before I noticed, the cleaning agent not only took off the goo but also some of the paint. Arbanas got to his locker at that moment to find white blotches on his red helmet. With a percussive curse, he threw the helmet past me into his locker, and I hurried off to other duties. Chiefs running back Mike Garrett walked past me on his way to the field and pressed something in my hand. It was a small packet of Pepto-Bismol tablets. He had swallowed a lot more trying to settle his nervous rookie stomach. The rest of my time was filled lugging equipment to and from the sidelines, offering players water along the bench, and cleaning up the ghastly filth on the locker room floor (my heroes could be pigs).

The most significant revelation from that night only hit me when I got home. My dad was waiting up to hear all about it, and when I marveled at the size of the players, he said, "Yeah, those are some big bucks on that team." While letting the racial slur pass, I realized that all night long I had only seen heroes, not color. I noticed the same thing three years later at a September 6, 1969, pre-season game against Atlanta after I had asked for another chance to work the sidelines. Both Chiefs squads went to the Super Bowl after those two seasons. All I got was a tee shirt from Hall of Fame defensive tackle Buck Buchanan as I left that gig.

Decades later, I realized that throughout my elementary, junior high, and senior high, my schools never had one black student. That was northeast Johnson County, Kansas, in the 50s and 60s—blacks were welcome, but only if they were famous or maids. I had an excellent education, but I was shamefully oblivious to the racism and segregation all around me until I went to college.

In my senior year, I lucked into the English class of Everett Rees, another imposing figure in my pantheon of educators. A bridge grand master and talented pianist, he brought alive the finer aspects of literature, but he struck a chord with me talking about the theory of language and the structure of English. I devoured *The Story of Language* and *How to Lie with Statistics*, as well as a textbook that introduced to me figures of speech as writing infrastructure.

He challenged my essay writing without disparaging it. For a final term paper, I explored the question of whether Shakespeare really wrote Shakespeare. The final grade was B-plus, not the A I had expected. I threw the paper on the floor in disgust in front of the class but waited until after class to ask why. He said it was too long; I had blown past the 3,000-word limit. I noted the lesson about word limits, tucking it away for later.

As graduation approached, choosing a university took precedence over studying. With good grades and placement test scores, my choice boiled down to Georgetown University or the University of Kansas. The former accepted me for its Maxwell School of Foreign Service with an assigned major of international economic affairs. Then my dad came up with an alternative. His business as a manufacturer's representative was thriving, but he could only promise me three years at Georgetown; a fourth might be beyond his means. (It turned out he was right.) If I chose Kansas, he would buy me a car. Georgetown was the obvious fast track to an international career, but Kansas would be close to home and give me time to find my true profession. I wrestled with the decision for a week. I got a 1964 Dodge Dart.

# CHAPTER 2
# University

*The Nerd Finds His Mojo*

The goals of any college student should be to excel academically while building the foundation for life's work. In my case, my four years at the University of Kansas were a dismal failure for the former and an unqualified success for the latter. I was a lousy student but a great student-journalist. I entered KU a cocky nerd not knowing much about my future. I did know I intended to exit academia and make my way somewhere overseas, eventually if not immediately.

As a student, I never really clicked. Even before I arrived, I suffered my first academic injustice. I earned a perfect score on a German language proficiency test. I expected 10 credit hours that would put me on a fast track to a diploma. Then I was

*1966: The author in high school German lab. The yearbook prediction of "a European disc jockey" was not far off.*

told that KU gave no credit hours for proven language proficiency; instead, I was required to take two semesters of another language. French was fun, but I felt cheated.

I cruised through my first semester almost on autopilot, earning acceptable grades. In the 1968 spring semester, I joined a fraternity, Alpha Kappa Lambda, where academic discipline prompted my best grade point average for any semester at KU.

Above all else, that spring semester lit a fire in me that never went out. The lecture hall class was called Introduction to Journalism, with a young instructor teaching verbatim from a mildly interesting textbook. But something in those twice-a-week sessions grabbed me. First, journalism was an international profession, so it could stamp my ticket to Germany. Beyond that, the profession in those days carried an aura of prestige and a touch of swagger. Telling someone you were a journalist often got an "Oh, wow," even with journalism's reputation as a seedy haven for asocial, insensitive ne'er-do-wells who drank and smoked too much. In the vernacular of the day, it sounded cool.

After a summer of driving a delivery truck (excellent motivation for staying in school), the first semester of my sophomore year featured a class with the bland title, Reporting I, where fate again guided me toward my life's work. The scheduled instructor got married and dropped out, forcing the school at the last minute to recruit Rick Dalton, city editor of the *Topeka Journal.* He looked like a city editor—tall, chunky, balding, with the furrowed face of someone always worried about something. This was no theoretical academician or burned-out retiree; he was an authentic, lifelong, day-job journalist

Rick was a godsend. On the first day, he dumped the textbook into a wastebasket and announced he would teach real-world journalism. Our classroom writing exercises involved news of the day so we could compare our work with his newspaper's versions. He sent us out on reporting assignments and spent class time assessing our work, holding us up to the kind of uncompromising scrutiny a professional could expect. Through it all, I discovered I had a knack for newspaper-style writing. It came easy to me, and he seemed pleased with my work. It was the best thing that could have happened for my professional career.

It was the worst thing that could have happened for my academic career.

Next semester, spring 1969, the Topeka papers were looking for a freelancer to cover the University and Lawrence. Dalton mentioned me to the hiring editor, Craig Chappell, and with absolutely no professional experience, I got the job. My first day as a paid journalist was Feb. 22, 1969.

That semester was a mélange of reporting for *The University Daily Kansan*, freelancing for the Topeka papers, and spotty class attendance except for journalism courses. My first assignment for Topeka sent me to Kansas City's Municipal Airport on short notice to interview civil rights attorney Florence Kennedy. She was known to just about everyone in America, except me. In the information dark ages before the Internet and Google, I only had time to find one brief magazine article about her. As we sat in an antiseptic airport waiting room, I mined that skimpy background for questions that I hoped were relevant to her work. She was patient and cooperative, and I suspect that she was on to me but didn't show it. After 30 minutes answering softball and generic questions, she caught her flight, and I hand-wrote a story that I dictated from a pay phone to a benevolent rewrite staffer in Topeka. The printed version was brief but readable, teaching me a deep and eternal appreciation for the skill of rewrite. I got my first check in journalism with a note that I was too wordy. It was not the last time I would hear that admonition.

As I waded deeper into journalism, I never considered the school's radio/TV classes. Its facilities were rudimentary, and that branch of the industry had not yet established its preeminence. Besides, I had a face for radio and a voice for closed captioning. I believed my future was firmly rooted in print.

Spring semester's Reporting II class made me a de facto staff writer for the *UDK*, as it was known on campus. I was eager and prolific.

Ethics, however, were a work in progress. I covered a major story on campus that semester while also being a participant. The university's ROTC program held a review in Memorial Stadium each spring. But that year, KU's growing anti-war faction decided to disrupt the ceremony. I belonged to a student organization that agreed to try to stop the disruption and report the names of any protesters we recognized. I went with them, rationalizing that it would put me in a prime spot for covering the story while also defending the right of the ROTC folks to hold their event.

It was an ethical atrocity. One role or the other was defensible, but to use one as a cover for the other was shameful. It didn't hit home until a student I had identified as a protestor was suspended briefly from school. I felt dirty, and I never let myself forget that feeling.

By contrast, my favorite project that semester was a series on the failure of most football and basketball athletes to earn degrees. The statistical research comparing rosters to graduation lists was tedious, but the fun came in the interviews with former KU stars to hear whether they regretted leaving the University before graduating. My roommate Monte Briley, a great high school basketball player, handed me the phone one evening looking almost pale. "It's Wilt Chamberlain," he whispered. I asked Chamberlain a few questions about his academic accomplishments, while Monte just stood like Moses listening to a burning bush. Chamberlain scoffed at the idea of needing a degree, saying he had attended enough classes since college to "earn seven or eight degrees." Part of that series won a national award, but I never found out why the school submitted just one part. Maybe it was too controversial. Or maybe the faculty wanted to hose me down a bit.

Professors began to notice that I was losing interest in classes. I showed up and worked just enough to save my grade average. In my defense, I was a model student for the reporting course and one other—copy editing. The professor, John Bremner, was another leading figure in my pantheon of educators. He was Australian, a former priest, a World War II veteran whose wounds had pulled him into drug addiction for a time, and a brilliant editor. He spent his summers as a guest copy editor at *The New*

*York Times*. He edited dictionaries. A hulking, deep-voiced classroom intimidator, he commanded respect, attention, and attendance. I soaked up everything he said.

My first exposure to the minutia of the English language had come from Everett Rees in high school. The sparks from Rees exploded in Bremner's class with a sometimes entertaining, sometimes torrential barrage of fundamentals and trivia that any good copy editor needed. He hooked a generation of his students on *The Careful Writer* by Theodore Bernstein, implanted the rules and art of headline writing, and instilled the fear of God for tolerating anything less than editorial perfection. He molded and mentored an impressive roster of copy-editing stars in his classes. It took me decades to discover I was one of them.

As that spring semester progressed, the *UDK* newsroom became my second home, often late into the night. I started sleeping later at the fraternity house and missing classes. I didn't care much, but my professors did. They took class-skipping personally, and as my academic work started to take a backseat to journalism, the needles started to come out when I did show up. A snide comment here, a rhetorical question about priorities there—nothing alarming, more like rumblings of a coming storm for what they viewed as a precocious upstart.

I created even more ripples at the end of the semester. Internships in those days traditionally followed the junior year. But at the urging of Associate Dean Mal Applegate, I applied for a *Kansas City Star* internship after my sophomore year—and got it. City Editor Matt Goree liked what I said in my interview and the clips I showed him, so he assigned me to the Kansas City, Kansas bureau for the summer.

KCK at that time was the armpit of the metro area. It was largely poor and a touch unsavory in the eyes of the rest of the area's residents, ideal for a cub reporter eager for the real world of newspaper reporting.

The bureau chief was an aging legend: Harry Hannon. A stereotypical ink-stained wretch—old for his years, lame in one leg, hard-drinking, profane and cynical—he was a hell of a reporter and a tolerant teacher. He was known as "Hanging Harry" for all the executions he had covered at the Kansas State Penitentiary in nearby Lansing. One story had him arriving late to a hanging as the condemned man was just finishing an eloquent final statement. Harry ran up to the scaffolding and asked him to repeat his speech. Instead, he gave Harry a short lecture on the virtues of punctuality, interrupted abruptly by the dropping gallows floor.

Another Harry tale involved the end of prohibition in the 1930s. *The Star* ordered Harry to cover the return of beer to Kansas City, and he felt obliged to partake of the newly legal brew as part of a reporter's due diligence. He hurried back to the newsroom close to deadline, only to suffer a sudden onset of what he called the "green apple quick step," which he blamed on some hastily brewed beer. Deadlines don't wait, but Harry had more pressing issues. In a classic newsroom solution, someone wheeled a typewriter into the men's room, and there Harry sat on his porcelain throne pounding out his story.

With me, it would be fair to say Harry suffered a young fool. My copy could lack clarity and correct spelling. But I was irrepressible, and Harry appreciated that. I loved what was called "police reporting," and there was plenty of mayhem in KCK to keep me busy. Every Thursday, Harry sent me to Leavenworth, Kansas to work a beat that included Fort Leavenworth and five prisons, including the notorious federal penitentiary and the even more infamous state pen. I was allowed inside both for tours, and my first front-page byline topped a final-edition story about a prison riot in Lansing. I had spent the day calling in snippets of information to the rewrite desk, but I hadn't actually written anything. That's when I learned you could get a byline by just contributing to a story.

I was making $80 a week but would have done it for free. Harry let me cover rock concerts on my own time, and I often landed post-concert interviews. The three singers for Three Dog Night were munching Oreos in a Holiday Inn lobby when they agreed to talk to me. They offered me some cookies with a warning that I would lose them if I asked the one question they hated. My first question: please explain the name Three Dog Night. They took away the Oreos.

After a Peter, Paul, and Mary concert, Mary Travers invited me and some friends to her birthday party, where she distributed cake and gave a long, eloquent lecture on the virtues of nonviolence. The Cowsills, often the butt of jokes for their wholesome bubble-gum music and squeaky-clean image, were hospitable and cooperative as they struggled to repair costumes backstage.

One Saturday night I covered the Byrds, but I couldn't get an interview, and my article about their concert was lame. I handed my copy to Harry along with a request for overtime pay. Harry took a quick look and was appalled. He said the story stunk and did not deserve overtime. He slid the copy and the overtime form into the bottom drawer of his desk, never to emerge again. I learned to file for overtime only after a story was printed.

With all that variety in coverage, police reporting was still my happy zone. Radio monitors in the bureau would constantly blare calls between dispatchers and patrol cars or fire stations, and we knew the code (10-47 was an injury accident, 10-48 a fatality, etc.). If something awful happened, I'd race off to the scene with a bureau photographer. One was Warren Liston, a dead ringer for Moe of the Three Stooges, but sharp and mischievous. He taught me how to place myself at a traffic accident scene so that I'd get in the shot of the TV film cameras for the evening news. Once in a while he'd stand behind the cameraman and look through his viewfinder to guide me to just the right spot. My parents marveled at the number of times they saw me on the news that summer.

One story taught me about the impact of newspapers and the hazards of unintended consequences. I found a guy who picked up stray and unwanted dogs and sold them to laboratories for research, and I wrote it up as a straight-up business feature. Good lord, what a reaction. Outraged readers called the bureau to protest, and some sent checks, demanding a balancing second story about the heinous nature of the business. Trying to put out the fire, Harry sent me to the local humane society to interview the director about the evil of puppy mills. I dutifully wrote the story, and in the process misspelled the director's name (Morris, instead of the correct Mouras).

He kindly let it pass. That's what internships are for. As someone said, you're going to be bad before you can be good.

By the time school started again in the fall of '69, I didn't care much about my attendance record. I was working on the student newspaper, showing up for the journalism classes I found interesting or useful, freelancing for the Topeka paper, dating, partying, and working just enough to keep my grade point average above the required minimum. I had a paying job at the *UDK* as make-up editor, meaning I would supervise the paper's composition every morning at the campus printing plant. I saw firsthand the transition of page composition from hot-lead linotype machines to easy-to-read black-and-white galleys pasted together for offset printing. I didn't realize that I was witnessing a revolution in newspaper production.

Too often I would arrive at the printing plant after being up all night and then, when the paper was "put to bed," go home and sleep until noon. Class attendance suffered, but I made it through the semester well enough to score a big *Kansan* job for the next semester—campus editor.

Spring 1970 brought national attention to the University of Kansas, none of it wanted. The semester started routinely, but national ferment for civil rights and against the Vietnam War was intensifying. As unrest percolated at KU, the *UDK* covered the increasingly common protests and visits by prominent radicals like Abbie Hoffman.

Then came April 20.

I was driving on campus at sunset toward Flint Hall, which housed the journalism school and the newsroom, when I saw a column of flames to the northeast. I rushed to the newsroom, where my colleagues told me the Kansas Union, the student union building, was burning. With the paper staff already on standby, I doled out the first pile of assignments to reporters and then hurried to the Union a half mile away. There was nothing to do but stare slack-jawed at the flames, so I rushed back to the newsroom to coordinate coverage of the most tumultuous week in Lawrence since Quantrill's raids. The *UDK* staff comprised college kids with little or no real-world experience, especially for something like this. That made their performance that much more impressive. Editors were planning a special edition, making calls for extra writers and photographers, watching the United Press International wire for any information it could offer, and generally doing their jobs with urgency but without panic or distraction. Writers worked their stories as diligently as their sources would let them. Faculty advisors were present if we needed their help but otherwise stood back and let us do our work. I have never been prouder of a newsroom group than I was of the *UDK* staff that night, and the school never produced a better group for disaster coverage.

Investigators quickly established the Union fire was arson but were never sure if it was the work of anti-war radicals or civil rights militants. The governor declared martial law, and National Guard troops were activated. Our college town became a battle zone.

The next morning, we were told to get special passes from the police department to exempt us from a dusk-to-dawn curfew. As I stood in line for my pass, I glanced at the guy next to me sporting an oversized helmet and a weapon at his side. It was Jim Czupor, a student reporter for the *UDK.* He worked part-time as a sheriff's dispatcher, but he had been deputized for martial law. He looked lost and almost goofy. It was deadly serious stuff, and I only stopped needling him about it years later when he admitted to being scared stiff during those three nights on duty.

The curfew pass carried an ironic image. It featured the Lawrence city emblem and the motto "From Ashes to Immortality," a reference to the city's devastation during the "Bloody Kansas" era more than a century earlier. Given what was happening, we thought it should add "and Back Again."

We assigned reporters to specific beats—police, fire, university administration, and so on. The students that semester included some interesting characters, such as running back and future NFL Hall of Famer John Riggins, who turned out to be a good writer. I assigned him to Lawrence Memorial Hospital with instructions to keep an eye on the emergency room. Then I forgot about him. At 4 a.m. he called and asked if he could go home. I was impressed that he had stayed at his post all night, and I thanked him. Later, I heard tales of how he amused himself with several nurses during the evening. I still refuse to believe them because I don't want to.

Another star student that semester was Jim Ryun, the Olympic miler and future congressman who was studying photography. A genuinely nice guy, he never behaved like the celebrity he was. But when I called him to report for curfew duty, he declined. No appeal to his sense of duty, his responsibility to the newspaper, or even his work ethic could change his mind. He stayed home.

The next day, I met him in a hallway outside the newsroom and expressed my disappointment in his refusal to come in. He paused for a moment, and then revealed that he and his pregnant wife had received death threats. I was flabbergasted and asked why he didn't say so when I called. He said he was afraid I would make too much of it. He was right; I would have insisted that he stay home and then called authorities. Several of the top editors, including me, also received threats during the week. But we shrugged them off as the work of kooks reading names in the *UDK*'s staff list.

That week is now something of a blur, with days of spotty class attendance giving way to near-constant newsroom work. Nights brought curfews, National Guard patrols, gunfire in housing areas on the east side of campus, and national coverage branding KU along with Wisconsin and Columbia as the three most incendiary campuses in America.

When martial law ended and the troops withdrew, the tension lingered. Chancellor E. Laurence Chalmers and his administration had succeeded to keep the university open despite provocations from troublemakers and inflammatory rhetoric from politicians.

We only had a week after martial law before the next shockwave hit.

On May 4, Ohio National Guard members killed four unarmed student protesters at Kent State University. The reaction nationally and at KU was instant and furious. Fearing a second, far worse wave of violence, Chalmers asked the entire student population to convene in the football stadium for a mass vote on whether to continue classes or immediately end the semester. The vote by the thousands present was nearly unanimous. The school year was over.

Even with the option of pass-fail grades, it was not enough to save my semester academically. My overall grade average fell below the *UDK's* required minimum. I began my senior year banished from the newsroom.

Fortune again smiled on me in the person of Mal Applegate, who had moved on to a recruiting role for the Gannett newspaper group in Rochester, N.Y. I received a second summer internship, this time with *The Rochester Democrat-Chronicle*, a flagship paper of the burgeoning media empire.

Never having been far from my family for any length of time, I now faced three months in a strange city 1,000 miles away. I found a small apartment with two other interns—tall, lanky Alan Koonse from Missouri and husky, red-haired Steve Hiney from Oklahoma State. They were amiable, and we had a lot of fun that summer. We worked different hours, with my overnight shift giving me mostly police and fire stories to cover—my favorites. Chasing sirens was exciting, seeing humanity at its tragic or violent worst was another kind of education, and the writing was easy. A fatal fire, nasty accident, or a robbery required quick and simple writing— "just the facts ma'am," the catch phrase tied to TV detective Joe Friday (which he never actually said).

I learned a painful lesson about deadlines while covering Rochester's Soap Box Derby. The annual competition featured boys in unpowered homemade racers barreling down a steep city park road marked up for racing. It was usually a day-long funfest, but that year's event didn't go so well. The chosen course proved too steep for some of the young contestants to navigate safely, and several were hurt in frightening crashes. Suddenly, I had a front-page story on my hands, but the primitive two-way radio in my company car didn't work, and no pay phones were in sight. So I stayed to the end to make sure I didn't miss anything.

When I drove to a pay phone to dictate my notes, the cigar-chewing assistant city editor, Dick Thien, cut me off in a voice I knew spelled trouble. I had missed the deadline for the first Sunday edition, and the paper had been forced to print the Associated Press story. Using wire copy for a local story is among the worst embarrassments a newspaper can suffer. Thien didn't want to hear my excuses and tore me a new one for breaking one of journalism's sacred principles—never miss a deadline. My only redemption was the front-page byline that topped my story in a later edition.

More enjoyable adventures helped to spice up the summer. I covered a two-day rock festival in Toronto, where I loitered backstage with the likes of Ten Years After, Delanie & Bonnie, the Grateful Dead, and Janis Joplin. I even intercepted Joplin at her hotel, where she shared some of her Southern Comfort with me before sweetly refusing an interview request. Other side trips that summer included my first look at Niagara Falls and my first horse race at Canandaigua Downs. Now *that* was an internship.

In the fall of 1970, I returned for my last academic year at KU with no doubt about what I wanted to do in life. Alas, studying was not on my list. I still covered KU for the Topeka papers, but I made it through my fall semester classes on cruise control. The bombing of the campus computer center reminded us that we were still on something of a powder keg.

As I contemplated starting a career without a college degree, I had a brief encounter with my idol, CBS News anchor Walter Cronkite. He came to KU to receive an award, and I schemed my way backstage to ask him about the importance of a sheepskin. After all, he did just fine without one. His answer: "Finish school. You'll need it."

I, of course, was sure I knew better and shrugged off class work. The journalism faculty did not block my work as a *UDK* editorial writer that final semester, but otherwise I had burned through whatever tolerance they had left. In addition to the perceived rudeness of my skipping classes, my two summer internships rankled them when better students had struggled to land one. They squirmed every time I won a national award, even though the school got a matching cash donation for each award. And they just didn't like my attitude.

The dean, Edward Bassett, taught a class titled Reporting of Civic Affairs. As a class assignment, I wrote a three-part series for the *UDK* on the increasing friction between student voters and permanent Lawrence residents. The series was one of the award winners. He gave it a C+.

The school inflicted its final wound at its year-end awards dinner. Each of the dozen or so *UDK* staff members received certificates of achievement—except me. My sympathizing friends tried to explain it away as a bureaucratic mistake. It wasn't. Later that night, my friend Kit Netzer sat with me in my car as I vented. She is still the only person in my adult life who ever saw me cry. Neither of us noticed the rise of a huge chip on my shoulder.

The copy-editing professor, John Bremner, saved his best shot for last. Years later, I got engaged to Beth Retonde, one of his favorites. When he heard the news, he called her into his office, closed the door, and spent 15 minutes listing all the reasons she should not marry me. My dad wanted to sue; her dad threatened worse. Beth and I let it pass.

Of course, none of this was my fault. Yeah, right.

I suffered from a chronic self-awareness deficit. I had no feel for the consequences of some of the things I said and did. The professors' dedication to journalism and education deserved more respect than I showed. Too often, I made self-serving references to my real-world experience, sounding as if I didn't need classroom instruction. My fellow students kindly tolerated my behavior, but the faculty didn't. They never realized that despite my spotty attendance, they had instilled a lifelong understanding and appreciation of the journalism profession in terms of history, practices, and ethics. They did their job.

I left KU with more professional experience than most students, but I wonder how much better I could have been if I had dragged my butt up Mount Oread to class more often. In the journalism-themed romantic comedy *Teacher's Pet,* Clark

Gable had a great line: "Experience is the horse, but education is the jockey." However, I also wonder what might have happened if the faculty treated me more as a challenge than a pariah. I didn't get all I could from KU; KU didn't get all it could from me.

My last day on campus ignited a family argument that spanned decades. I left KU needing a semester's worth of credit hours to complete my degree. Nevertheless, I exercised my right to take "the walk" with my journalism pals at commencement. I rented the cap and gown and invited my parents to Lawrence to share the moment. We were walking to the ceremony when I casually announced that I was leaving KU without a degree. My father gritted his teeth; my mother was devastated. She had been planning a grand party celebrating my achievement. No diploma, no party.

My father tried to argue that he had not gotten what he paid for. Not so. If college was meant to help a person identify and prepare for a career, KU had certainly done that. Now I was ready to go to work.

# CHAPTER 3
# Sun Newspapers

*The Dawn of a Career*

I walked away from the University of Kansas in May 1971 with a decent resume, overflowing confidence, and not much else. No degree, no job, no money, and no clue about the next phase of my life. It was not an auspicious start to a career. Typical, maybe, but not auspicious.

I tried to leverage connections from my internships at *The Kansas City Star* and Gannett. *The Star* was a dead end. Gannett had more than 30 newspapers nationwide, including seductive destinations in California and Florida. They offered Rochester. No thanks.

Stan Rose had been publishing semi-weekly suburban Kansas City newspapers for decades. Stan was that rare breed of solid newspaperman and shrewd businessman. He also had the guts to take on the monopolistic *Kansas City Star*. By the time I came hat-in-hand, he had carved out a solid niche in a lucrative suburban market with papers delivered free on Wednesdays and Fridays to homes in the *Star*'s advertising sweet spot. I never figured out or even cared about his business model, but his journalism was street-level storytelling that filled a lot of news holes ignored by the behemoth downtown.

For someone with aspirations for stardom as a foreign correspondent, the Sun Newspapers were not a particularly attractive option. For someone with no work and living with his parents, they had potential. At least I knew the coverage area—the comfortable middle- and upper-class suburbs of my youth.

I met Stan in his efficient Overland Park office, and the conversation started with his recollection of my mother as one of his early advertisers. He didn't remember that I had interviewed him for my junior high careers project. He had reviewed my resume and writing samples and asked me what kind of job I wanted. I told him that I just wanted to report and write. After a little more chatting, he offered me a job as a reporter. $110 a week. I said yes on the spot and started the next Monday. It wasn't *The New York Times*, but I had a job doing what I wanted to do.

I went home and broke the news to my mom, who was annoyed I had not consulted with her first. "Mom," I said, "when a grown man is offered a job, he doesn't run home to his mother to ask for permission." My KU J-school buddy Jim Czupor and I agreed to share an apartment, and I went to work.

Stan had a broadsheet newspaper to fill twice a week. He had no news services to help him fill the news columns, so the half dozen writers and editors plus freelancers had to come up with enough news to fill the blank spaces around the ads. (Newsroom wags would say that was the purpose of all editorial content in every newspaper.)

The variety of assignments made this the perfect first job. I had to cover local governments, schools, zoning boards (a woefully under-reported civic institution), police departments, courts, politics, community affairs, religions, social organizations such as the Rotary and Lions' Club, local and pro sports, and more. I'd write at least two or three stories a day. Saturdays off were rare, Sundays off more common.

After a month on the job, Uncle Sam tried to ruin everything. In 1971, the Vietnam War was winding down, but the draft was still harvesting young men, including those like me whose draft deferments ended when they left school. One sunny June day I answered the summons for my draft physical at the black glass-and-concrete induction center downtown near Kansas City's Union Station.

I got through the preliminaries, but my first trouble spot was the test station for hearing. The technician ordered me into a soundproof booth with a window facing his work panel. I was to put on headphones and punch a button when a tone stopped and again when I could hear it. But I knocked my glasses off as I put on the headphones and bent down to feel for them on the dark floor. The technician saw the tone getting louder and louder, and when he looked up at the window, I wasn't there. He barged into the booth expecting who knows what, and he wasn't buying my excuse for messing up his precious test.

More trouble came when the security test asked if I had ever associated with anyone seeking to overthrow the U.S. government. KU hosted plenty of controversial characters while I worked there as a reporter, and fearing the existence of a file photo showing me near Abbie Hoffman or some other troublemaker, I didn't know how to answer the question. So I pleaded the Fifth. Off I went to another room to fill out an exhaustive "History of Life" questionnaire. When it asked where I had traveled abroad, I asked for an extra sheet of paper to cover my two summers in Germany.

Finally, they took my fingerprints, squirted cleaning glop on my hands, and ordered me to a restroom down the hall to clean up. I rubbed my hands as I went, dropping greasy black globules on the shiny vinyl floor that a janitor had just polished. Then I ran into the janitor. His indignant scolding chased me into the restroom, and I left a clean man. The Kansas draft board never reached my number (161), so I was spared military service. If you're wondering, I would have served if called.

Free to concentrate on my work, I was having so much fun that I never noticed the extra hours I was piling up each month in unpaid overtime. When the Labor Department investigated Stan's operation, he had to promote me to City Editor to exempt me from overtime. I got a raise to $125 per week that I didn't even ask for. I shrugged, took it, and went back to having fun.

As I progressed, I started picking up lessons in real-world newspapering. Stan was a civic star in the community, and he had his causes and preferences. As publisher, he had every right to use his newspaper as a platform. His front-page column sometimes offered commentary about an issue covered in a front-page story. To me, that tested the bounds of journalism school ethics, but it was real-world newspapering, warts and all.

Another lesson taught me how a newspaper could damage itself with a poorly chosen editorial position. A local police chief had a running argument with the county district attorney. The chief was popular, handsome, and articulate. The prosecutor was a bit rough around the edges, plain-speaking, and hardly charismatic. I was covering the feud, and Stan printed an editorial siding with the police chief. That immediately made me a hero at the police department, with one secretary thanking me for "telling the truth." The county prosecutor's office maintained a professional but chilly attitude toward me and the paper. A few weeks later, the chief was arrested after an inebriated tirade from the balcony of a local hotel room—in his underwear. We reported the incident and let the community come to its own conclusions. The district attorney and his staff never gloated and never heckled me or the paper. They didn't have to. The lesson was learned. I never fully trusted any newsmaker after that.

Of all the lessons learned in that one year with Stan, perhaps the most indelible was the impact of a journalist's work on the readers. Since I wrote about the area where I had grown up, my work not only reflected on me, but also my parents. The feedback I got from or through them gave me a sense of how people might react to what I wrote. I learned that sensitivity had a place in journalism, as long as it didn't lead to self-censorship.

Our impact grew throughout the Kansas City area when we reached a deal with a local station, KCMO-TV, to share our news on Tuesday nights. Stations were not covering Johnson County much, so this let KCMO broaden its scope while giving *The Sun* a weekly plug. One anchor I worked with was Don Harrison. Our paths crossed decades later at CNN, where we had fun recalling the "old times."

Once I dragged my father into the fray. As the 1972 election season approached, I decided to test the county's system for preventing voter fraud. I asked my dad (a real estate appraiser at the time) for the addresses of seven vacant homes. Armed with those addresses, I registered to vote in seven different jurisdictions. Same name and personal info, just different addresses.

However, being a good boy and thinking about possible consequences, I first told the district attorney, Margaret Jordan, about my project, thus proving I had no criminal intent. She gave me clearance to conduct my experiment, although nothing in writing.

About a week after registering, I got a call from my father. He was not pleased. The election commissioner had called the first Ted Iliff he found in the phonebook to ask why he had registered to vote in seven cities. When my dad said the commissioner had the wrong Iliff, the commissioner congratulated him on not being the one who had seven felony warrants out against him for voter registration fraud.

I hung up on my dad and immediately called Jordan's office to claim my get-out-of-jail card. She was on vacation, and nobody else there knew anything about our little agreement.

I called the commissioner, confessed, and told him about my deal with the district attorney. He didn't care. He wanted justice, but he settled for a deal: He would tear up the warrants if I would do a story on how his election security system had worked. That's what I had planned anyway, so I wrote a front-page story about the sanctity of the Johnson County voting system. The commissioner was mollified, Jordan was amused when she got back to the office, and I think even Stan got a kick out of it. My dad, on the other hand, was not to be denied his moment of indignant wrath. The next family dinner dissolved into a blistering oration about reputation and taking stupid risks and challenging authority and so on and so on. I thought about reminding him that challenging authority was part of my job, but I let it go.

Stan was a tolerant and patient boss and mentor. He kept a close eye on my work and often reviewed the front-page stuff, more as an editor than a critic. He was a great editor. With such a great boss came occasional burdens outside the realm of reporting and writing. As a leading light of the community, Stan had plenty of social and professional obligations befitting a man of his stature. Sometimes, he was overbooked.

Stan had been asked to speak at a synagogue's bar mitzvah ceremony. (Stan was Jewish.) He couldn't make it, and he asked me if I would cover for him. I'm a 22-year-old Roman Catholic nobody with a German mother, and I'm supposed to take his place as guest speaker at a synagogue?

Don't worry, he said. It will be a small crowd. They're nice people. Talk about what newspapers can do for a community. It'll only last 15 minutes.

I was still at that age when I thought I could do anything (or fake it well), so I agreed. I jotted notes on index cards, rehearsed a couple of times, and went off to my first appearance as a public speaker. Jim, my roommate, came along to share the portentous moment.

I entered the synagogue at the appointed time and froze. There had to be a hundred people in there—parents, the boys, and lots of relatives. It was a full house. I realized my breezy chat would not suit the occasion. I needed to make a from-the-podium formal speech. I remember all those people sitting down in unison and all those faces looking at me. Most were neutral, some were friendly, some were skeptical. "Where's Stan Rose, and who's this putz?"

I don't recall exactly what I said, but I remember sounding pompous. My lecture on the virtues of local newspapers sounded like a homily. The faces never changed expressions. I lasted for 15 minutes, wrapped up at the first opportunity, and made way for the joyous part of the festivities. As I endured the long march to the lobby, I saw Jim, head down. He couldn't look at me. He tried to be gentle, but it was no use. I was pathetic. It took years before I agreed to speak in public again.

Another humiliation Stan assigned to me sounded like a lark. Every spring, Kansas City would hold a boat, sports, and travel show. Part of the tradition was a beauty contest to select "Miss Boat, Sports, and Travel Show." Stan was invited to serve as a judge but asked me to fill in. Beauty contest? Sure. What could go wrong?

The Saturday morning started with introductions to my fellow judges. One was Bruce Rice, a likeable veteran TV sports anchor. The other was Bruno Bernard, introduced to us as "Bruno of Hollywood." He was a renowned photographer of the stars, so presumably he could spot potential that Bruce and I might miss.

About 50 contestants, all over 18 through early 20s, sauntered in swimsuits across the stage one after the other as we sat at the judges' table trying to decide which ones had the looks to match the show's theme. After just a few contestants, I started to squirm. They were all attractive, but there were no opportunities to learn more about them and their interests other than what they wrote on their brief application sheets. I felt like I was judging a sporty meat market.

To appear fair, we had to preside over several rounds of contestant parades, even though we agreed we had recognized the two finalists in the first pass. Bruce and I liked a high school senior with short brown hair and natural-looking tan who would fit into any outdoor setting. Bruno liked the other one, a petite, pale platinum blonde. He said she was photogenic and "he could do more with her," whatever that meant. Bruce and I thought she had the look of an anorexic shut-in. We prevailed; the high school senior reigned over that year's show. Our reward for sacrificing our Saturday was a free dinner at a fine Italian restaurant. Too bad I wasn't hungry.

A more serious and consequential escapade capped my year with Stan. In April 1972, Stan was approached by an acquaintance who told of a strange business proposal he had received from a perfect stranger.

The acquaintance was sitting at a lunch counter when some guy next to him started pitching an idea that sounded too good to be true. The stranger gave his prospective pigeon a phone number. Stan gave it to me and said I could investigate if I had time.

Consumer protection stories were a favorite of mine. They served the public, stopped bad guys from doing bad things, and saved people money. I made the call, and a male voice on the other end asked some routine questions. I told the truth, except what I was doing for a living. I said I was working for my dad but wanted something better. We scheduled an appointment, and I met him at few days later at a Holiday Inn near Kansas City Municipal Airport.

The visit was brief. This middle-aged, well-tanned character identified the enterprise as a cleaning supplies outfit called Willex, and he summarized its supposedly unlimited earnings potential. When he decided I was a legitimate prospect, he offered me an all-expenses-paid weekend trip to Omaha for a Willex "recruiting conference."

The following Saturday morning, with Stan's blessing, I took the flight to Omaha and checked in to the downtown Hilton. I was introduced to my "sponsors," a fresh-faced midwestern couple, and was hustled to the first of two presentations, which turned out to be sales pitches.

Willex was a classic pyramid sales scheme. You could buy a distributorship and sell Willex products in your local area for a decent profit, but the real money was from signing up other distributors. You got a share of their distributorship fee plus a slice of their profits. The more distributors you signed up and they signed up, the more money you made. You could rake in a small fortune just leeching the distributors in your pyramid. No sales were necessary.

During a break, I met a young man who was just as skeptical of the presentation as I was. I asked him to keep his ears open and to share his experience with me later. He gave me a few useful nuggets for the story.

After an afternoon session, we were guests for dinner and had the evening free to hobnob with Willex pitchmen and other distributors and recruits. During small talk in the bar, I learned that my "sponsors" paid for my flight and hotel. The Willex sharks had assured them that if they signed me up, they'd get their money back and more. I felt sorry for them, but any expression of sympathy would have blown my cover.

The next morning, I flew back to Kansas City. The story turned into a three-part series. The first covered the issue of pyramid sales schemes, their popularity, and their illegality. The second described my Omaha adventure. For the third, I interviewed the attorney general of Iowa, where Willex had been expelled for illegal activity. Stan vetted every word.

The series got plenty of positive reader reaction, but not from Willex. Executives demanded a retraction, then threatened a lawsuit. Stan stood his ground and told them to get lost.

This episode has two postscripts. Several months after the series ran, and after I had left the *Sun* newspapers, Editor Anne Canfield sent me a clip of the *Sun* story on how the Kansas attorney general had thrown Willex out of the state. Later that year, Stan asked me to drop by the office, where he gave me a plaque from the Suburban Newspaper Association of America. It read: "Editorial Award presented to Ted Iliff, Johnson County Scout [the paper's original name], First Place, Best News Story, 1972." It remains my sole individual national award.

The Willex series was the high-water mark of my tenure at the *Sun*. As I approached my first anniversary, I developed itchy feet. The job was still fun but had its frustrations. Before I could even start looking around, a cold call took me up my next step.

# CHAPTER 4
# United Press International

*Three Helpings of Salad Days*

Within a week of my anniversary date at the *Sun*, I decided to call the United Press International bureau in Kansas City. I had fed them information during the "troubles" at KU and a few other times, and I hoped they would remember my name.

Did they ever. The bureau executive, Paul Haney, said he remembered how I had helped UPI. I told him where I was working and asked if he had an opening. Paul invited me to the bureau for an interview, where I met bureau manager Jim Kidney. Days later I accepted an offer to be a writer for UPI. Stan knew there was no way he could counteroffer, so he wished me well. In one move I leaped from local to global journalism. Or at least I thought so.

I knew nothing about wire service work, other than having read UPI at the *Kansan*. I saw the word "international" in the company title and assumed I was on the fast track to my ultimate career goal. I fantasized that a short apprenticeship could lead to a foreign posting at a UPI bureau.

Wrong. In so many ways.

In those days, UPIs sent news via teletype to contracted "clients." On the receiving end, newspapers and broadcast stations watched their clacking teletype machines for news from across their state and beyond.

I knew almost nothing about all that on the May day when I entered the bureau on the second floor of a downtown building also housing a movie theater and a TV station. I was pumped. Then I walked into the bureau, with its dirty floors and windows, decrepit furniture, musty odor, and thundering wire machines. No glamor here.

Jim Kidney, a gruff, somewhat rumpled stereotype of a wire service guy, ran the place. Others in the bureau could have come straight from central casting: Carl Christensen, the curmudgeonly bureau sage; John Braden, the mercurial do-it-all writer; Pat Malone, the long-haired intellectual I knew at KU; Charlie Smith, the quick-witted and quick filing sports writer; and a few blue-collar types with the official title of teletype operators who quietly and capably added proofreader to their duties.

And then there was Margaret Richards. Maggie. The UPI legend. She was just a few years away from retirement when I got there. She trained me, just as decades earlier she had trained a United Press rookie named Walter Cronkite. She was short, trim, white-haired, and could be mistaken for anybody's favorite grandmother, but there was nothing matronly about her. She was a tough veteran of the wire service wars dating back to the 30s.

Her most famous exploit was on June 17, 1933, at Kansas City's Union Station, where a mob gang tried to free Frank Nash from federal custody. The resulting gunfight left three federal agents and Nash dead. Maggie rushed to the scene to report on the massacre. In her haste she walked through pools of blood, ruining her new white tennis shoes. When she filed an expense report to get new shoes, it was denied.

Fast forward four decades. When Maggie decided to retire, the bureau held a dinner in her honor at a fancy downtown restaurant. Walter Cronkite called to offer congratulations, and UPI sent a senior executive from the New York headquarters. After dinner, he gave Maggie her retirement gift—a gleaming new pair of white tennis shoes.

One other claim to fame stemmed from her long tenure covering local politics. A close friend was Bess Truman, Harry's wife. She knew them from the early days in Independence, Missouri. As Truman was dying, Maggie did not trade on her friendship with Bess, but her reporting featured an extra sparkle that nobody else could match.

My first task, Maggie announced, was to learn writing styles for newspaper and broadcast clients. Print style matched how I had always written for newspapers. Broadcast style was another matter. Writing for radio required present tense, conversational wording, and short sentences. Taking a 300-word story and boiling it down to a 30-second radio item required a new skill set. I picked it up fairly quickly and learned to enjoy it. The write-for-the-ear style brightened my print writing as well.

The scope of line bureau work was a letdown. Instead of writing big stories for big audiences on my way to international stardom, I was writing about fatal wrecks, state politics, commodity prices, fishing conditions, weather forecasts, and other mundane news for Kansas and Missouri. Sometimes things would perk up with a plane crash or tornado, but a routine day could be a hectic bore.

Bureau writers relied on the teletype operators to "punch" ribbons of yellow tape, which was fed through a device that translated the tape's holes into printed wire copy. As the words typed out on the bureau's machine, telephone lines carried signals that would reproduce the copy on client wire machines. When no operator was available, a writer worked the teletype machine to get the story out.

I've had scary moments, but nothing terrified me more than the first time I had to operate that smelly, inky, clacking contraption by typing on a resistant keyboard. So many things could go wrong, and hundreds of readers at the other end of that circuit—clients and other bureaus—could see the error and know the perpetrator's identity by the sign-off code. ti1220p. Any typing mistake would play out on the machine's yellow or white paper for all the world (sometimes literally) to see, requiring a humiliating correction.

Those infernal contraptions weren't satisfied to drain my sweat glands. They needed to be fed. They devoured paper, ticker tape, and inked ribbons. The paper on rolls or in boxes went into the machine with little effort, but if the new paper tore, the keys would pound on the roller. It could jam, mangling the copy and requiring another run. The yellow tape could tear, jam, or get loaded upside down or backwards—each requiring a restart.

Worst of all were the spooled ink ribbons. They had to be threaded by hand through the gaps and slots of the ribbon carriage. Anyone who guided a ribbon through the carriage wore proof of their effort with inky fingers, hands, face, clothes, coffee mugs, and anything else they touched. The ink, by the way, was indelible; disfigurement lingered long after cleanup. Dry cleaners must have loved the stuff.

Despite all this, I started showing proficiency in bureau operations during the slow news days of summer. Sports never stopped, and the bureau's sports writer, Charlie Smith, produced crisp, accurate copy. But he did present one challenge: Charlie stuttered. Taking dictation under deadline pressure from a stuttering reporter required patience. If Charlie got stuck on a word, he didn't want help, but the result was always worth the wait.

The typical apprenticeship in a wire service line bureau was three months. By August 1972, I was feeling fairly comfortable with the pace and diversity of writing and reporting in Kansas City, even though I wasn't going out to cover many stories. It was mostly phone work and rewrite.

In early September, the world was watching the appalling massacre at the Munich Olympics. I followed the story as best I could on my car radio, but I had more immediate concerns. I was being transferred.

In late August, UPI's state editor in Topeka, Pat O'Connor, announced he was leaving for a public relations job in Ohio. He didn't give much notice, so the bosses were in a bind. The state editor worked alone, covering state government and political news plus some news and sports outside the state capital. The Kansas City bureau helped when it could but not often.

With little time to fill the vacancy and no obvious candidates, UPI took a gamble. Jim Kidney called me into his office and, without any warning or set-up, offered me the job. Or, more to his style, he told me I had the job.

I had a surplus of self-confidence, but this was daunting. I had no idea how that job was done, and I didn't know much about state government or politics, other than what I had covered for the *Sun*. And then there was the issue of living in Topeka, a sleepy, vanilla kind of town my father had grown up hating. The city was a perfect fit for the old line, "I spent a whole week there one night."

Nevertheless, this was an opportunity to pad my resume, learn a new facet of the profession, and escape the comfortable obscurity of line bureau work. During the first week of September, I loaded my 1966 Ford Galaxy 500 with my few possessions and moved to a furnished apartment a few blocks from the capitol building.

In professional terms, it was a good move.

The UPI statehouse correspondent was responsible for reporting anything of interest in the Kansas capital city. I had a small office off *The Topeka Capital-Journal* newsroom and a desk and dedicated teletype machine in the capitol's press room. Everything out of Topeka was written in print style.

I spent almost all my time at the capitol press room to stay close to whatever action deserved coverage. Newsmakers would casually drop by to chat, spin, gripe, and schmooze. And why not? The press room cast of characters was irresistible. John Petterson, Ken Peterson (an old KU buddy), Leroy Towns, Roger Myers, and Laura Scott comprised an eclectic cohort that was at times hilarious, contentious, therapeutic, or inspiring.

The two leading inmates in that asylum were Lew Ferguson and Elon Torrance, the Associated Press tag team and my direct competitors. We were in separate rooms to shield our stuff from the other side. Lew was hitting his stride, and Elon had been there forever. Together, they knew everything and everybody of importance in Kansas. Early on, they cleaned my clock. Regular calls from Jim Kidney asked me why I didn't have a match for an AP story, or, when I did have one, why it was late.

I had to learn from scratch how to scrounge for news. I also learned the meaning of the journalism slogan "speed kills." The pressure to be first was constant in the wire service business. AP was the older, more widely used wire service in the United States, so UPI marketed itself as faster, nimbler and better written. Or at least tried to.

Alf Landon, the former governor and 1936 GOP presidential nominee, lived in a white mansion on a ranch west of Topeka. Long retired, he was still a respected voice in Kansas and national politics. I went to his home every year for the obligatory birthday interview. The story never amounted to much, but he did enjoy bumming cigarettes off me when his wife was out of the house. In our first meeting he was nice enough to mention that as governor, he had regularly ridden to work on a street car with my grandfather.

One Friday his office circulated the text of a speech he was making that weekend. As on every Friday, I was in a hurry to start my weekend when the transcript landed on my press room desk. I gave it a quick glance and banged out a story leading with Landon's endorsement of nationalizing America's passenger rail system.

The next morning, I happened to be at home and got a phone call from Landon himself. "There's a story about me on the front page of the Wichita paper this morning, and I think you wrote it," he said in his usual measured, conversational tone. "It says I favor nationalizing the railroads. I don't know where you got that, but I didn't say it and don't favor it."

I can still feel the sting of the blood rushing to my face. I rushed to the statehouse press room and checked his speech transcript again. Yep, I had screwed up. I had seen railroads and nationalization in the speech and had somehow fused them. I immediately filed a corrected story and then called to apologize. He accepted my apology and still granted me annual birthday interviews. My bosses were amazingly tolerant, preferring reprimand to dismissal. Lesson learned—slow down. That's easy to forget when the fires of competition are frying your tail.

In December I was pulled me back to Kansas City for a few weeks. Harry Truman was dying. The former president was admitted to Research Hospital, drawing a media death-watch crowd that filled the nursing school's gym. What started as a stakeout spot grew into an indoor media camp featuring cots, phone banks, folding tables for typewriters and other equipment along with generous supplies of sandwiches, cookies, and coffee from local stores. It wasn't a pig sty, but it wasn't fit for surgery either. I stayed with my parents.

On Christmas Eve, Truman's daughter Margaret went home to New York to spend Christmas Day with her family. We thought this was odd; some called it callous. But the end was near, and rumor mongers speculated the former president was kept alive artificially for a day or two for the sake of his daughter's holiday.

Meanwhile, bureau chief Jim Kidney got an idea that ruined my Christmas. We didn't know when Truman would die, but we knew where his body would go—a funeral home in his hometown of Independence, Missouri, east of Kansas City. Jim's wire service imagination spun up the idea that if Truman died on Christmas Day, his family might send the body to the funeral home and hold the announcement until the next day. But if UPI were there when the body arrived, we'd have a historic scoop.

Jim ordered me to stake out the funeral home and report the body's arrival, if it happened. At around 8 a.m., I parked on the back row of the funeral home's parking lot and waited. And waited. The weather was sunny but cold, forcing me to run the engine for heat. My Christmas breakfast was the same as my Christmas lunch—Hostess Ding Dongs. To pass the time, I carefully read *Playboy*. The articles seemed extraordinarily attractive in that edition. Around noon, people started showing up for visitations. Some would stare at me, and I'd put down the magazine. I wondered who would hold a visitation on Christmas, ignoring the fact that it wasn't Christmas for everybody. Jim sent me home after dark.

The day after Christmas, I was back in the crowded Research Hospital gym around 6 a.m. to rejoin the death watch. Radio and TV news crews were sleeping on the cots; other journalists and technicians were chatting almost in whispers while sipping coffee and wolfing down free goodies.

Then all hell broke loose.

A commotion on stage alerted everybody that an announcement was coming. It could only be one thing. Sleepers bolted from their cots, snackers dropped their treats, and everybody hurried to their assigned positions.

An official came to the microphone and announced that Harry Truman was dead at age 88. I was at the UPI table and snatched the phone linked directly to the New York desk while Paul Haney called the Dallas regional hub. I told the editor in New York that Truman was dead. He asked for the authentication code—May 8, Truman's birthday. Out went the 10-bell flash, and we were the first in the world to report the news. My one regret is that I never got a copy of that flash.

The next day my duties shifted to the Truman Presidential Library in Independence, where Truman's body lay in state. I was there in case anything out of the ordinary happened. Nothing did. The day of the funeral, with CBS correspondent Ike Pappas, I climbed onto the roof of a flower shop and watched the procession go by. Again, nothing.

The morning after the funeral, I was ordered to stake out the library garden where Truman was buried. My assignment was to interview the first person to visit the grave site. I was late. A few people were already in the garden, so I phoned in quotes from "some of the first" to visit the grave. That's called a "fudge" in the business, vague but accurate.

After the holidays, another real-world news clinic awaited me in Topeka. In early January, the Kansas legislature convened its annual session. My sleepy beat overnight exploded into too much news to handle. Kansas City sent a "legislative relief" reporter to help out. In 1973 it was John Braden, an enterprising reporter who always seemed to be running. A year later, it was Frank Cook, an irrepressible fellow Jayhawk hired from a small Missouri newspaper. He could be irreverent, boisterous, and really funny, but he was also a crackerjack reporter. Braden and Cook covered the Senate, and I took the more populated and complicated House, including committees where legislation was born and most of the news was generated.

In the ornate, wood-paneled House, reporters sat at a bench to the right of the speaker's chair facing the chamber. The press corps had a ringside seat to a political circus—members ranging from old to young, competent to laughable, ambitious to burned-out, rural to urban, smart to silly. It was hard to believe some of them could win an election. Being Kansans, some would quote the Bible for validation, and others would misquote it for effect. You could hear rants against the evil of fluoride in water. Some would denounce the sin of the bottle with liquor club cards in their vest pockets. When the members weren't cracking us up, we would mumble one-liners to each other. To be fair, Kansas was well governed in those days, sometimes in spite of itself.

We were nothing like the press room gang in *Front Page*, but we kept things loose. Many legislators, aides, and lobbyists played along. Some mornings we'd shuffle into the House chambers after a night of hard partying. A governor's aide surveyed us one morning and shook his head, saying, "Looks like you boys fell into a thicket of whizbangs." We'd find the Rev. Richard Taylor, leader of the Kansas United Dry Forces, and ask for a card to take the pledge. We didn't take it seriously, and neither did he.

One Saturday morning each month, the state Supreme Court would release a stack of decisions. Thumbing through opinions covering anything from criminal law to divorces to financial disputes was not how I wanted to start my weekend. I would pick two or three that seemed to speak to the masses and write them up, then nervously wait to hear if I had missed a truly important case the AP was reporting. To ease the selection process, I made a rule for myself. I tossed aside any decision using the words "fiduciary" or "escheat." I didn't know what they meant and couldn't imagine how they would have any real-world relevance. To my knowledge, that rule never got me in trouble.

The fall of 1972 threw me into yet another news arena—elections. I never had a chance to cover a presidential candidate; my reporting stuck to speeches and statements from Kansas candidates. It was a yawner, but it eased me into the art of covering campaigns.

The 1974 midterms were another matter. In the early months of that campaign season, state capitol managers decided to honor Kansans missing in action in Southeast Asia by planting three memorial trees on the statehouse grounds. One of the MIAs was Terry Murphy, a UPI freelancer lost somewhere in Cambodia. As the UPI representative in Topeka, I was asked to make a few remarks for a small crowd at the planting ceremony. U.S. Sen. Bob Dole, then running for his second term, also spoke. I talked about journalists having a duty to report the truth even if, as Americans, it hurts. Dole spoke less like a politician and more like the wounded World War II veteran he was. We shook hands afterward, and that was it. I thought.

A few days later, a member of Dole's campaign staff invited me to dinner. Expecting some sort of news tip, I accepted. As we sat at Poor Richard's eating salads, the conversation took an unexpected turn. Dole had been impressed with my remarks at the planting ceremony, and he wanted me to work for his campaign. I was too surprised to answer, so I said I'd think it over.

I knew I wouldn't and couldn't accept the job. The salary was less than my meager wire service pay, and I loved reporting too much to leave it. The final reason exposed my pathetic political instincts. I thought Dole would lose. He won a second term and went on to serve as GOP leader in the Senate, Gerald Ford's running mate in 1976, and the party's presidential nominee in 1996.

No instincts were required to cover Vern Miller, the state's attorney general. He was a small, pugnacious dynamo with fire in his eyes and a forward lean when he walked. He was a reporter's dream. On a slow news day, you could nose around Miller's office and eventually find something to write about. Moreover, his stunts would have fit nicely in any of the *Lethal Weapon* movies.

Miller waged a personal war on drugs that stretched the scope of his job description. He was determined to rid his state of mind-altering substances, starting with marijuana. His signature stunt started with investigators setting up a sting. When the perps showed up with the goods, Miller would jump out of a car trunk to make the arrest. More than once, journalists were invited to the show, just in case Kansas voters might want to see their attorney general and would-be governor in action.

When he cast his gaze on the state's prohibitionist liquor laws, he found novel ways to bring attention to himself and Kansas, with unintended consequences. After studying the state constitution's ban on liquor by the drink, Miller decided that the law extended up into Kansas air space. With great fanfare, he barred liquor sales to airline passengers over Kansas. The state was an instant laughingstock and fodder for late night TV comedians. Miller didn't care.

One of Miller's escapades ended in embarrassment for him and a professional black eye for me. Miller had heard about illegal gambling at a social club in Salina in central Kansas. He sensed an easy conquest, and his team invited me to string along. Miller's agents barged into the smoky, seedy clubhouse announcing a raid. Then the front door flew open and in walked this cigar-chomping, leather-jacketed mountain of a man with a star on his chest. He was the local sheriff, and he was not pleased, bellowing, "Who the hell comes in to my county to do a bust without telling me?" Hearing Miller's name inflamed his rage. He ordered the agents out of the club and out of the county. The agents, who had a legal right to operate in Salina, slinked out and left town, but not before calling Miller to report the fiasco. This, of course, was a way better story than the one I had expected.

My trouble started when Miller asked me not to do the story. I couldn't agree to that, so he then asked me to wait until he could talk to the sheriff and smooth things over. Then, he said he would give me an exclusive statement. Like an idiot, I agreed.

Later in the evening, I got a call from a reporter in Salina who had heard about the blow-up. He was just nosing around, but I knew I was about to lose my beat on the story. I tried to contact Miller to warn him that I had to file the story, but I couldn't find him. I filed it anyway.

The next morning, as radio news announcers all over Kansas read my account of the Salina fiasco, Miller ordered me into his office and, behind closed doors, called me a liar, a fraud, and a few other things (no profanity, though) and said he and his staff were through with cooperating with me forever. All I could do was apologize and explain why I did it. He didn't accept my apology, nor should he have. I had betrayed a source; I had broken a promise to the Kansas attorney general that I should not have made.

In the aftermath, I learned that in those days politicians and public figures did not hold grudges for long, or at least they tucked them away. Miller and his staff were soon talking to me as if nothing had happened. Maybe public officials tolerated bad behavior by reporters as a professional hazard. Maybe they felt reporters were essential for good public relations, even if they screwed up once in a while.

The Miller blow-up was unique. Usually, I enjoyed cordial relations with state government and political sources. It was not a social exercise; I needed them to compete with the AP guys. Lew and Elon were hooked into everyone and everything important in Topeka.

Away from politics and government, the Topeka area didn't have much news to offer. I did score an exclusive interview with the reclusive Linda Brown marking the 20th anniversary of the U.S. Supreme Court's landmark Brown vs. Board of Education of Topeka that struck down segregation in schools. Even though her name was on the decision, she didn't want to talk about it. I coaxed a few comments from her, so it was a story, but nothing special.

To survive the AP dominance, I had to be creative. I compiled a list of state agencies that dealt with topics I considered of interest to average Kansans. The insurance department, the transportation department, the revenue departments dealing with such things as taxes and vehicle registration, offices involved with public safety—populist journalism, if you want to call it that.

Take the director of the state health department. His portfolio included disease prevention and treatment, child and elderly health, and public sanitation—

responsibilities that touched the lives of nearly every Kansan at one time or another. I'd call to ask if there was anything new. The stories I got from this habit were not earth-shakers but were newsworthy: a new health program for schools, a new illness prevention campaign, a new health product in the state worth mentioning. These generated little 200-word stories that fit easily in a newspaper and, more importantly for UPI in Kansas, could be easily boiled down into short radio stories. Clients loved them, and just as importantly, they drove the AP guys nuts. Their bosses in Kansas City would hear one of these little gems on the radio and fire off a message to the Topeka bureau asking why AP didn't have the story. Lew Ferguson told me decades later of the irritation those simple little stories inflicted.

This trick also won me a bit of vindication at the KU journalism school. Dean Ed Bassett was still teaching a class on reporting public affairs (where he gave me a C+ for a national award-winning series). A student told me that in one class session Bassett praised me as a "master at massaging sources." That felt good.

One thing did not—Topeka. It was fine for raising a family, but for a single guy in his 20s, it was a social wasteland. Weeknights were so desolate I found time to teach myself to play a five-string banjo. I had a cluster of friends in the press corps, but after spending all week with them, I needed something and somewhere else for the weekends.

I spent most weekends in Kansas City. I'd stay with my best friend Mark Retonde, unless I was with my parents to protect my place in the will. Even in the big city, my social life was spotty, but anything was better than Topeka.

With the legislature out of session and other newsmakers on vacation or taking it easy, summers in Topeka were snoozers. In July 1973, I was recalled briefly to the Kansas City bureau to fill vacation vacancies, just long enough to embarrass myself in front of the President of United States.

Clarence Kelley, a former Kansas City police chief, was Richard Nixon's choice to head the Federal Bureau of Investigation after J. Edgar Hoover died. Nixon and Kelley came to Kansas City for the formal swearing-in ceremony at a downtown hotel near the bureau. I walked over to watch the arrivals and departures in case something broke.

Nothing did, except for my pants. As the limo carrying Nixon and Kelly rolled up to the hotel's entrance, I decided to climb onto a short stone wall for a better look. As I raised my leg up to the top of the wall, the back seat in my suit pants let go. It was an epic fail. I finished my climb and turned to see Nixon at that moment emerging from the limo. I doubt he saw me, but that didn't matter. I was mortified. In the modern age of security cameras and social media, the moment could have gone horribly viral. But in those days, all I had to worry about was standing very still until Nixon and Kelley entered the hotel and then walking with a mincing gait two blocks back to the bureau. The staff, mercifully all male that day, had their fun with my predicament and then sent me home.

Heading into 1974, my life had settled into a cyclical routine of weekdays in Topeka and weekends in Kansas City.

Then came a seismic shift in my career and my life.

On March 18, 1974, The Wire Service Guild, a branch of The Writers Guild, called a strike at UPI. I was not ready for this professionally, emotionally, or financially. I liked working and didn't want to stop.

Caving to peer pressure in Topeka, I had joined the union just before the strike. Assuming I was a member, I showed up at the Kansas City bureau on strike day and joined a four-person picket line. The bureau being in the same buildings as KMBC-TV, its evening news carried a brief report on the strike, including a shot of us picketing. My conservative parents were aghast.

The next day I asked the local union leader why I had never received a card. A check of union rolls found no evidence of my membership. That's all I needed to rationalize my way off the picket line and back to work. I hated the term "scab," but that's what I was.

With Frank Cook covering Topeka, I spent the next 23 straight days with Paul Haney, Jim Kidney, and a few other staffers grinding out stories to keep news flowing to clients. Our output required both routine news plus "enterprise" pieces to show clients we didn't need the strikers. We did, but that's how the game was played.

I came up with a story about an organic farmer before most people knew what "organic" meant. South of Kansas City I visited the boyhood home of Fred Funston, a national hero in the early 20th century who, as military commandant in San Francisco, is credited with saving much of the city after the 1906 earthquake. My story noted that historians later blamed Funston for inept fire control measures that spread the inferno. These and other stories were little more than pot-boilers to keep the wires humming.

A routine news day turned ghastly with word that a plane had crashed in southeast Missouri. I called the county sheriff's office for confirmation. A dispatcher told me it was a small airliner, and the death toll was nine with no survivors. The dispatcher could not identify the plane's owner, but she did have the registration numbers from the tail. I called the Federal Aviation Administration and used the number to learn who owned the plane.

Without thinking, I asked information for the number of the Maryland company listed as the owners, and called. A man answered, naming the company in his greeting. I told him who and where I was and started asking questions.

"Does your company own a plane?"

"Yes."

"Where is it now?"

"Flying company employees to Las Vegas."

"Is the pilot experienced?"

"Yes."

"Have you ever had any trouble with the plane?"

As the answers became increasingly short and tense, the gentleman finally asked, "Why are you calling? What's this about?"

They didn't know.

Paul Haney was standing behind me listening. He rushed out the door, refusing to hear any more.

I faced an agonizing choice: hang up or tell him. I told him. Each "Oh my God" got louder, and I could hear others around him scream as he blurted the news. All I could do was express my sympathy, tell him who to contact, and give him a phone number. He hung up without another word, and I was left with the task of writing that story. I wanted to include everything—my breaking the news, his reaction—but Paul wisely vetoed that idea.

So many lessons from those few minutes. There are times when the rush to gather news needs a limiter. Unintended consequences can ruin far more than a story. In a tragedy or disaster, journalists should be among the last people survivors talk to, not the first.

My capacity for compassion was tested again two weeks later in the waning days of the strike. A freelancer called in a story about an 18-year-old woman's first attempt at skydiving. The parachute never opened.

Chasing more information about the victim, I found her home phone number and called. A woman with a pleasant but subdued voice answered. I identified myself, expressed my condolences, and asked for confirmation of the victim's name and age. The woman on the line was her mother.

Out of respect, I planned to make the conversation as brief as empathy would allow. However, the mother started describing her daughter—pretty, red-haired, adventurous, popular. She told of other pastimes, of small and larger achievements in school and elsewhere. She rambled on for nearly a half hour. When she finally stopped, all I could do was repeat my sympathies and thank her, fighting the lump in my throat. I wrote a careful portrayal of the young victim's life and her mother's grief and then put it on the wire. I don't know if any client ever used it. I don't care.

On April 10, 1974, the 23-day strike ended with nobody winning. The union accepted a small raise and a few other minor concessions. Our strikers came back to work, and the local's leader filed a complaint against me for strike breaking. A quick investigation sided with the local and fined me one dollar. I never paid, and was never asked to. The professional atmosphere in the bureau returned to normal in a surprisingly short span of time. Credit goes to the union guys; they could have poisoned the workplace. It was not my last encounter with a strike, but the next outcome would be far different.

Other outcomes fermenting that spring had a little to do with work and everything to do with my life.

I had known Beth Retonde for years. Her brother Mark had been a fraternity brother in college and was my best friend. At first, Beth didn't like me much. We met when she was 17, skinny, cute with long blonde hair, whip-smart and contemptuous. I didn't pay that much attention to her when our paths would cross at the Retonde family home on Kansas City's south side.

After years of infrequent contact marked by mutual indifference, our paths converged in early 1974 as Beth was finishing her senior year as a journalism major at KU. She was an excellent student and a born copy editor. Graduation was approaching, and she was looking for a job. She deigned to ask me for help; I was glad to, but I considered Mark's little sister off limits for anything but networking.

A couple of lunches to talk about job-search strategy led to a few dinners to talk about more than job-searching strategy. She started showing up with me at parties in Topeka, drawing curious glances from the press room gang. If you must know, she always stayed overnight with friends.

By the time of the UPI strike, her employment outlook was not improving, but that didn't seem to matter much. We spent as much time together as strike and studies would allow. About two weeks after the strike ended, Beth and I capped a date with a late-night chat in the den of her parents' new home in another Kansas City suburb, Leawood. We weren't even sitting together when I suddenly lost my mind and asked her what she thought about the institution of marriage. That's not how she heard it. She asked if I was asking her to marry me. Truthfully, I had not planned to ask her at that moment, but I did. She said yes.

Paul and Jim knew about Beth, so they weren't surprised when soon after our engagement I asked to stay permanently in the Kansas City bureau. Frank Cook was doing a fine job in Topeka, so the UPI hierarchy approved the change and made Frank my permanent replacement.

By graduation day in May, Beth had a job as copy editor at a trade publication in Kansas City. We were married on September 14, 1974 by a priest who'd been a lifelong friend of the Retondes. Before the wedding, he scolded us for missing church prenuptial classes and reminded us of our duty to bear children for the Church. Years later he was convicted of pedophilia, was expelled from the priesthood, and was banished to his mother's home wearing an electronic anklet. And he had presumed to tell *us* how to live.

As we settled into married life, my work settled into an easy routine. An active sports market, Kansas City gave me the opportunity to cover pro and college football (Chiefs, Kansas, and Kansas State) and pro hockey (the short-lived Kansas City Scouts NHL franchise); I was an avid sports fan and a fast writer. That came in handy when a game seemed settled and everybody in the press box had started writing, only to have a late score change the outcome. Obsolete copy was ripped from typewriters, and keyboards rattled from frantic writing under sudden deadline pressure. I learned I could handle it.

Not long after I had settled down again in Kansas City, Jim Kidney left and was replaced by Dan Taylor from Denver. Jim and Dan were not polar opposites, but they came close. If Jim shaded toward the Lou Grant style of newsroom management, Dan brought a more relaxed style befitting the former ski bum he was. Jim was a better manager, but Dan made the bureau a lighter place to work.

Another change that spring heralded a revolution in wire services and the entire news industry. We got our first computers. These beige beasts with small green screens hogged the entire surface of a desk. They were hot, finicky, intolerant of ambient heat or static electricity, and had a bad habit of swallowing stories when almost finished. But they eliminated the need for teletype punching. The new devices sent stories directly to the wire, freeing writers from the drudgery of wire filing while also, sadly, eliminating any need for teletype operators. Some filled special needs for a while, and a few showed they were qualified to write. But most succumbed to technology, just like linotype operators at newspapers.

Those contraptions may have saved my job. The regional hub in Dallas was directly hooked into state broadcast and newspaper wires and could file stories to them when the local bureaus were closed overnight. My shift at the time started at 4 a.m., with the first broadcast copy of the day due on the wires by 5 a.m. An hour was plenty of time in normal circumstances, but I was often late and had to work with my hair on fire to get everything ready on time. A few times I was too late, and Dallas had to cover. But instead of firing me, Dallas took over the 5 a.m. filing duties and not long after that the 6 a.m. slot too. Those two extra hours of sleep were a life saver.

Early in 1975, I started agitating as best I could from the hinterlands for a shot at a bureau of my own. After all, I was approaching three whole years in the wire business, so I considered myself ripe enough to take the next step. Top management in New York didn't agree. In addition, I failed to recognize that my new ambition risked a dangerous schism in my career ambitions. The news business had far more staff jobs overseas than management postings. By feeding my ego with fantasies of management, I could be narrowing my chances for Germany.

By summer, headquarters had found a solution that didn't excite anybody. They offered me Detroit, but only as an assistant bureau manager. That meant staff status with just a few unspecified supervisory duties. I wasn't enthralled with a move to the Motor City, and I later learned that the incumbent bureau manager didn't want an assistant at all.

My wife had her own qualms about Detroit, but as we pondered the move, it grew on us. Beth expected plenty of career opportunities in that job market, and it would introduce us to what was still an exciting and thriving city. We shrugged, and I said yes.

In September, we left our hometown behind and moved into a modest townhouse in down-river Taylor, Michigan. A half-hour freeway drive ended at the Detroit Free Press building. The bureau on the 11th floor mirrored the Kansas City office, but with more desks, more space, more wire machines, and nearly double the staff. Bill Bell, the bureau manager, had years of experience in Europe. The business manager, Pat Harden, had shared time overseas with Bill, and they often traded insider one-liners that left the rest of us clueless. I thought their European connections might help me get a posting over there. That was a pipedream.

Bill was UPI's most cherished maniac. He was a news dynamo, notorious for shepherding a major story 24 hours a day, sleeping on or under a bureau desk for a few hours. Under stress, his bald, round head would turn red with veins popping out. His rapid-fire monologues were often meant for nobody in particular, and sometimes he would spray more than say. I never worked with a more competitive and perceptive journalist. Meanwhile, he stonewalled every mention I or his superiors made about the assistant bureau manager title. We got along, but he was in no mood to suffer any meddling from some snot-nosed interloper from the prairie.

The bureau staff was an easy-going collection of solid pros. Melanie Deeds was the secret glue holding the place together. Jim Higgins could cover anything well. Frank Lazari was a former teletype operator who had proven he could write for radio. Reliable Chris Mead handled the night desk. Jerry Wolffe was the disabled overnight staffer who was as courageous as he was capable. Others included auto industry writers Ed Lechtzin, Micheline Maynard, and Jeff Sheler.

Bill's stonewalling of my title did not spoil the job. Detroit and Michigan featured interlocking layers of economic and social diversity that generated a variety of news unimaginable in Kansas City. My byline started appearing on a regular basis on the A-wire, UPI's front page carrying only the most important national and international news of the day. A few of those first bylines topped stories about James Hoffa. The former Teamsters leader had vanished from a suburban Detroit restaurant five weeks before I arrived, and every day seemed to produce a major story about the mystery, even if most of them chronicled investigators' futility in trying to find out what happened.

In November, the ore carrier Edmund Fitzgerald sank in a Lake Superior storm. Being a Kansas boy, I was slow to understand the disaster's impact in Michigan, particularly the maritime community. I wrote about the memorial services, the investigations, and the recriminations that followed the loss of 29 men aboard a Great Lakes icon immortalized in Gordon Lightfoot's ballad.

Even though the bureau had a writer dedicated solely to auto news coverage, I got my share of exposure to that industry. I was in the press room of Ford headquarters in suburban Dearborn on September 14, 1976, as company and United Auto Workers negotiators were trying to avert a strike that started anyway the next day. Between periodic updates from spokesmen reporting no progress, the assembled journalists dined on lobster Newburg and napoleons courtesy of Ford management.

When I got home late that night, my stomach was gurgling as I told Beth about the fine Ford cuisine. Then she coldly reminded me that it was our second wedding anniversary. While I had pigged out at the Glass House, she had settled for McDonald's. The next 21 days of overtime strike coverage were a blessing both in terms of good experience and a cooling off period.

A shock wave rocked the bureau itself in 1976 when Bill, a self-declared wire service lifer, was lured to *The New York Daily News* to serve as its religion editor. I hated to see him go, but I worried about his health and hoped the slower pace at a newspaper would suit him.

The logical successor was a young UPI stalwart running the statehouse bureau in Lansing, Paul Varian. The selection made few waves in Detroit or beyond, but it had the force of a tsunami on my career.

Paul, 28 at the time, was a stocky, handsome, gruff-speaking Irish-American with no college degree, but he didn't need one. He was born into UPI; his father Harry was a career executive with the company. He was a natural for wire service work and was being groomed for greater things. He later rose to assistant managing editor and then foreign editor.

He moved in two doors down from us in Taylor with his fun-loving Scottish wife Sandra and their three young children. Having your boss as a neighbor and friend can be tricky, but it worked for all of us for many years and beyond Detroit.

One of his first declarations as bureau manager was to make me assistant bureau manager. Finally, I had a management title, and Paul delegated some of his duties to me as well. He put me in charge of staff scheduling, not much of a challenge in a bureau of 12. I also administered the bureau's network of freelancers. Most worked for UPI client newspapers and broadcast stations, and they would call in stories from their localities that they thought would be of wider interest. I kept a record of their submissions and compiled a monthly tally of what they were owed.

My role required weekend work with Tuesdays and Wednesdays off. Weekends featured a tidal wave of sports news that hit the bureau every Saturday from September to March. During their regular seasons, college football and basketball games ended roughly at the same time, and I would file up to a dozen stories in a two-hour span with no help. It was a test of my writing speed, work flow management, and sports expertise. I never worked harder in my life than on football and basketball Saturdays.

The bureau's sportswriter was Rich Shook, an effervescent character who could never sit still. Much of his work was done at game sites, so the bureau staff had to take his dictation and then file his stories. He made it easy. Paul also insisted on having him work every election night, and I saw why. Sports news is mostly verbalized numbers with quotes and context added. That's pretty much what election coverage is as well. Those sports coverage skills catapulted other journalists into far bigger jobs. ABC's Roone Arledge and Robin Roberts and HBO's Bryant Gumbel are just a few who come to mind.

But Shook couldn't do it all. When he needed help, I jumped in. I covered Michigan and Detroit Lions football, Detroit Tigers baseball, Detroit Red Wings hockey, and a PGA event, the Buick Open in Flint. Each sport produced memorable experiences, not all positive. I was surprised by the spartan (no, not Spartan) conditions in the Michigan Stadium press box, with its cold, utilitarian work spaces, bland food, and apparent indifference to the comfort of the men covering the games. I don't think sports reporters need luxury accommodations like they have today, but Michigan fell short of the norms in that era.

The PGA event was a boring day sitting under a steamy tent waiting for scores. I did manage to insult golf legend Sam Snead, attending as a VIP guest. He was wearing a blue blazer similar to a Johnny Miller number I had at home. I asked Snead if his was also a Miller jacket, and he snapped back that he would never wear anything with Miller's name on it. I don't think he meant to insult Miller; he was probably incensed that I would suggest he wore budget-brand blazers.

I covered baseball games at old Tiger Stadium when Shook had a conflict or needed a break. The press lounge atmosphere was always congenial and welcoming, even to a young stand-in like me. The Tigers' revered announcer Ernie Harwell treated me like a regular. The funniest man in baseball, network announcer Bob Ueker, shared his feelings about a recent ABC game broadcast that had gone terribly wrong. During the telecast, Ueker and his broadcast partners had relayed their best wishes on air to a boy who was battling terminal cancer. Later they found out the boy's parents had kept him unaware of his condition. While watching the game, he learned he was dying. Weeks later, Ueker was still having trouble talking about it.

One of the greatest baseball nights of the age was on a Monday in 1976. The Yankees were in town to play the Tigers, and rumors were flying that Yankees owner George Steinbrenner was about to fire manager Billy Martin. On the other side, the Tigers were riding the wave of national fascination with their phenom, pitcher Mark "The Bird" Fidrych. The mop-haired marvel known for talking to the baseball was that year's American League All Star starter on his way to rookie of the year honors. The pregame buzz was almost deafening.

That morning, as the Martin story was percolating, Paul asked me to canvas any Yankees I could find in hopes of getting an early tip on Martin's future. I called the team's hotel, the Pontchartrain, identified myself, and asked to speak to Yankee coach and national treasure Yogi Berra. Without any hesitation, the hotel operator connected me to his room. The phone rang, and the voice that answered was unmistakable. Masking my surprise, I asked a simple question: "Mr. Berra, do you know anything about Billy Martin's future?"

I heard a sigh, and he replied, "Look. I just got up. I'm sitting on the can, and I don't know nothin'."

What could I say? I thanked him and hung up. I wrestled with whether to use that gold-plated quote in my story about the buildup to the game, but I had too much respect for Berra. I paraphrased that he had heard nothing new.

My most extensive sports writing involved the Red Wings. In the late 70s, the franchise was emerging from years of mediocrity to become a playoff contender. My work was mostly limited to game coverages, but a few times I tried to spread my wings, only to get them clipped.

During the 1977-78 season, a young group of overachievers hustled the Red Wings to their first Stanley Cup playoff appearance in eight years. As the season progressed and they earned national attention, I wanted to take a closer look at General Manager Ted Lindsay, a Hall-of-Fame hero from the team's glory years. I thought a night-in-the-life feature on Gordie Howe's former line mate would make a good story.

Lindsay agreed to let me follow him around during a game but soon grew to regret the decision. I tailed him into the press box, into the high-priced seats, and into the general admission stands, eavesdropping on his conversations to get a feel for how the boss spent game nights. At first he ignored me, then started glancing over his shoulder at me as he talked, then glowered at me, and eventually tried to hide from me. He'd hurry from one spot to another without signaling where he was heading, and I labored to keep up with the still-fit Lindsay as he flitted around the arena. I gave up after the second period, having enough material for what turned out to be an okay story, but not what I had hoped.

Another inglorious moment came courtesy of another hockey deity, Scotty Bowman. At the time, he was head coach of the indomitable Montreal Canadiens. I don't remember much about the game, but I remember everything about my locker room interview with Bowman after his team had won.

I had formulated what I thought might qualify as one of the greatest hockey questions of all time. It involved tactics, player matchups, and more. Then I got to the locker room. After talking to the only other reporter in the room, he turned to me. On cue, I let fly with my monumental testament to hockey insight. I got through the preliminary thesis, then on to the main point, and then named a player whose actions validated that point, and then noticed the souring countenance of a future Hall of Famer. "Hey," he interrupted, "you like to talk a lot." My deflation was almost audible, and he was right. I finished with one quick sentence, he gave me a useless answer, and I left. Lesson learned: My job was to prompt sources to give compelling answers, not to regale them with brilliant questions. From then on, I always mentally rehearsed questions, even under stress, to distill them for brevity.

While sports offered an entertaining and welcome diversion, my day job was straight news. And Detroit throbbed with it. The Jimmy Hoffa case never seemed to lose the public's interest. Once a year, I drew the onerous assignment of trudging four blocks to another downtown high-rise housing the law offices of his son, James P. Hoffa, for the time-honored news gimmick, the "anniversary story." On or about July 31, I would sit down in his wood-paneled office and ask the obligatory questions: Do you know what happened to your father? How's your mother? How do you feel about what happened to your father? (A particularly loathsome thing to ask.) Will you ever try to lead the Teamsters Union? (He said no but later did.) Hoffa was always pleasant and cooperative. I always left with the ingredients for a decent story, but I hated doing it. It felt like a rude imposition on a still-grieving family.

Another national story with an odd twist involved future General Motors Chairman Robert Stempel. In November 1975, two men snatched his 13-year-old son Tim while the boy was skateboarding near his home in trendy Bloomfield Hills. The idea was to grab some rich kid for ransom. They had no idea their hostage's father was a top GM executive, and they got no hint from the news. Authorities wanted a news blackout to deny the kidnappers any information about their intense search for the boy, and local media complied, a remarkable concession in Detroit's dog-eat-dog news arena. It lasted four days until Stempel paid the ransom and his son returned home unharmed. Police caught the hapless kidnappers and recovered most of the $150,000 ransom. Then the public got the news.

Authorities said media cooperation helped save the boy, and we were all feeling pretty good about ourselves as a small gaggle of reporters gathered at the Stempel home seeking a statement from the family. For more than an hour we huddled in the snow and the cold. No invitation inside, not even into the garage to stay warm. We were miffed; after all, we had helped to assure their son's safe return home. We later heard second-hand that Mrs. Stempel feared we would soil her carpets. I don't recall ever hearing a thank you from the family.

I managed to scoop my own organization for one story. A Romanian-American Orthodox bishop, Valerian Trifa, had been holed up in Grass Lake, Michigan for years, fighting deportation as a suspected Nazi collaborator in his native Romania. A new legal turn in the case motivated New York to try, again, to interview Trifa. National writer Richard Gross asked us to find a phone number for the secluded cleric. I got on the case and found a promising number. I dialed it to see if it worked, and a man answered. It was Trifa. I identified myself but worried he wouldn't cooperate later when Gross could call. So I started asking questions, and he answered them. He repeated his claim of innocence, recited his sanitized version of his wartime record, and described his life under what amounted to self-imposed house arrest. I wrote the story and filed it to New York, where the exclusive appeared on the A-wire. Paul and others editors were impressed; Gross was livid. He accused me of disobeying instructions, of stealing his story, and probably a few other things I never heard about. Federal authorities later deported Trifa to Portugal, where he died in 1987.

I covered several court cases that drew nationwide interest and taught me some things about American justice. One involved John Swainson, a former governor who had lost both legs in World War II. Federal prosecutors had charged Swainson and two others with bribery, and I covered the trial daily. In the end, the jury acquitted Swainson and his two co-defendants of bribery but convicted him of perjury. He got a short sentence, but it ruined him. I never understood how he had lied about something he didn't do.

The most notorious case ensnared two Filipina nurses working in the intensive care unit of the Veterans Administration hospital in Ann Arbor. After a series of sudden deaths in 1975, federal prosecutors built a case alleging that the nurses had injected patients with poison to induce respiratory failure. The summer trial in 1977 was ugly, based mostly on circumstantial evidence and tinged with allegations of racism. The jury found them not guilty of murder but guilty of poisoning patients. I couldn't figure that one out either. The trial judge, however, had seen too much that bothered him, and he tossed out the verdicts the next February. The case was never tried again.

Both trials were cautionary tales. Federal prosecutors coaxed guilty verdicts from jurors using evidence that was sketchy at best. Since then, I have suspected that if the federal government really wants to get you, it will find a way.

I faced a personal trial in early 1978 when I decided to end 10 years of smoking. I was up to three packs a day, and cigarettes were giving me chronic headaches. One night when I complained, Beth said I should quit. The next day I had five smokes, and on February 22 at 1 a.m. I borrowed a Benson & Hedges from her for my last cigarette ever.

Cold turkey is not the recommended method for quitting, but that's what I did. Some people use gum or candy to replace the habit's oral component. I started with toothpicks, but they were too flimsy, so I switched to a pacifier. For three weeks I worked at my desk sucking a binky. When I explained, my colleagues kindly accepted it. Visitors stared but didn't say anything. After work I would spend an hour at a gym and, after dinner, go to the basement to listen to sports on the radio while tinkering with my model railroad. It all worked, and I've never had any tobacco product since. If I did, I know I'd start smoking again.

The rumbling of another UPI strike heralded a tectonic shift in my career. In the spring of 1978 negotiations between the Wire Service Guild and UPI were going nowhere. This time, I was a card-carrying union member. Detroit was, after all, a labor town, and I valued office harmony far more than I had four years earlier.

In May, talks broke down and the guild called a strike. On the appointed strike day, we showed up at the bureau armed with picket signs and ready to walk out at noon. Around 10 a.m., a call from the union stunned all of us. The strike was off. We were told that the parent Writers Guild had decided to pass on a UPI walkout to preserve its strike fund for an expected strike at *the New York Times*. We put away our signs and got back to work. With no leverage, the Wire Service Guild accepted a tepid contract offer from management, and the crisis passed.

But it bothered me. The company's offer had shown little appreciation of its workforce, and the union had shown that its priorities did not include protecting Unipressers, as we called ourselves. Added to that frustration was the company's continuing inability or refusal to find me a bureau of my own. I suspected I was being kept in Detroit to succeed Paul whenever he moved on, which he did in 1979.

All this led to one conclusion: It was time to leave. By this time Beth had switched careers to trust department work in a bank. With two incomes and a nice townhome in Detroit's southern exurbs, we were the most comfortable we had been in our marriage. Paul called us the first yuppies he ever knew. Beth had once volunteered without being asked that my career would always take precedence, so she agreed that our Detroit days were numbered. I don't know why, but finding another job in the area never entered my mind. I started looking.

I was invited to an interview at *The Charlotte Observer*, where I botched a wire editing exercise and then tanked the weirdest test I had ever taken. It had questions like whether I'd rather be a flower or a bush, my favorite color—all touchy-feely stuff that had nothing to do with journalism. This apparently was a trendy new way to vet prospective employees, favored no doubt by personnel offices (not yet called human resources) indifferent to the skills of the profession. The test room was three-sided with one wall of floor-to-ceiling glass, perhaps to watch me. I sat at a school desk, and the only other person in the room was a woman about 20 feet away. She was taking a test as well, but she whispered each question to herself. I was tempted to say something to her, but then I stopped myself. What if this is part of the test? Is this some way to see how I handle stress and distractions? I kept my mouth shut, finished the stupid test, and left. Understandably, I never heard back.

Another long-distance opportunity was in Corpus Christi, Texas. *The Caller* was looking for a city editor. Nice town, but the job wasn't for me.

In November, I spotted a cryptic classified ad about a job in Germany. It didn't identify the company, but its criteria seemed to fit my resume, and it was *Germany*, still my dream destination. When I was summoned for an interview in Washington, I learned whom I was dealing with—Radio Free Europe/Radio Liberty. All I knew about them was TV ads in the 50s asking viewers for donations to help the organization broadcast "the truth" to people behind the Iron Curtain. That didn't stop me. We were talking about Germany here.

The bureau manager, Tom Bodin, was friendly and encouraging. The writing test was easy. Then Bodin threw me a curve, handing me a German-language story (the fatal poisoning of a Bulgarian in London with an umbrella), which I translated into English copy. Bodin explained that RFE/RL was based in Munich. A central newsroom wrote stories in English that were translated into various languages for news broadcasts to Eastern Europe and the Soviet Union. The pay was good, the benefits sounded too good, and I was stoked. I went home and told Beth that I was expecting an offer. She had established herself as a bank trust department officer and enjoyed the work. Nevertheless, she agreed to it if the opportunity arrived.

It finally did, in early February, with a Bodin phone call. I accepted immediately, but I said I needed a written offer before I could resign from UPI. No problem, he said, but he mailed it first class, and it took five agonizing days to reach me. I guess it hadn't been urgent for Bodin, but it was life-changing for me.

When I told Paul, he was disappointed. When he relayed my decision to UPI Vice President H. L. Stevenson, his reaction was, "Well, if he wants to go write propaganda, I guess that's his choice."

We might as well get this out of the way now. The word "propaganda" will appear in several passages of this narrative. In America, propaganda is a dirty word for dishonest or misleading information. That's too narrow and simplistic.

If the goal of news is to inform, the goal of propaganda is to persuade. Propaganda is the selective use of words and images to promote the source or disparage an adversary. Advertising, particularly political advertising, can be labeled propaganda—accentuating the positive attributes of a candidate or product or the negative traits of the competition.

Some dictionaries list both advocacy and disinformation as synonyms for propaganda. All propaganda is advocacy; not all propaganda is disinformation. The most effective propaganda features a credible core, *real or perceived,* augmented by supporting facts and observations.

Hitler may have been the world's first master of mass propaganda. All he needed was the traditional anti-Semitic *perception* of Jews in Germany and elsewhere to build ideological scaffolding for the Holocaust. The Soviet Union used the inequalities in American life (racism, poverty) to "prove" the evils of capitalism. The West did the same with the economic failures and suppression of human rights under communism. Both sides provided ample foreign policy hooks for easy propaganda—Hungary and Czechoslovakia, colonial Africa and Vietnam, to name a few on each side.

Dishonest propaganda used to be bad propaganda. That has changed. Information framed to fit the tribal worldview of a particular audience is now often rebuttal-proof. Some segments of societies in America and elsewhere are mired in a post-factual fantasy land. Nobody knows how to make someone believe something they don't want to believe or reject something they perceive as true. That is the fundamental challenge for journalism in the 21st Century – how to make facts matter again.

For those with open minds, what differentiates news from propaganda are balance and context. A story can fight off the propaganda label if it presents all sides of an issue with some explanation of its background and meaning. All a journalist can do is present an accurate story that is as comprehensive as time or space allows, then let it go.

As we headed for Munich, I didn't care one way or the other about propaganda. Fiddle dee dee. I would worry about that later. I was moving to Germany! And on generous terms I could have never expected. Beth and I sold what we could, tossed more, and exploited RFE/RL's moving allowance to stuff what was left into a 20-foot container.

On March 16, 1979, we boarded our one-way flight and headed off to fulfill my lifetime goal, and I wasn't even 30 yet.

# CHAPTER 5
# Radio Free Europe / Radio Liberty

*To the Mountaintop and Beyond*

During my early days at Radio Free Europe/Radio Liberty, I confronted a chasm of ignorance yawning before me. The headquarters building gave no hint of the challenges waiting inside. The bland two-story stucco structure with its main core and six wings flanked the eastern side of Munich's sprawling English Garden. The interior was just as utilitarian until the broadcast studios and master control room betrayed the real purpose of the place.

Radio Free Europe spoke to the Soviet satellites—Poland, Czechoslovakia, Hungary, Romania, and Bulgaria—plus Albania. Radio Liberty, which Congress merged with RFE in 1976, targeted all 15 Soviet republics. In all, RFE/RL broadcast in 25 languages, but not English or German.

The RFE/RL mission was unique. The Voice of America, BBC, and other government-funded broadcasters spoke to the world, as did Radio Moscow and its Warsaw Pact clones. RFE/RL, however, spoke to audiences inside the Soviet Union and its allies, presenting itself as the radio service they would have if they were free democracies. While all foreign radio broadcasts annoyed Communist governments, the programming originating in Munich drove them nuts. Most of their expensive jamming efforts were directed at RFE/RL, but they could never completely block the multiple shortwave signals carrying what Moscow called "black propaganda."

The nexus of this operation was the central newsroom, a rectangular room about half the size of a basketball court with large windows looking out into the English Garden. Each desk had a computer terminal connected to a primitive server, the concentrator, in its own glass booth. It was new and temperamental and required the only air conditioner in the building. Clustered in the center of the room were four desks facing each other in a square. They were for the supervising editor who served as shift boss, a slot editor monitoring news agency copy, a German news desk looking at German media, and a central monitoring desk with printers spewing English-language news from more than a dozen Communist countries. Behind this cluster were desks for writers. An adjacent room separated by a glass partition held more desks for feature writers and special projects. It was efficient and unpretentious, and for the language services it was omnipotent.

House rules required precise translation of Central News copy. If a language service wanted to air a story it had found on its own, it needed Central News authorization first. A broadcast analysis unit ensured compliance, and violations, though rare, carried devastating repercussions for the perpetrators and their supervisors.

My initiation into Central News was as a writer of brief new items similar in length to UPI broadcast items and written in a matter-of-fact style that would be easy to translate. Nothing to it, I thought.

That's when I discovered the depth of my ignorance. Editors patiently guided me into the world of international news writing, particularly for our target countries.

A random short list of what I had to learn included:

"Soviet" and "Russian" were not synonymous. Russia was just one Soviet republic.

"Billion" was 1,000 million in some places, 100 million in others.

What I called wheat was corn to others, and what I called corn was maize to others.

In some legal systems, a suspect was "detained" before charges. The status moved to "arrested" after charges were filed.

There was a difference between president (head of state) and prime minister or premier or chancellor (head of government). A summit meeting involved only heads of state.

In many countries, buildings have a ground floor and then a first floor.

A "two-source" rule was rigidly enforced. Writers scoured multiple news agency stories to find verification for every line of their stories. Attribution rules were just as stringent; we learned that who said something could be as important as what they said. If an interior ministry said it was deploying its forces (i.e., internal police) to quell unrest, that was one thing. If a defense ministry said it was deploying its forces (i.e., the army) that was far more serious. The entire list of what I had to learn could fill an encyclopedia and should for any journalist serious about meticulous writing. Central News veterans, including me, would argue that their work never faced more rigorous editing.

Central News exposed us to so much background and context in news that we took pride in our ability to argue all sides of an issue with facts and without emotion. We were encouraged to dig deeper into source material to find that morsel of balance or rebuttal to make our writing journalistically bulletproof. Accuracy was not enough. We sought precision to the point that any expert on any topic would have had no issues with a Central News story on their specialty.

Above all, our copy was to be impartial in content and tone, which might seem odd when stacked up against RFE/RL's mission as an anti-Communist radio operation. We could not write anything that listeners would perceive as insulting or condescending to their countries or communities. On the other hand, we routinely reported news that put the United States and other Western democracies in a bad light. Offending a target audience or protecting the image of the West eroded credibility and therefore trust, as verified by audience research.

Looming over the entire organization was the shame of 1956, when the Hungarian service encouraged rebels to keep fighting with a false promise of outside help. RFE/RL was determined to never repeat an episode like that. Subsequent broadcasts to Czechoslovakia in 1968 and Poland throughout the 1980s proved that the lesson had been learned.

As I waded through the morass of my ignorance, I started to understand what was expected of me. And just in time, because 1979 turned out to be a helluva year for news. The Three Mile Island nuclear plant melted down just a few days after I arrived. Later in the year, newscasts often led with regime change in Iran and the seizure of diplomatic staff at the U.S. embassy. In different ways, both were black eyes for America, but they were examples of our "warts and all" coverage mandate. In late December, the Soviet Union invaded Afghanistan, prompting creation of Radio Free Afghanistan. Our news stories regularly chronicled the messes both superpowers created for themselves.

By this time, I was acclimating to the newsroom managers and staff, an eclectic, iconic, sometimes irascible, sometimes engaging and always fascinating collection of talented characters.

Jim Edwards was the boss. An RFE/RL veteran, he had left his beloved Paris to take a job he didn't really want. A compact, mustachioed Englishman, Edwards's focus was external, dealing with the top bosses and the heads of the language services to meet their demands and needs while zealously protecting the political independence of his newsroom. His deputy was Canadian Barry Griffiths, an opera-loving and chess-playing editor's editor. He was a patient and friendly mentor, never tolerating any violation of newsroom standards. He was the only superior ever to tell me to slow down.

And then there was Indianan Larry McCoy, the senior supervising editor. An avid basketball player and skier, Larry had interesting people skills. His critics said he had none, but that's way too harsh. His journalistic skills were unmatched, his standards were Olympian, and he applied them to everyone. His critiques could be loud, sarcastic or eviscerating—sometimes all three—but never malicious. He baffled some colleagues, entertained most, and intimidated a few. He motivated me to challenge my work before he could. I thought he was a hoot.

The writing staff ranged in age from under 30 to over 60 and comprised mostly non-Americans: English, Scots, Welsh, Irish, South Africans, Australians, New Zealanders, and a few Germans. The small American contingent was, like me, there mostly for the experience of working in a foreign country.

In July, I got a painful introduction to Germany's world-class health care system. Running for a bus after a night shift, I slipped on a wet leaf and fell on my right elbow, snapping the end of a bone off like a stalk of celery. I stumbled my way back through the rain to the building and had a security guard call a cab, which took me to Krankenhaus Rechts der Isar, the main teaching hospital in Munich. A doctor told me there were no operating times available and I would have to wait three weeks. Then he asked to see my insurance card. It was a private plan, not the government-paid public one. Well, that was a different story. He checked the operating schedule again, and I went under the knife three hours later. They put me in a private room, much nicer than the ward designated for public insurance holders. Until then, I had not known that Germany's vaunted universal health care featured upper and lower tiers.

As I adjusted to the newsroom's functions, I started getting special tasks beyond routine writing. I worked the slot, monitoring the major news services, collecting news agency copy for writers and editing their stories before sending them to the broadcast services on an internal network. Editing was something new for me, and I liked it. I could see how other writers worked, and checking their writing improved my writing.

Juggling all that news content, I learned how to recognize all sides of an issue and the role critical thinking can play in writing, as opposed to rote regurgitation of information. Working with copy from a half dozen news agencies taught me the dangers they posed. Their product could be the journalistic equivalent of processed cheese. An international story could change in wording and meaning as it passed through a reporter, translator, rewrite editor, and desk editor before reaching the client newspaper or broadcaster.

Like processed cheese devoid of nutritional value, processed news may not have much journalistic value unless a skilled writer handles it carefully and skillfully by seeking a second source, hunting for background and context and then writing only what is evident, not just apparent.

With more frequent editing shifts, my preference slid from writing to editing. I had already pretty much left reporting behind, but not entirely.

In November 1980, Edwards sent me to Madrid to cover the Conference on Security and Cooperation in Europe, an early East-West attempt at nuclear arms control. I was to assist Rolie Eggleston, a Central News mainstay who had covered all the previous sessions and knew more about the process than the diplomats. Eggleston, an Australian, walked as if none of his parts fit, but he was an intrepid scribe.

Nobody in Munich ever said anything, but I think my Madrid stories stunk. The subject matter was obtuse, and I tried to write stories with a brevity that suited radio news. I was never told that the language services wanted longer pieces for feature programs. It was my only road assignment for Central News.

I managed to pick up a case of intestinal flu that kept me in my hotel room for the last two days of the conference. (Rolie didn't need me anyway.) Having never been to Spain, I took a couple of extra days to look around. The highlight was the Prado, one of the world's great art museums. Still feeling the flu's aftermath, I walked gingerly through the galleries, and turning one corner, I came face to face with Griffin Bell, the U.S. attorney general and a delegate at the conference. Just as I made eye contact, my gut cramped, forcing me to bow. Bell, not sure what to make of this, returned my bow. He walked away, and we never said a word to each other.

Bell's boss, President Jimmy Carter, was no fan of RFE/RL. He and other Democrats in Washington worried that RFE/RL interfered with efforts for better East-West relations. We had heard that the administration might even close us down.

*1981: Aftermath of the RFE/RL bombing in Munich, orchestrated by Carlos the Jackal. (Courtesy RFE/RL)*

This underscored the different attitudes of the two major political parties regarding international broadcasting. Democrats tended to see it as a dirty business unworthy of a liberal democracy. Republicans viewed it as a tool for hammering the world with information emphasizing the superiority of Western political systems and values and the evil of America's adversaries.

That contrast came into play after Carter lost to Ronald Reagan. The new Republican administration wanted more funding for RFE/RL to rattle communism's cage. Most Central News staffers liked the idea of a bigger budget but worried about the new ideology.

About a month after Reagan's inauguration in 1981, RFE/RL took a gut punch. On February 21, a Saturday, only 40 people out of the entire staff of 1,000 were at work. In the newsroom, four were finishing the evening shift—supervising editor Roy Fairbairn, Terry Willey, Breffni O'Rourke, and myself.

At 9:47 p.m., a soul-shaking explosion hammered the building. A remote signal had touched off at least 20 pounds of sophisticated explosives. The blast rattled windows a half-mile away and was heard throughout Munich.

The detonation pulverized the building's phone center. Roy, an unflappable Scot, told me to run to a pay phone down the street and call the on-duty executive, RFE Director Jim Brown. As I hurried out the front entrance, a middle-aged woman staggered past me, slowly climbing the steps and clutching the railing. Blood covered her face. She could not cry but managed a pitiable whimper as her trachea dangled from a gash in her throat. It was Maria Pulda of the Czech service. The bomb had been placed against a wall outside her office. Terry didn't wait for an ambulance and drove her to a hospital, probably saving Maria's life. Three other employees were wounded that night, but nobody died.

I reached the pay phone, made the call, and rushed back to help. That was when I saw the extent of damage. The blast had disintegrated a load-bearing column where a wing was attached to the main core, leaving a huge hole partly clogged by debris. Across the street, the shock wave had popped a tennis court canopy like a balloon. About 100 yards to the east I could hear glass still falling from dozens of windows that had been shattered in apartments facing our building. Two people there were hurt by flying glass.

First responders were arriving as I returned to the newsroom. My reporter's juices started flowing. Without any authority I went to our newsroom teletype machine and typed out two quick lines about the bombing, fed the tape into the reader, dialed up UPI (of course), and hit send. After the message was out, I started to dial up the Associated Press when a Bavarian policeman in a standard green uniform walked in with a gorgeous German shepherd on a leash. In a very proper, controlled Bavarian dialect, he told me to leave the building. Speaking German, I tried to explain that I only needed a minute to send the news bulletin. He frowned and jerked the dog's leash. It was not a particularly vicious growl, but it worked.

I joined colleagues in the freezing cold in the front circular driveway, where we stood and watched until well past midnight. As I was about to go home, a U.S. Army major drove up in a Jeep, hopped out, and tried to ask questions. When nobody paid much attention to him, he started pacing back and forth, mumbling to nobody in particular, "The President isn't going to like this."

It took a while to know whether the President cared at all. On Monday, the administration finally issued a rather bland statement condemning the attack, but it came from Secretary of State Alexander Haig, not the White House.

More than a decade later, documents found among secret police files in East Germany pinned the attack on none other than Carlos the Jackal, who was hired by agents of Romanian leader Nicolai Ceausescu. The Carlos henchman who planted that bomb was eventually tried in Berlin. Maria Pulda was in the courtroom for his sentencing.

The bombing forced construction of a high concrete wall around the building with a remote-controlled metal entry gate. There had been earlier attempts to sabotage RFE/RL, such as the time someone put poison in the café's salt shakers. None had altered the station's open, park-like setting. Now it had more of a fortress feel. It couldn't be helped, but it was depressing.

At the time of the bombing, RFE/RL was deep into coverage of its most significant and perilous story. The previous summer, food price hikes and other grievances in Poland had proven too much for workers along the Baltic coast, notably in Gdansk. Strikes broke out at the Lenin Shipyard, spawning a protest group called Solidarity headed by an electrician, Lech Walesa. The regime tried to keep a lid on the crisis, but enough news leaked out for RFE/RL to broadcast news, analysis, and international reaction. On West German television, we saw men walking among the strikers with boom-boxes blaring RFE/RL broadcasts that had pierced the jamming.

The pressure on Central News was immense, due in part to the legacy of Hungary. The Polish service was under strict orders to broadcast only news produced and approved by the news division. All of us knew that one mistake, one inflammatory or poorly crafted story could cause tragedy in Poland and maybe even beyond. What we wrote could get people killed.

A couple of Polish broadcasters used obscenities to describe Polish government leaders; they were fired. On the rare occasions when something needed correcting, help came from sources within Poland, from ordinary citizens to high-ranking officials taking risks to contact us. Once a deputy prime minister went to the U.S. embassy in Warsaw with a clarification to be relayed to Munich.

Walesa, Poland's first post-communism president, was asked what role the Polish service played in bringing democracy to his country. His answer: "Would there be an earth without a sun?"

Another constant headliner in those days was the Soviet invasion and occupation of Afghanistan. It was hard to know what was happening with sketchy information from official Soviet pronouncements and periodic tips from inside the country.

That's when British Prime Minister Margaret Thatcher decided to play editor. Having forged a conservative bond with Reagan, her influence trickled down one day into the newsroom log book, a journal of routine newsroom matters. A note announced that we were to identify the Afghan mujahedeen fighting the Soviet occupiers as "freedom fighters." In normal times that loaded label would have never been allowed in Central News copy, but now it was mandated. Fast forward 20 years. Calling the Taliban, Osama bin Laden, and various war lords "freedom fighters" was an atrocity. I'm glad it was the only such interference I experienced in Munich.

Life in Munich away from work had gone from good to ideal. The start had been rough for Beth, who sat alone all day in our small apartment, not speaking the language, afraid to go out, and passing the time mostly with books and American Forces Radio. It didn't help when the container carrying our household goods arrived with a hole in the top, where sea water had leaked in during the voyage across the Atlantic. Not much of value was ruined, and the hurt was eased when a stuffy insurance adjuster from Lloyds of London arrived to appraise the damage. He came right out of central casting, with a gray raincoat and bowler hat. We had laid out damaged items on a table, and the first item he picked up was a small, rusting wrought iron wine rack worth $10 at most. "So this was an antique," he noted, holding it in the air for emphasis. When we tried to correct his assessment, he persisted. "No, it looks like an antique to me." He proceeded to appraise nearly every damaged item as an heirloom, collector's item, or treasure of some kind. Turns out he felt sorry for us (mostly Beth). We made a nice profit from that "disaster."

When Beth found work at the Stars and Stripes bookstore in the RFE/RL basement, that's when we started really having fun. We traveled whenever we could.

Visits to my German relatives and weekend trips to Florence and Vienna were just the start. After thinking we didn't want a car, we couldn't resist an orange 1976 MGB for sale on the street. The next three years we drove all over Western Europe, mostly France and Italy. We learned to ski, which made Munich's long, gray winters tolerable.

There were adjustments to make, of course. Religion directly affected secular life in ways Americans would never expect. In heavily Roman Catholic Bavaria, church holidays were bank holidays. The ribald pre-Lent party season called Fasching was tolerated, but anyone displaying any form of frivolity on Ash Wednesday risked a police citation. The tranquility of the Sabbath was sacrosanct; no car washing, apartment vacuuming, or any other noisy activities were allowed.

Stores closed every weeknight at 6:30 p.m., 2 p.m. on Saturdays, except for the first "long" Saturday of each month and every Saturday during Advent. Sundays were for families, not shopping. Stores in train stations were open for travelers, who had to show tickets before they could buy something. Convenience stores along major routes were open for motorists needing fuel or refreshments on their journey. By law, stores could hold sales twice a year—the summer closeout sale and the winter closeout sale. The government dictated which items were to go on sale. It all felt like restraint of trade to me, but we learned to adjust.

Life in Munich had plenty of bright spots. The city itself was a jewel; every day we walked out of work and into a world-class tourist destination full of recreational and cultural opportunities. We never had time to see all of the city's museums and art galleries. Concerts catered to every musical taste. We listened to Germans quietly humming along with Pavarotti at the Nationaltheater and lustily singing along with Johnny Cash at the Olympiahalle. He had served in the Air Force in Germany, earning a devoted German following. World championships in boxing and ice hockey were among the endless sports attractions.

In the summer of 1981, I qualified for home leave—an extra month of vacation with air fare and expense money thrown in. We started and ended in Kansas City, but a ridiculous airline deal took us to San Francisco, Las Vegas, New Orleans, Denver, and Utah for a three-day float trip.

In December I launched my movie career. It lasted all of one scene. *Inside the Third Reich*, a TV film based on Albert Speer's memoir, was filmed in Munich. When the Armed Forces Network station said the producers were looking for extras, I had to try. An outdoor filming session at studios south of Munich put me in a crowd threatening Adolf Hitler, played by Derek Jacobi. I must have been too tame because I was cut out of that scene. My role in the other session, however, is preserved for posterity. A scene filmed at Munich's luxurious Hotel Bayerischer Hof was set in a dining room, where Speer's wife, played by Blythe Danner, and Speer's father, played by Sir John Gielgud, discussed trouble in her marriage. Every time Danner was on camera, a mustachioed fellow eating steak and drinking wine (actually grape juice) graced the shot over her left shoulder. After eight hours of good eating and watching how films are made, I walked away with 80 D-marks in my pocket and immortality assured.

Heading into 1982, life was good, but I couldn't leave well enough alone. Expatriates tend to get nervous about when and how they will get back home. They worry that staying abroad too long will eventually erase their career paths and leave them exiled. I got that twitch in the early months of 1982, a sign of my inexplicable penchant for needing a change about every three years. In May, I booked a flight to Detroit, ostensibly to attend that city's first Formula One race. But I also had arranged a few job interviews in Atlanta and Washington, just to see what was out there.

In Atlanta, I stopped by a new enterprise called CNN. I was offered a writing job, but the pay killed that idea. National Public Radio in Washington was looking for a Morning Edition editor. The 3 a.m. start time derailed that discussion.

My third stop was at the temporary headquarters of a national daily that was being launched by Gannett Corp., the nation's largest newspaper group. I had interned at the Gannett newspaper in Rochester, New York, and a few of the people I had met there were now involved in the new project, which was named *USA Today*. I was fascinated by the concept—a colorful national daily with easy-to-read short stories catering to the presumed shorter attention spans of television news consumers. Even the boxes for street sales looked like TV sets. Most importantly, despite its U.S. focus, it would offer international news in its front section every day.

I met with several editors, including John Walter, whom I knew from Rochester, and it all felt right. They wanted an editor for what they called the World Page, and they thought my experience would dovetail nicely with their writing philosophy. For a start-up, it paid well.

This was my career zipline back to the U.S.A. I was sure it would succeed. If not, I would be in the Washington area, where I'd surely have no trouble finding something else to do. Another landing zone could be somewhere in the burgeoning Gannett empire.

First, I had to persuade Beth. Once again, I was ripping her out of a comfort zone. She had come 180 degrees on Munich and loved it. A year earlier, RFE/RL had found us a bigger apartment in northwest Munich within walking distance of the Olympic Park. It even had a garage. She had a fun job, and we had friends. But it didn't take long for her to agree to the move.

My bosses said they were sorry to see me go, and the staff threw us a nice farewell party. By the end of July, we were gone.

# CHAPTER 6
# USA Today

## *Launch It, Love It, Leave It*

I arrived at *USA Today* with unshakable confidence in the future—both the paper's and mine. Even at 33, I could envision spending the rest of my career as a founding staff member at The Nation's Newspaper.

After some time in temporary offices, we relocated to the 14th floor of the gleaming USA Today tower in Rosslyn, Va., across the Potomac from the Lincoln Memorial. Production of prototype issues started before all the furniture was in place. Founder Al Neuharth and his team had given the staff a clear mandate: *USA Today* was to be colorful, readable, and interesting with plenty of "positive" news to offset the normal news diet of gloom and doom.

National editor Nancy Woodhull asked me to write templates of news briefs that would fill the left edges of inside pages. What I produced were in effect radio briefs in newspaper style. She used my examples as teaching tools for other writers, some of whom struggled with it. Most staff members were on temporary loan to *USA Today* from Gannett newspapers around the country. I heard plenty of gripes that stories couldn't be properly told with the paper's insistence on brevity. Most staffers came around in time, but outside critics took longer to be convinced.

As launch day approached, the staff started filling up, and the World Page crew took shape. I had arrived thinking I would be World Page editor, only to be told the title was co-World Page editor. I guess they weren't sure I could manage the page. Enter Don Kirk, an experienced foreign correspondent who had spent a lot of time in Asia. He was a published author, so the bosses decided he should be the page editor. I had to settle for assistant editor. I'm not sure why it didn't bother me much, but we all had too many other things to worry about. The page staff was fleshed out with David Bauman, Juan Walte, Paul Hoversten, and John Brinkley (David Brinkley's son). We all had experience that fit the needs of a foreign news page, and we worked well together. We were tucked away in a corner of the newsroom, and I suspect we were viewed as an oddball collection of repatriated expatriates.

In the early days, morning editorial meetings were unnerving, but not for editorial reasons. Our conference room's floor-to-ceiling windows faced northeast, and we watched airliners glide by on their approaches to Ronald Reagan National Airport. If the planes drifted a bit to the right, we could see faces in the windows. After a Gannett call to the Federal Aviation Administration, airlines were ordered to adjust their flight path farther over the Potomac.

Those morning meetings were similar to the ones held every day in every newsroom. Stories were discussed, priorities set, and coverages assigned. The meetings at *USA Today*, however, featured something I had never seen and didn't much like. Editorial meetings I had attended elsewhere picked a topic to cover but left the focus and particulars to whatever the reporter learned from working on the story. At this newspaper, the morning meeting specified topics as well as what the story was about. Reporters were then expected to confirm the premise—in effect starting their work with a preconceived idea of what to write. I squirmed but said nothing. Nobody else objected, and who was I to raise my hand?

*USA Today* was to roll out city by city, with Washington up first on September 15, 1982. The night before, as the staff put together that first edition, the World Page team was expecting to lead the historic first front page with the assassination of Lebanon Prime Minister Bashir Gemayel. Around 6 p.m. Nancy Woodhull was walking past our desks when bulletins popped up from all the news agencies. Monaco's Princess Grace, the American former actress Grace Kelly, had just died. She had been badly injured in a car accident a few days earlier, but she had been expected to recover. I told Nancy, who started to say that wasn't possible, froze in mid-sentence, and hurried off to tell Neuharth and the other top editors.

What followed was an editorial debate that is still discussed in journalism classes. The World Page crew, of course, argued that Gemayel's death would have far-reaching consequences in the eternally unstable Middle East. Neuharth and others countered that the death of Grace Kelly was essentially about an American goddess and deserved to lead the front page. He won, and the inaugural edition hit Washington streets early the next morning with a headline screaming "America's Princess Grace dies in Monaco." Gemayel was relegated to the World Page.

Neuharth was right, of course. For this newspaper's first edition, the story about the shocking death of America's fairy-tale princess had to be the lead. Years later Neuharth would confess that on its first front page, the newspaper's headline violated a major style rule. Whenever possible, the paper would use USA for all things American, a nifty bit of brand reinforcement. That first lead headline should have read "USA's Princess Grace dies in Monaco." Another front-page headline was arguably worse. Over a color photo of an airliner crash in Spain, the headline read: "Miracle: 327 survive, 55 die." Think about it; there was nothing miraculous about 55 deaths.

Everything went as planned that first day. At 25 cents a copy, the newspaper was a sellout. Then we had to do it again, every weekday. Each Monday, *USA Today* showed up in a new city. Atlanta, Minneapolis, Pittsburgh, Seattle, San Francisco and so on. New York met *USA Today* on April 24, 1983. Staggered launches continued for almost two years. By that time, it was a historic success, making a profit in less than five years while the industry mimicked its use of front-page color and other innovations.

*The Columbia Journalism Review* took notice of the paper's success in its March/April 1983 edition. Interviewing me in the newsroom with official permission, the author asked me to talk about the paper's tight writing style.

Here's what appeared in her article:

*The stories are short. They rarely contain more than one idea.*

*The (internal writing) guide advises: "KEEP IT TIGHT. Propel the story with punctuation. Colons, semi-colons, bullets and dashes can replace some words. Condense background information. Don't prattle on for several grafs explaining what happened at Love Canal, or spend an entire graf telling who Phyllis Schlafly is. Our readers are well informed.*

*One enthusiastic proponent of these points is Ted Iliff, assistant world editor, who came to USA from Radio Free Europe in Munich. "This is one of the few newspapers I feel comfortable working with," says Iliff. "In radio, you learn to keep it tight; you learn what to keep out. The first thing that goes is tedious background." The second thing is "tedious attribution." (Of course, Iliff hastens to add attribution is needed in stories about a claim or an allegation or a theory.) Quotes, he says, are often "too much of a crutch." But don't quotes lend credibility to a story? "If people are suspicious," Iliff replies, "they won't see a quote as back-up. They'll think you made it up anyway. I'm asking the reader to trust me. The point is, why force a reader to go through two grafs when one will do. That's the whole point here... to fit into our format, we cut the living hell out of everything."*

Ahem.

First off, she got it right, and a CJR editor called me later to confirm what I had said. The first hint that something was amiss came when she said, "Well, that's an interesting perspective."

The minute I read that passage, I realized that I had botched the interview, especially the part about quotations. What I meant to say was that too many newspaper reporters paraphrased what someone said and then added the full quote, a needless redundancy. I intended to advocate using one or the other, whichever is more effective in communicating the thought, but not both. Where that "crutch" thing came from I'll never know. And that "trust" idea was naïve.

A few colleagues dropped by the desk to say they had read my comments. Their words were not critical, but they acted as if someone had died. None of the bosses ever said a word to me about it, but it probably didn't do anything for my stature in the newsroom. Nor should it have. Lesson learned: Rehearse before an interview, even if you aren't sure what you'll be asked.

I will always be proud of my role in the creation of *USA Today*. I'm not so proud of how the World Page staff lost its cohesion in the months after launch. Don Kirk was a fine writer, a convivial drinking partner, and told great stories from his colorful past. Copy editing was not a strength. He succumbed to the temptation good writers can suffer by trying to recast every story into his style. Writers would stand behind him as he edited their story so they could protest his more drastic changes. Sometimes they had a point, sometimes not.

My duties were mostly as another copy editor. My writing was often limited to the World Page briefs, and Don left them alone. Nevertheless, the World Page staff lost harmony, and the most energetic arguments distracted the wider newsroom. We became a side show to some and a leper colony to others. Adding to the frustration was the inconsistent space for international news—some days just a quarter page. A few executives wondered whether we were overstaffed. I was glad to have a long drive home to Manassas, Virginia every night to calm down.

Beth noticed the strain but seemed content staying at home managing the house and gardening. Then, at our New Year's Eve dinner at a downtown Manassas restaurant that had been a church, she confessed that she missed Munich. I almost fell out of my chair. I asked her if she missed it enough to go back if we could, and without hesitation she said yes. My head was spinning the rest of the night, and it wasn't from champagne. With conditions souring at work, I had toyed with the idea, but I had assumed Beth would never go for it.

We let the idea ferment for a few weeks to make sure we really wanted to go back. The awkward conditions at work helped to lock in that conclusion. We had to strategize my approach to RFE/RL for learning whether a return was even possible.

I asked one of my best friends in the Munich newsroom, Kevin Foley, to broach to Barry Griffiths the idea of me returning to Central News. Kevin called back a few days later to say that Barry liked the idea. That grew into a quick back-and-forth with an offer even better than I expected. I would move back to Munich, all expenses paid, with the same compensation package as before. Furthermore, RFE/RL would treat my time at *USA Today* as a leave of absence because I had been gone less than a year. In effect, I would pick up as if I had never left, minus a year of service credit.

We jumped at it. When the paperwork confirmed the offer and our acceptance became official, I served notice to Bob Dubill, who had succeeded Nancy Woodhull as national editor. He was a no-nonsense straight-shooter; he didn't try to keep me, and I didn't expect him to. Nor did Don. We've exchanged cordial emails since then, so there's no lingering grudge.

I gave the newspaper four weeks' notice, giving us plenty of time to prepare for the move. The house sold for our price on the first day it was listed. Some things are just meant to be. After Memorial Day, we headed for our Munich encore, featuring a fine apartment Barry personally selected for us in the prestigious Bogenhausen neighborhood a short walk from work. RFE/RL would prove to be similar to the first act in some ways, far different in others.

# CHAPTER 7

# Return to RFE/RL

*Back on the Not So Merry-Go-Round*

Not much had changed in Central News while I had been gone. Terry Willey, a fine self-taught journalist with a boundless intellect who had been in the newsroom the night of the bombing, had risen to assistant news director. A few more Americans sat at the writers' desks, but the facility, the system, and the daily routine had not changed.

In the executive offices, plenty was changing. The Reagan administration had given control of U.S. government-sponsored international broadcasting to loyal conservatives, who wanted a more aggressive tone toward the East bloc. Frank Shakespeare, an ardent anti-Communist who headed the U.S. Information Agency under Richard Nixon, was recruited from CBS News to be chairman of the Broadcasting Board of Governors, overseers of all government-funded civilian media. The board's choice for RFE/RL president was James Buckley, a former U.S. senator and brother of conservative columnist William Buckley.

Buckley was no strident ideologue. He was charming and by no means aloof. Early in his tenure, Americans in the newsroom organized a Fourth of July softball game and picnic in the English Garden. As a courtesy, we invited Buckley and his wife Ann. Not only did they show up, but they played. Buckley, then 61, did his best at first base; Ann was a star of the game. With Jim Edwards as a firewall, we never knew whether Buckley ever tried to affect the newsroom.

Buckley did order changes that had nothing to do with broadcasting. The company restaurant in the building's basement had featured a staggering selection of liquor. Drinking was rampant at RFE/RL, with cultural traditions cited as an alibi. A basement men's restroom had a vending machine dispensing small bottles of Jägermeister, Doornkaat, and other gut-busters. By 7:30 a.m. empty bottles would line the top of the machine. In a nod to local customs, the newsroom allowed beer consumption during work. Some writers insisted a beer or two didn't hurt their work and might even have improved it. If I had one beer at work, I was worthless.

Friday nights in the canteen were always lively, with workers from the various broadcast desks congregating at tables according to nationality. Old rivalries would flare, and one night the Russians and Ukrainians went crazy. Combatants broke chairs and glasses, and some suffered cuts and bruises. Buckley was appalled. He ordered an immediate ban of all hard liquor sales in the canteen, allowing only beer and wine. There was no appeal.

The newsroom made its own impression on Buckley another way during a brutal summer heat wave. The staff suffered through day shifts in a room full of hot computers with no air conditioning other than in the glass booth for the precious server. Arthur Breslauer, a beloved stereotypical New Yorker who had worked there forever, told how his family kept cool in the old days by placing a block of ice in a room and blowing a fan on it. Desperate to try anything, staff members miraculously found a block of dry ice and what had to be the last electric fan in Munich and placed it all on a table in the middle of the newsroom. The fan proved to be useless. Foggy wisps blew off the ice and collected on the floor. Someone asked if we should get a canary to warn us of impending asphyxiation. The experiment failed, but the ice served another purpose. Staffers stacked bottles of beer and other refreshments on the ice for convenient cooling. That's when Buckley walked into a newsroom full of men and women in summer skivvies working around a block of ice stacked with beer and juice bottles as a white fog rose from the floor. He just shook his head, turned around, and walked out.

Buckley may not have managed with a heavy hand, but others in charge were trying to lower the boom. In line with the Reagan administration's abhorrence of communism, broadcasters were being urged—sometimes ordered—to take a harder line in their programming. Dissidents were given more prominence, and negative portrayals of regimes in target countries were allowed to air more frequently, particularly pertaining to Poland, still under martial law. The new broadcast philosophy led to several high-level resignations. Edwards shielded the news division from all of it. We heard about the pressure, but we never felt it. His greatest legacy at RFE/RL was defending and preserving the news division's standards and independence.

Frank Shakespeare visited the station periodically. He stayed at an exclusive downtown hotel that gave each guest a box of fine chocolates. One day he walked into Buckley's offices (Beth was a secretary/receptionist) and with a "Here ya go, girls," tossed the box onto the front desk. The women stopped picking through the chocolates when they saw he had poked a hole in the bottom of each one. They were his rejects.

Shakespeare's only meeting with the Central News staff was epic. He regaled about 30 of us with right-wing talking points, but for each one a staffer would interrupt to offer a rebuttal based on the facts of international relations—not arguing, just balancing. That back and forth lasted almost an hour. Afterward, we heard that he had stormed into Buckley's office raging about those liberal bastards in Central News and demanding Edwards's head. It wasn't his politics that bothered us; some probably agreed with him. We resented his condescending lecture that lacked any feel for the sensitive nuances that shaped Central News writing. We knew more about the world than he did.

Reagan's attitude toward the Soviet Union seemed to soften as he won a second term in 1984. Aging Soviet leaders kept dying, clearing the way for Mikhail Gorbachev in 1985. His new watchwords, *perestroika* and *glasnost* (restructuring and openness), signaled a new era in domestic and international policies. At the same time, the hardliners guiding U.S. international broadcasting were losing the war of ideas within the administration. By 1985, Buckley had moved on to the 2nd U.S. Court of Appeals, and Shakespeare was ambassador to Portugal.

Their successors were no less committed to democracy and the ideals of RFE/RL, but their tone and style were far less strident. Steve Forbes, son of media magnate Malcolm Forbes, took over the board, while respected broadcast journalist Gene Pell came from the Voice of America to be president. Politically, the storm seemed to have passed, but in terms of internal politics, not so much.

I would never pretend to understand all the machinations going on between top management and Central News at that time. But the departure of Shakespeare and Buckley did not seem to reduce the heat on Edwards. There always seemed to be friction, and in time some of the sparks burned me.

Beth was working in the president's office, and Pell liked both of us, so we socialized once in a while—a couple of dinners with his wife, a Kansas City native, and a visit to his home, where he showed off his model railroad. That had been my hobby in Detroit, so we had more than broadcasting in common. Beth's role also had us sharing time away from work with other executives, including holdovers from the previous regime and no friends of Edwards.

Gradually, things Edwards did and said led me to suspect he viewed me as a management mole, which of course was ridiculous. One tipoff was a summons to his office after I had been seen having lunch outside the building with one of his internal critics. He told me how harmful the guy could be to Central News and to watch what I said to him. We hadn't even talked shop.

That was politics. In terms of journalism, Edwards would go out of his way to compliment my work. He stood behind me as I wrote our first story of the Challenger disaster in January 1986 and said "Nice work," with a pat on my shoulder. For the Olympic Games in 1984 and 1988, with Edwards's approval, I was an Olympics editor, monitoring news agencies and five TV networks to report medal results and anything that pertained to our target countries. Eight hours a day for two or three weeks, watching television at work. Not bad.

Barry, meanwhile, was consistently supportive. He would assign me shifts on the features desk to write longer analysis pieces and then edit them, sharing expert insights into the structure and flow of long-form journalism. Most importantly, Barry started assigning me regular shifts as supervising editor. I wasn't getting paid extra to do it, but I craved every chance to show what I could do. Edwards was not pleased, but the shifts kept coming. I learned from an employee handbook that if a staff member worked a shift above his pay grade for a certain number of days, he was entitled to an automatic promotion to the higher position. I did the math and realized I had passed that threshold.

I approached Edwards in his office in early 1987 and showed him the paperwork confirming my eligibility for the job. His response: "That damn Griffiths." He snatched the papers from my hand and said he'd consider it. Weeks later I was in the supervisor's chair one night when he walked by, threw a folded document onto my keyboard, and quietly snapped, "There, you have what you wanted." It was confirmation of my promotion. I had fulfilled and even exceeded the dream that started forming at that Black Forest picnic in 1956. I was a journalist in Germany supervising a talented staff in a world-class newsroom. Edwards couldn't even manage a handshake.

The enigma of Jim Edwards could also reveal unparalleled grace and dignity. One example involved newsroom colleague Brian Mullins. Brian had brought us a bottle of wine the first night we were in our Gentzstrasse apartment in 1979. We found out later he was not happy to have us in the building. Brian was gay, and he was afraid we would see him bringing someone home with him. We didn't notice, and we didn't care. We just appreciated his hospitable gesture.

Brian died of AIDS in 1987. He was English and had said he wanted to be laid to rest in the soil of his homeland, but his brother did not approve of his lifestyle and refused to pay for the coffin's shipment, forcing a Munich burial. Edwards led a Central News delegation at the burial. After a brief service, we approached the grave site for the traditional scooping of soil onto the coffin. Edwards went first, lifting the scoop and filling it with dirt. Then he put it down without emptying it into the grave. He told us that if Brian wanted to be buried in England, he would not be a party to covering Brian with German soil. We all followed Edwards's lead and walked out to the strains of Verdi's *Requiem*. I almost cried.

In the newsroom itself, the atmosphere was loose but serious. With more Americans in the mix came more teasing banter with Anglos, Brits mostly. I never heard it turn acrimonious. But there were underlying currents. The non-Americans were understandably envious of the better pay and benefits enjoyed by the Yanks. On the other hand, some Anglos' mild criticisms of America and Americans drew mumbling about hypocrisy considering who was signing the checks. Again, these issues did not disrupt the newsroom routine, so in all it was a great place to work.

When Beth and I weren't working, we traveled. Visits with the German relatives were frequent, and vacation itineraries read like travel brochures. Name a western European country other than Scandinavia, and we were there. Add China, Tibet, Egypt, India, and Nepal. Home leave in 1985 featured long drives through New England and the Southwest. We rented a vacation apartment in the Austrian Alps for a year. We never had it so good.

On summer Sundays with good weather (never a sure thing in Munich), we played softball at 11 a.m. in an English Garden meadow. We started with batting practice, sending softballs into centerfield to encourage nude sunbathers to relocate. Our games would draw a small crowd of Germans, including policemen, with no clue what we were doing. Some spectators joined in anyway. Afterward a short walk would take us to the Chinese Tower, Munich's favorite beer garden, for liter mugs of beer and giant pretzels. Then it was on to someone's apartment for dinner and a spirited game of Risk, or, when it became a fad, Trivial Pursuit.

Among our best friends were Dan and Susan Williams. We spent a lot of off time together, including antiques shopping in the Alpine foothills, skiing, and periodic champagne runs to France. They had a station wagon to haul around their kids Gretchen and Martin, so we would go to our favorite vintner and load up. One of those runs started in late April 1986. On our way, we heard something about a nuclear accident in the Soviet Union. We went on to Epernay in the Champagne region and returned home in time for a Sunday softball game on the dew-covered field.

We didn't know that the radioactive cloud from the world's worst nuclear disaster at Chernobyl had already drifted our way. The next day, the news was scary. Munich store shelves emptied of dairy products, produce, and other radiation sponges. Warnings mentioned the danger in precipitation; we kicked ourselves for letting the kids play in that dewy field. The hazard passed in a few days, but its consequences lasted far longer. The disastrous Soviet response to the emergency gave Gorbachev a pretext to accelerate his reform efforts. You could argue that Chernobyl was the beginning of the end of the Soviet Union and of RFE/RL as we knew it.

The beginning of the end of my time in Munich came in 1988. Until then, I had harbored a belief that I had a future in management. A series of events unraveled those ideas, starting with a puzzling chat with Barry. After a summons to his office, he suggested that I might want to, in effect, curb my enthusiasm. As I said in a letter to my parents, "I've been told I'm doing such a good job that I'm attracting attention and making some colleagues uncomfortable. So I've been told to cool it. I don't know what I'm supposed to do. So I'll keep working the way I always do. If others feel threatened, that's their problem. It's a temporary problem and it will pass, but it's still annoying."

I tried to figure out what was happening. Maybe it had to do with different work ethics. A few English colleagues viewed ambition and initiative as bad form. Instead of drawing attention, they felt it was better to blend in and patiently wait for managers to notice and reward good work. The American style of workplace comportment was collegial but more assertive.

For example, Tom Todd, a scholarly supervising editor from Yorkshire, told me a story extolling the virtue of patience:

"A reporter was interviewing the head groundskeeper at Wimbledon and asked how the tennis mecca had created its pristine grass surfaces. The groundskeeper explained that they started with the finest seed and best soil, applied just the right amount of fertilizer and water, rolled it gently... and then waited a hundred years."

My somewhat inelegant reply: "And while you wait, you lose an empire."

Tom could also wield the needle. While editing a story by Tom, Larry McCoy turned to him and asked with some impatience, "Tom, what the hell does that second line mean?"

Tom's earnest reply: "You know, Larry, I was wondering that myself."

That kind of gentle banter did not rise to the level of a culture clash. But then, as the English say, I blotted my copy book. In other words, I made a helluva mess.

My first blunder was a social faux pas. Griffiths and his hospitable wife, Inge, invited Beth and me to join them on a ski trip to France's Three Valleys region. We had skied there before and were looking forward to the great runs and fine cuisine. But it didn't go as planned. Barry and Inge were excellent skiers; we were not. The only good snow was at higher elevations on runs out of our league. Barry and Inge limited their skiing to the lower slopes, but mushy snow made things worse. After two days of struggle and a third of rain, we were sure we were ruining the trip for Barry and Inge. That night at dinner, we told them we were leaving in the morning and driving to Paris for a few days. They tried to persuade us to stay, but we were sure this would save their ski week. We left the next morning.

It took me years to understand the enormity of that decision. Barry didn't invite just anybody to a ski trip. Our bailing out midweek, even with the best of intentions, was rude. We could have taken day trips to surrounding towns and then met for dinner each evening. From that time on, Barry's tone at work lost its conversational warmth. The social interaction stopped. Unfortunately, I barely noticed.

That fall, I managed a far greater blunder—this one hurting newsroom friends. I'll fudge the details to protect the actors in this sordid drama. Let's just say that a buddy got out of line with several women linked to the newsroom. One case in particular upset me, but when Beth accused this fellow of hitting on her, that was it. I felt it was no longer just a social problem but had risen to a workplace issue. I forewarned the individuals involved that I was going to tell Barry, spurning their fervent pleas not to. When I walked into Barry's office and told him what was going on, he looked at me as if I had two heads. He said he would look into it and turned back to the paperwork on his desk. That was it. In the #metoo age, management might have had a different reaction, but not then. I told the key players involved what I had done, costing me one friendship and tarnishing others for years.

Word got around the newsroom, as I had expected. Nobody spoke to me about it. Nevertheless, this was the beginning of the end of my time in Munich. By telling the principals about my chat with Barry, I ensured the newsroom would know what I had done. I considered my handling of the matter professionally prudent. Instead, it was naïve stupidity spiced with a dose of sanctimonious arrogance.

I have never stopped thinking about this episode. When I do, I wince. This was the single worst mistake of my career and my life. I had put my employer ahead of my friends. My employer didn't care.

A few months later I was called to the office of Executive Vice President Bill Marsh at a time of growing speculation about changes in newsroom management. My work was still getting good reviews, and I still had plenty of friends in the newsroom and executive offices. I thought Marsh might want to discuss a role for me in the new hierarchy.

Not exactly.

Closing the door, he informed me that he had received a petition signed by 10 senior newsroom staff members demanding that I never be given a management position in Central News. I asked to see the petition, and he refused. I never saw it. This, of course, was a slobber-knocking haymaker. Blinded by my self-awareness deficiency, I could not imagine what I had done to deserve this.

The dots now were spread all over the page. Barry's warning to curb my enthusiasm, his aloof indifference toward me after the ski trip, the corrosive undercurrent from the tattle tale disaster, not to mention Edwards's enduring suspicions of my priorities and loyalties. And I *still* didn't connect the dots.

The petition's timing could not have been worse. Leadership changes in Central News were indeed coming, and I was ready to move up. Sure enough, an announcement confirmed that Edwards was out and a news director would be sought from outside. Edwards left with little fanfare, which was sad. He deserved much more. He retired to his beloved Normandy, where he lived until his death three decades later.

A new vice president for corporate affairs, Ken Taylor, came to RFE/RL around time of Edwards's departure. He was given a role in filling a new Central News position, director of current affairs. I wanted it, and I invited him to dinner to present my case. As we stood on the RFE/RL front steps waiting for a taxi, he mentioned that he had just filled the position with a broadcast news veteran who had worked for CBS in Moscow. I still bought him dinner, but I had lost my last shot at management. The guy he hired was Gary Thatcher. Years later, it turned out to be one of the best things that ever happened to me.

With no more rungs to climb on my career ladder in Munich, I started discussing an exit strategy with Beth, now working in the station's early version of a computer center. We had thought RFE/RL's days might be numbered ever since a weekend trip to Hungary, the first Warsaw Pact country RFE/RL allowed its employees to visit as tourists.

We checked into Budapest's upscale Hotel Duna on the banks of the Danube, handed over our passports, and went to our room to freshen up. We returned to the desk an hour later to retrieve our passports. An attractive young woman with excellent English handed them to us, saying, "So you work for the radio station in Munich." There was no way she could have known that from our documents. Seizing the moment for impromptu audience research, I asked her if she listened to RFE's Hungarian broadcasts. "We used to," she said, "but now our radio stations are much more interesting."

That encounter and others that weekend led us to suspect RFE/RL might not last long. If radio stations behind the Iron Curtain were starting to take listeners away from our broadcasts, how long would it be before Washington decided RFE/RL was no longer worth the cost?

This awakening plus my personal dead-end status in Central News gave us compelling reasons to think hard about the future. As in 1982, Beth loved Munich, her life, and her work, and did not want to leave. She conceded that she had promised to give my career precedence, but this time she extracted a promise that the next move would be hers. We were due for home leave, so we would use it as a cover for job hunting.

As I started to check job postings and reactivate my professional network, I ran across a stunning piece of good news. CNN had recently hired its first senior editor.

It was Paul Varian, my old boss and friend from Detroit. A former UPI colleague of his father was a top CNN executive and had lured Paul to Atlanta. Paul and I hadn't talked in 10 years, and I wasn't even sure he wanted to. I wrote a cautious letter of reintroduction, and the response was electrifying. He wanted me to visit him in Atlanta during our home leave, and to be sure to bring Beth.

We flew to Atlanta from Kansas City and had a delightful reunion dinner hosted by Paul and Sandra at Atlanta's posh Bones steakhouse. The next morning Paul ushered me into CNN Center, a contemporary concrete and glass mausoleum kind of place in downtown Atlanta. He showed me around and explained how the newsroom worked. Most of it went way over my head. I breezed through a mandatory writing test, and we were done. I left him with my updated resume, which lacked TV experience but was spiced up with two new entries.

The previous year in Munich, dinner with our friends Cindy Emmans and Dr. William Byxbee had produced a tip for how to earn a college degree. He told me about a program run by the State University of New York called Regents' College. It would count credit hours from my Kansas transcript toward a liberal arts degree and then let me fill in the missing hours with tests and correspondent courses. I lacked 18 hours. A German proficiency test earned me 12, and the last six came with a general science correspondence course. My diploma arrived in the fall of 1988.

About the same time, my first book project was published. Brian Deming was the husband of Central News colleague Carol Damioli. Sharing beers at a downtown gasthaus one summer evening in 1985, Brian and I started talking about Munich's history, particularly its role in Adolf Hitler's life. We agreed it would make a great book. Instead of leaving it there, we started researching.

Brian looked at English-language sources, and I studied German-language ones. Over the next three years, we used our new personal computers to write a manuscript that detailed, with a map, where Hitler lived and worked, the sites of his early exploits, including the 1923 failed putsch, and other landmarks from the era. Over two days we walked Munich streets to check our descriptions of every site in the book. Some were untouched from Hitler's time; others had changed, and a few were gone. We added chapters on Dachau and the anti-Nazi resistance, and in early 1988 we decided we were ready to find a publisher.

We were so naïve. We wanted a German publisher to buy our English-language book that detailed a part of Munich's history that the city wanted the world to forget. We looked for publishers who already had English-language travel books in stores. The first didn't respond. The second said he wanted no part of a book that could turn into a pilgrimage guide for neo-Nazis.

We moved our search out of town and found Plenk Verlag, a publishing house in Berchtesgaden, the Bavarian alpine town where Hitler had built his Berghof retreat. It had published several English-language travel guides. Anton Plenk, the son of the founder, said he had never heard about anything described in our book. He bought it and even agreed to pay for the rights for photos and graphics. He saw a market for it in the *Stars and Stripes* shops at U.S. military bases, and perhaps beyond. We hired a lawyer to write our contract that called for a 10-percent royalty split evenly between Brian and me for every $20 copy sold. He tossed in a demand for a 500 D-mark bonus for each of us, which we didn't even ask for. Plenk signed without any changes, and the book, *Hitler and Munich*, came out in September 1988.

Stories about it appeared in *Stars and Stripes* and *Abendzeitung*, a Munich daily. The first 10,000 hardback copies sold out within a year, followed by another 10,000 in paperback. The end of the Cold War drained Germany of most American military personnel, so *Stars and Stripes* bookstores closed, and we lost our primary market. We didn't care; we were published authors.

The new and improved resume helped Paul sell the idea of hiring me to his CNN superiors, even though I had no television news experience, had not lived in the United States for most of a decade and was coming from what some dismissed as a government-funded propaganda mill.

In early June, I returned to Munich with a job offer from CNN as a copy editor. I could think of no better way to return to work on American soil. I served notice, giving Central News plenty of time to plan our move and recruit a replacement. We had no office going-away party, no parting gift (I got a nice pewter beer stein for my first departure), just private farewells with friends. Some of the non-Americans were glad to see my backside; most Americans were hoping their return home would be as promising.

Of course, all the jealousy, suspicion and resentment that some of my bosses and colleagues directed at me were not my fault. I had done nothing to deserve any of this.

Yeah, right.

It took me years to recognize and accept my share of responsibility for all this – primarily from my critical shortage of self-awareness. I went through most my time in Munich not perceiving the effects of my words and actions on those around me, even when bosses and coworkers tried to warn me. This is not about wallowing in self-pity or regret. I learned, eventually.

As my last day approached, I was invited to the daily meeting of department heads and executives. I remember a few complimentary comments about my time there, and then I was invited to make farewell remarks. "Well," I said, "there's an old saying that silence is golden but sometimes just plain yellow. I think I should leave it at that. I've enjoyed my time here very much. Thank you."

What a disgusting thing to say.

For the record, this is what I should have said:

"Working as a journalist in Germany was my life's dream. RFE/RL allowed me to fulfill that dream. The invaluable lessons I learned here as a writer, editor, and student of the world will serve me forever. My supervisors were cordial and tolerant despite some unintended provocations, and my colleagues were a fascinating and enlightening group of journalists who would excel in any newsroom. Life the past 10 years has been a marvelous adventure. I thank you and RFE/RL for the opportunities you created for me. I will be forever in your debt, and I wish you all well, individually and collectively."

Too late now, but there it is. I had reached my life's goals before I turned 40. Everything after that was luscious icing on the cake.

# CHAPTER 8
# CNN

## *Basking in the Glow of a Golden Age*

In the 1987 romantic comedy-cum-docudrama *Broadcast News,* one brief scene signaled the coming ethical train wreck in American broadcasting. Neophyte anchor Tom Grunick (William Hurt) was reporting live breaking news when he adlibbed a line: "I think we're all OK." Staring up at Grunick's image on a control room monitor, producer Ernie Merriman (Robert Prosky) scowled and spoke the line of the age: "Who the hell cares what you think?"

While that film was in production, a parallel drama with historic consequences was wrapping up in Washington. On August 4, 1987, the Federal Communications Commission under President Ronald Reagan abolished the Fairness Doctrine, a policy adopted in 1949 at the dawn of TV news to require stations to air balanced and fair coverage of controversial issues. In effect, it ended the longstanding consensus that the airwaves were protected public property and opened them to anything short of obscenity.

The following year, Rush Limbaugh's nationally syndicated radio talk show premiered on Aug. 1, 1988. In time, the genie slithered out of the bottle; fairness was out, opinion was in.

Fortunately for me, that tectonic shift in broadcast news took more than a decade to inflict its lasting damage. It had hardly registered on July 27, 1989 when I strolled into CNN's newsroom for my first day with no way of knowing that I was entering at the dawn of the network's golden age. By the time my CNN adventure ended 13 years later, the broadcast news landscape would feature Fox News and the Internet in the upheaval of a profession and industry.

As in previous jobs, I couldn't just walk in, sit down, and start working. I was the dumbest guy in the place. The setting alone was intimidating. The all-in-one production center housed the anchor set, the circular writing and editing stations called pods, the supervising producers' elevated work space, the national and international newsgathering desks, the tape library, and the kaleidoscopic monitor wall of the video intake center. Because it all served as a background for newscasts, everything was tidy and presentable, including the staff. The dress code was strictly business; one young man in the video intake area almost lost his job for wearing a hockey jersey that briefly flashed on air.

I was hired as a copy editor, but Paul Varian asked me to keep it under my hat so I could blend in with the writing staff. As the new guy, I drew a fair share of curiosity because of my previous employment, my past association with Paul, and my age. At nearly 40, I was one of the oldest employees in the newsroom, as I was reminded early in my tenure when one morning I walked in to find a confused production team. A congressman had compared South African's Nelson Mandela to H. Rap Brown, a black power advocate from the 60s. In those pre-Google times, nobody could figure out who Brown was. Executive producer Susan Merritt saw me arriving, pointed to me, and said, "Let's ask Ted. He's old. He'll know." I rolled my eyes and explained that H. Rap Brown was considered a founding father of rap music. Some actually bought it for a second. Old, indeed.

The writers worked at the three round pods behind the main set. The rim had space for five or six writers facing the elevated work station of the copy editor. It was a classic journalism layout, but it didn't last. It was abandoned years later when tests showed that the pods were circular firing squads dousing copy editors with radiation from backs of the computer monitors surrounding them. For a time, editors wore protective lead aprons before being relocated away from the pods.

A newscast's preparation started with a producer drafting a rundown. This meticulous document included instructions for scripts—topic, time allowed, video and graphics to use, and other elements. Writers would look at the video and write matching words that told the important elements of the story. A copy editor would check the text for accuracy and to make sure the script matched the producer's instructions. The editor would print the script, and entry level staffers called video journalists would separate the copies and distribute them to the anchor, teleprompter operator, director, associate producer, font operator (typing the words appearing on the screen), audio board operator, and producer.

It didn't always work that way.

Rundowns changed with the news throughout a show's two-hour preparation period. Video would not arrive or would change, forcing hasty revisions. A script (or five) could be too long or short, messing up the rundown's timing. If a show was running too long, the producer had to cut something to end on time. If too short, something was needed to precisely fill the time gap. A math error in timing the rundown could blow up the newscast. Live shots or phone reports could fail. Guests might not show up. And of course, breaking news could trash the entire plan. In crunch times, the script distribution system looked more like a frantic relay race than a well-oiled machine. The script copies were almost as messy as the old UPI teletype machines, and newbies trying to dress for success paid some hefty dry-cleaning bills before learning to choose more durable working duds.

The script itself was split vertically down the middle. The right side was the anchor's copy as it appeared on a teleprompter. Tucked between some of the lines were instructions, such as when the anchor was on camera and what was on screen when not. Embedded in the copy were phonetic pronunciations of uncommon names and words. The system had its potholes. Bobbie Battista was reading a script and came to the cue line (TAKE FULL SCREEN GRAPHIC). She read it word for word and kept on going. Someone forgot a pronunciation guide for "chihuahua" (chee-WAH-wah). The poor ambushed anchor gave it her best shot. "Chuh-HOO-uh-HOO-uh." I've heard that a binge-worthy compilation of CNN bloopers exists somewhere. Seeing that video is one of the few things left on my bucket list.

As if the right side wasn't enough of a challenge, the left side looked like a Rosetta Stone of words, numbers, and abbreviations. That side was the show's guide for the technical staff in the control room—directors, audio operators, tape playback operators, and font operators. It listed anchor cues, videos, graphics, and fonts and at what point in the story they should appear. And that's just the basics. As I struggled with these hieroglyphics, I realized that in TV news, good writing was only part of the game.

There were a million variations of all this, and the learning curve was steep and precarious. One requirement I was slow to honor was viewing a story's video before writing the script. A computerized tape index described what the video showed, but it was not always reliable. The only way to know for sure was to look at the video. The goal was to match the images with the words so what the viewers saw was in sync with what they heard. When it worked, it was art. When it didn't, it might go unnoticed. Or be confusing. Or cause a disaster.

Of course, I had to learn the hard way. Producers tended to assign new writers like me easy, lighter stories called "kickers" for the end of the newscast. For one prime time newscast, I was assigned the story from Ohio of a dog lover's wedding with her pets among the guests. Instead of getting my lazy ass up and going to the viewing station to look at the video, I glanced at the shot list in the tape index and wrote the story from that. Trying to be clever, I wrote this lead (the name is changed): "A good-looking crowd showed up for Mary Smith's wedding, but some of the guests were real dogs." Then the video started, showing the bride, the minister, and plenty of other humans, but no dogs for 15 agonizing seconds. I had in effect defamed an entire wedding party, in prime time. After a quick post-mortem with the copy editor, all I got was a mild scolding from the producer.

The true editorial heroes were the copy editors. Viewers never realized how many mistakes they caught; they only saw the ones that the editor missed. In my prime time writing phase, my editor was Kim Engebretsen. She never seemed to miss anything, from language mistakes to factual errors to wrong script elements. In terms of policing copy, Kim was the best.

When I was assigned a script about the Tucker Torpedo, a futuristic but short-lived car from the late 40s, I started with this: "You may not have heard of the Tucker Torpedo…" Kim didn't get past that line. Looking down from her editor's perch, she smiled and said, "You've been gone, haven't you?" The Tucker Torpedo and its creator, Preston Tucker, had been the subject of a 1988 Francis Ford Coppola film. Lots of folks knew about the Tucker Torpedo. Except me. Kim not only caught the error but also understood why it happened.

Even though I was new and somewhat mysterious in terms of my background, the staff was quick to treat me as a peer. They even accepted me on the CNN softball team. I was useless, but I still played a few innings each game. The team was friendly, but that gang could wield a mean needle. They gave me jersey number 42, my age and the team's highest number. At bars and cafes away from work, the chatter was lively and upbeat, with topics ranging from office gossip to world affairs. Working conditions and schedules drew gripes, but they were never bitter or sustained.

Reasons for joining CNN were as diverse as the staff itself. Some saw CNN as an entry into the TV news business after failing to penetrate the professional walls around networks and local stations. Others were true Ted Turner believers who wanted to hitch their careers to his dream. Still others just liked living and working in laid-back, affordable, diverse, and thriving Atlanta. Money was rarely discussed, at least around me. Nobody at CNN, not even the anchors, came close to earning the salaries paid at the major networks. That didn't seem to matter, or at least it rarely came up in office banter. It was an exciting and fulfilling place for anyone hooked on news.

When I moved to prime time, my stock rose as the Berlin Wall fell. My three shows were the International Hour at 3 p.m. ET and the 8 p.m. and 10 p.m. newscasts. Unprecedented political ferment was roiling Eastern Europe, so much that even CNN executives famous for disparaging foreign news as "a ratings killer" mandated coverage.

Producers realized that Eastern Europe was my editorial wheelhouse, so they assigned me the "European stuff." One prime time producer, Mark Bauer, went so far as to hold the entire second block of his rundown open for me. I decided what stories we should tell, what video we had to illustrate those stories, and in effect produced the entire segment. Those assignments sealed my status as a trusted CNN writer. I recreated my Central News writing style—crisp, easily understood language and rigorous accuracy—always matching the words with the images. I was in my happy zone.

Throughout that first year, I solved the TV writing puzzle with the patient guidance of Paul Varian, Kim Engebretsen, and an all-star battery of editors, producers, and writers. The newsroom was as relaxed as the work allowed, and the staff and supervisors were friendly and supportive. When I was ready, Paul started easing me into copy editing. The writers and other editors still did not know I had been hired with that job title. They noticed the relatively quick elevation, but I never sensed any backlash.

I was sailing along in prime time when a change at the top brought Tom Johnson to the CNN presidency. The erudite, easy-talking Georgian was publisher of *The Los Angeles Times* when Ted Turner twisted his arm to take over his pet project. Some executives, including those hoping for the job, turned up their noses at someone with no TV news experience. The choice was brilliant and just in time.

Johnson moved into the president's sixth-floor office with a window overlooking the newsroom on August 1, 1990. Less than 24 hours later, Iraq's Saddam Hussein launched a surprise invasion of Kuwait. CNN was already a household name because of its pioneering coverage of live breaking news, from a child rescued from a Texas well to the 1986 Challenger disaster. Now, CNN had its first major international crisis to cover.

Johnson, a former aide to President Lyndon Johnson, offered a new perspective to CNN while leaving coverage matters to his TV news-savvy executive team. He kept close touch with the George H.W. Bush administration to make sure CNN reporters and crews in the Persian Gulf region were not in harm's way. We knew a military response was coming, and we expected to be tipped off when it started.

The network's collective imagination ran wild with what it needed to cover the Kuwait occupation, the build-up for a military response and the war. A comprehensive library of lists, maps, and special reports enhanced constant live, global coverage. I was ordered to compile a list of historic sites in Iraq that a war could endanger, and then I helped to prepare maps and other graphics and write matching scripts. I was almost ashamed at how much fun I was having getting ready for a war.

By that time, Paul had been moved to other editing duties, and Kim had succeeded him as senior editor. She devised a special schedule for writers and editors to be activated when the war started. She moved me to a 4 a.m. start time, putting my shift in sync with daytime in the Gulf. That meant that if the war started after dark in the United States, I'd be on the sidelines.

Sure enough, the first air raids of Desert Storm were launched during U.S. prime time on January 16, 1991. The White House had sent Johnson and all other network chiefs the expected warning code hours earlier, so we were ready. Sitting at home when the first breaking news aired, I called Kim, offering (more like begging) to come in. She told me to stay home, so I settled down and joined the world watching coverage unprecedented in the history of journalism.

The "boys of Baghdad," Bernard Shaw, John Holliman, and Peter Arnett, were taking turns giving live, real-time coverage of the war at ground zero. Defense Secretary Dick Cheney told the world that most of what the Pentagon knew was coming from CNN. The major networks eventually gave up trying to compete and took CNN's coverage without permission. We didn't care. That night CNN claimed its place as the world's news leader.

I hurried to work early the next morning to start three weeks of tedium, writing scripts that never aired because most of the coverage was live. We also scoured news agencies and other reputable sources for information we could use in our coverage. When the ground phase started on February 1, CNN was among many news organizations with reporters "embedded" with coalition forces. In four weeks, it was over. CNN would never be the same. As NBC's Tom Brokaw said, the days of CNN standing for "chicken noodle news" were gone.

A few weeks after the war, senior executive producer Bob Furnad pulled me aside for a quick chat. In the newsroom, Bob was revered and feared as the maker and breaker of careers, particularly for producers. He gained a permanent place in broadcasting's pantheon in the ubiquitous video of him barking "I need Amman, I need Saudi Arabia..." into a control room microphone in the war's first minutes. He could be brash and even harsh, but more importantly, he was innovative and brilliant. If CNN's first 20 years were its golden age, Bob deserved much of the credit.

Everybody talked about him, but as a new writer I had little reason to notice him. During one of my early prime time shifts, he walked by my seat, tapped me on the shoulder, and pointed to my sportscoat. "Your coat tail is on the floor," he said.

"That okay," I replied, "it's not much of a coat anyway." To a man who demanded a fastidious newsroom, those words could have doomed my CNN stay. But they didn't, and I remained in what I assumed was secure obscurity.

Our quick chat was in a dark corner of the production center, an intimidating spot if Bob Furnad is talking. Without any preface, he said he thought I would make a good supervising producer, and he wanted to make that happen. He said we'd talk more about it and walked away. I couldn't move; I wasn't even sure I had heard right. A supervising producer shouldered full responsibility for a shift of CNN programming, day, night, or overnight. All producers had to clear their ideas and rundowns with the supervisor. The supervisor alerted the control room to breaking news and decided when to go live and when to dump out.

And here I was, less than a year on the job with no producing experience, being offered a shot at one of CNN's most coveted titles. Later, I heard that Bob liked my news sense and background as well as my way of handling pressure (thank you, UPI), key traits of a supervising producer. The mechanics of show production could be learned soon enough.

For the first time, I realized that I was being noticed. I never shied away from the chance for a little self-promotion, but this was way beyond the pale. I started sorting through recollections of previous conversations with others. A disappointed vice president who resigned after losing out to Johnson was in his last days when I walked by to say goodbye. "Thanks," he said, "and I really hope we can work together again someday." Huh? I was just a writer, a nobody. In my early days as a copy editor, Lou Waters, a CNN original and a demanding anchor, sent a message to me from the set during a show I had edited. "You're a great editor." I thanked him but didn't know why he had said that. I had hardly settled in as a writer when the International Hour's new executive producer hand-picked his writing staff, and he wanted me. At our first show meeting, he said he had demanded "the best writers we have." I remembered other compliments from higher-ups and wondered whether they were more than random comments.

Recalling how I had chafed some of my Munich colleagues, I kept my mouth shut and didn't tell anyone, but word got around. Bob assigned producer Eric Gershon to teach me the art and science of preparing a rundown. One of Bob's lieutenants started talking to me as if I already had the job. There was one complication—it was for the overnight shift. My wife worked days, and being over 40, I wasn't sure how I would handle those hours. After a few weeks of waiting, I wandered into Bob's office and confessed that I wasn't sure I wanted to work overnights. Bob said he understood and would take that into consideration.

That was the deal-killer. There was no way he would elevate me to the rank of supervising producer and then give me preferential treatment ahead of others with more experience and seniority. All talk about supervising producer stopped, and another candidate, Henry Schuster, got the job. It was perfect. I avoided getting sidetracked or even derailed in a job I wasn't ready for, and Henry was a star who went on to produce for *CBS 60 Minutes*. Not bad, for both of us.

Meanwhile, Bob found out that I shared his fascination with motorsports, particularly NASCAR. Over the next decade, he invited me to go with him to races in Atlanta, Charlotte, Talladega, and Daytona as well as several smaller tracks in the Atlanta area. He and his classy wife Barbara became warm and generous friends. When my father died, the only time I choked up was when I saw the flowers they had sent.

In 1996, my NASCAR infatuation dovetailed with my Turner ties for an innovation ahead of its time. TBS broadcast on two race weekends each year from the Lowes Motor Speedway in Concord, North Carolina; I came up with an idea for linking viewers real-time through the still developing concept of email. Working with a TBS executive and World Sport, the race production company, we set up an experiment.

For the Memorial Day weekend races, TBS urged viewers to email questions as they watched. Bandwidth was not robust enough yet to do so directly to our trackside communications trailer, so TBS staff in Atlanta had to read the emails over the phone to our experts in the truck, NASCAR driver Phil Parsons on Saturday and racing legend Buddy Baker on Sunday. If a viewer asked specifically about a team or driver, we radioed the question to two reporters in the pits who would chase the answer and radio it back to us. We'd get it to Atlanta, where it was emailed back to the viewer. It sounds complicated, but it worked. I was told both days were successful, and World Sport tried it once more at the fall races. A scheduling conflict kept me from participating that weekend. The concept became routine with the advent of the Internet.

After the Gulf War, Kim Engebretsen kept me on the early shift and moved me into the editing chair responsible for the 6 a.m., 8 a.m. and 10 a.m. newscasts. I was ready, but I still had a lot to learn, mostly involving the people skills that I had fumbled in Munich.

A seminal experience in my management of writers came courtesy of a talented and TV-savvy writer, Carol Brooks, whom we occasionally socialized with outside work. This Caribbean lady had an easy laugh, sardonic sense of humor and did not suffer fools, especially editors. I brought a lot of supervisory habits from RFE/RL, and they were hard-core old school. The boss was the boss. Civility should never be misunderstood as weakness or indecision. CNN supervisors had a different approach in the workplace culture inspired by Ted Turner himself. But I was too busy with the nuts and bolts of editing to notice. One morning Carol wrote a script that I didn't like. I explained my objections and told her to rewrite it. I turned my attention to other scripts until I noticed show time was approaching and Carol's rewrite was missing. When it showed "done" in the script queue, it was not what I had wanted. Time pressure forced me to print it.

After the newscast, as she was going for a coffee break, I headed her off at the escalator and let her have it. I wasn't yelling, but towering over her (I had her by almost a foot) I told her I didn't approve of her handling of the script, and I wasn't going to tolerate any insubordination or disrespect as long as I was editing. As I prattled on, all of a sudden, I heard the voice of Scotty Bowman ("You like to talk a lot"). I finished my thought, and Carol looked at me as if I had grown horns. "Why are you talking to me like that?" she asked, more quizzical than defiant. As she headed down the escalator for coffee, I stood there frozen. Why, indeed. What was that really about? What was I trying to prove? Carol came back and wrote for the next show as if nothing had happened. I sat down to edit, but my mind wasn't entirely on the scripts on my screen.

My behavior, not hers, was the problem. For days later, I thought about that moment and how I needed to adjust my handling of this talented, dedicated, and diverse group of writers. I had never seen any CNN editor treat any writer, including me, that way. Having missed all the cues in Munich, this was an epiphany. CNN wasn't your daddy's workplace anymore. If I had any hope of succeeding there, I had to change. At the end of every shift from then on, I would emulate other editors by reviewing the show with the producer and writers, praising good scripts and critiquing without rancor those that had missed the mark.

That morning shift was tough because of the 4 a.m. start time. At first, I tried to go to bed around 8 p.m., but that was a waste of time, particularly when the Atlanta Braves got good in the 1991 season. I stayed up to watch every game if I wasn't at Atlanta-Fulton County Stadium. Surrendering to reality, I switched to a later bed time and slept again from 1 p.m. until Beth got home from work. The main benefit of the early shift was that I had weekends off.

Another benefit was the morning crew. It was a bright and talented bunch at all levels of production. Nothing seemed to faze them. The writers were a chatty group who shared their opinions on various issues probably more than they should have in a newsroom. But they kept them out of their copy.

They socialized among themselves, and I would join in when invited. I joined a few on the golf course, where my game was more vandalism than sport. I even was inducted into two poker groups, the tightest social units on the planet. I had more tells than William's momma, so I was easy to read and sure to lose. The evening of good food and good times was worth it.

The morning crew broke character only once that I can remember. We had finished our 6 a.m. newscast, and the team typically strolled to the café for coffee. But this morning the whole gang rushed to the escalator as soon as the last script was read on air. I was the last to find out why: Ted Turner and Jane Fonda were having breakfast down there. Ted was a common sight around CNN Center, but this was breaking news. Ted and Jane had just started dating and sometimes would stay in Ted's penthouse apartment. The staff lined up for refreshments with all eyes on the famous couple. So much for aloof professionalism. After a while the staff drifted back to their work stations buzzing about their celebrity encounter, and I had a moment to get coffee. As I walked out of the cafe, there they were, walking just ahead of me, chatting quietly and seemingly oblivious to all the stares. She had her arm around his back, not a very intimate gesture. Nothing to see here, folks. Weeks later they were there again, and I again walked out behind them. This time her hand was on his butt. Now, I thought, we're getting somewhere.

So was I, although I didn't know it right away.

**CNN International: The Whole World Is Watching**

Seeing the worldwide reaction to CNN's Gulf War coverage, network leaders suspected there was a market for a separate version of CNN that would cater to the different needs of international viewers. CNN International had been available by satellite around the world since 1985, but with limited programming, it was marketed as a service for hotels. Within months of the war's end, rumors swirled that a true international CNN network was coming.

I wanted in, for the obvious reasons. (It was also three years since I had joined CNN. Just saying.) Vice President Peter Vesey headed the project, so I let him know, often, how interested I was in participating. He was supportive but non-committal. In the summer of 1992, he posted job openings for two titles, senior producer and writer/producer. I aimed high, trying for one of the senior jobs. This was of course an overreach; that job involved shift supervision, and I was no more qualified than when Bob Furnad had floated his offer. Executive Producer Donna Mastrangelo, an intense, energetic NBC veteran with a solid international news pedigree, picked Sid Bedingfield, a CNN producer who had been a writer when I arrived; Rena Golden, an imaginative India-born producer of CNN's International Hour; and Jeff Ofgang, a CNN supervising producer whom I had worked with in Munich. No argument there.

Donna chose me as a writer/producer, a vague title with a flexible job description depending on network needs. A small staff of producers, writers, and anchors already was in place, and in September, we all squeezed into the cramped fourth-floor newsroom across a walkway from the even smaller control room and a tiny set. We were "the network under the stairs." Nearly everyone had international credentials. To give the network a global flavor, the anchor corps included Bulgarian Ralitsa Vassileva and German Bettina Luescher. We also carried a newscast from London anchored by Hillary Bowker and another from Washington featuring the venerable Reid Collins.

The London crew was easy to work with, but Collins was a challenge. A product of the all-star CBS radio news stable, Collins jumped to CNN in 1985 to get a crack at television news anchoring. He was already a D.C. bureau mainstay when CNNI gave him a half-hour daily newscast. Collins was notorious for resisting change. In a computerized newsroom, Collins demanded and won the right to retain the use of a typewriter; a minion would type his copy into the computer. He was finicky and strenuously professional. His mannerisms and personality mirrored the Ted Baxter character that Ted Knight had played on *The Mary Tyler Moore Show*. Talking to Collins could be intimidating because of his stature in the profession, but our chats were always cordial, even when we disagreed. He often sported a faint smile, hinting that he wasn't taking anything, including himself, too seriously.

It was easy to shrug off his idiosyncrasies as long as they didn't affect his on-air work. For domestic CNN, he was solid. For CNNI, with its international writing and editorial style, it was a struggle. He chafed at rules against American slang and cultural references that were a common ingredient in his scripts, whether written by someone else or rewritten by him. After trying long distance coaching and cajoling, Donna dispatched me to Washington to try to convert him to the CNNI way. Our meeting didn't solve much. His qualities on air were valued just enough to outweigh his editorial resistance.

Donna soon made me de facto chief editor, not only editing scripts but also handling staff schedules and dictating style rules. Scheduling was a singular challenge because of Vesey's egalitarian shift rotations. Every six weeks, everyone moved—overnights to days, days to nights, nights to overnight. It was a noble concept but an administrative can of worms. Allowing for turn-around time, vacations, and other variables, the staff was constantly churning. Some handled it better than others, and the complications only multiplied as we added staff for our expanding newscast lineup.

I managed the writing style by drawing on my Munich experience, but that only went so far. Our audience spanned 24 time zones and two hemispheres, so we had to be careful with time and seasonal references. When talking about New Year, we had to respect the fact that China, Iran, Israel and other places marked their own New Year days. Christmas and Easter were a week later for orthodox Christians. When did something happen? Tuesday in the United States could already be Wednesday in Japan, so identifying the day of the week was discouraged unless necessary. Even foreign spellings could be minefields. When an airliner crashed off the California coast, we fonted the location as Ano Nuevo Point. A colleague from CNN's Spanish network hurried into the control room demanding an immediate correction. It should have been Año Nuevo, with the tilde, meaning New Year. Our version on screen translated to New Anus.

Graphics caused chronic headaches. Creating an acceptable generic map of the Kashmir region required a tedious back and forth between the embassies of India and Pakistan, both having complicated "lines of demarcation" illustrating their claims to the area. China complained about our illustration that gave a segment of disputed territory to India. Our weather list for international cities generated its own turbulence. It had room for only so many lines, so I had to decide which cities made the cut. The reaction was swift and intense. Copenhagen's mayor offered me an expenses-paid trip to show why it deserved a place on the list. A Brazilian city offered to pay for a slot. Later we created regional lists, placating those left off the world list.

I saw nothing wrong with using Sea of Japan and Persian Gulf to label those bodies of water, until South Korea and Saudi Arabia complained. They preferred the East Sea and the Arabian Gulf. We pointed to accepted international maps to defend our choices.

As countries changed city names to match their cultural preferences, Bombay became Mumbai, Alma-Ata became Almaty and so on. When we changed Ulan Bator to Ulaanbaatar, a U.S. diplomat wrote me a thank-you note, adding that the change had set off a party at the embassy.

*1994: The CNNI editorial meeting on the last night in the old newsroom. (Courtesy Bruce Jacobs)*

We did not, however, compromise on spelling. I insisted that all spellings follow American rules, not British. Labor not labour, defense not defence, theater not theatre. The only exception was for proper nouns. Some of my British and Australian colleagues chafed at this, arguing that Oxford English was the world standard. I countered that American English dominated entertainment and technology. Brits used plural verbs with collective nouns (Arsenal have won again). We followed American usage requiring singular verbs (Arsenal has won again). The British billion equaled 100 million; we stuck with the U.S. billion equal to 1,000 million. When provoked, I played my ace of trump: We were an American network. That's the way it was, as long as I was there. Two unavoidable exceptions: the metric system and temperatures in Celsius.

In terms of the news, our editorial decisions catered to a world audience. We didn't pay as much attention to U.S. politics as CNN/US, and we focused on stories from remote parts of the world that the domestic network ignored. When CNN aired wall-to-wall coverage of the O.J. Simpson trial, CNNI cobbled together a one-hour special each day to show highlights.

When viewers outside the United States talked about CNN, they mean CNNI. The world watched us, and the feedback was gratifying. In airports around the world, it was our anchors—Riz Kahn, Jonathan Mann, Sonia Ruseler, Jim Clancy, Michael Holmes, Rosemary Church, Colleen McEdwards, Anand Naidoo, Joie Chen and others—who were stopped by admiring viewers. When newsmakers made themselves available, it was to CNNI. Sponsors lined up for special shows on Africa, on sailing, and other specific topics, only on CNNI.

Coinciding with the network's growing stature was a grand plan for a new production facility tailored to CNNI's needs. Located in space on the third floor across the atrium from our increasingly unworkable workspaces, this complex featured multiple sets, more offices, an expansive newsroom, and a unique suite of four master control rooms for our four regional program feeds: Asia, Europe and Africa, South America, and North America. Each had a program schedule tailored to the peak viewing times and specific interests of each region. The idea was driven mostly by business considerations—advertisers preferred targeting their spots to specific regions rather than scattering them around the globe. The control room was twice as big as our cramped version upstairs. In April 1994, after a gala opening featuring Ted Turner and President Bill Clinton, I supervised and Natalya Ferguson produced the first newscast from the new digs.

At that time, I was expanding my duties and learning new skills. Now titled senior producer, I spent more time in the control room supervising newscasts and sometimes live breaking news. I was soaking up principles of news production that I had lacked when Bob Furnad made his astonishing offer years earlier.

My expanded role gave me a new insight into a troubling pattern in live breaking news coverage. With a "Breaking News" banner on the screen, we would take as long as was necessary to explain what was happening, as far as we knew. Then, the news flow would stall. The way I put it, a "crap gap" would foul the coverage with unfounded speculation, fatuous babbling—anything to fill air time and hold the viewers until we had more real news to talk about. The "vamping," as it was called, was deemed better at holding an audience than switching to other news or just repeating ad nauseum what was known.

The event that inspired my "crap gap" metaphor was the 1995 bombing at the Murrah Office Building in Oklahoma City. I remember standing in the control room with CNN Supervising Editor Earl Casey as we both stared at the monitors trying to figure out the cause of the blast. I mentioned to Earl that I hoped CNN didn't speculate on Islamic terrorism or any other cause before authorities offered their assessments.

Our coverage was coming from the D.C. studios anchored by the meticulous bureau manager, Frank Sesno. Moments after my comment to Earl, there was Frank on screen talking to an FBI expert on—what else? —Islamic terrorism. I understood how the producers would be desperate for anything to keep the coverage going, but raising that issue dragged CNN coverage into the crap gap. As it turned out, the murderous atrocity was the work of two home-grown American terrorists.

While having little involvement with the business side of CNNI, I did make the network some advertising money. I had done advisory work with a nonprofit called the International Foundation for Electoral Systems (IFES), which helped countries plan and stage fair and safe elections. CNNI needed informational spots to fill commercial breaks devoid of commercials, so I approached IFES for their help with what I called Election Watch, a 30-second billboard of upcoming elections around the world. IFES fed us the data for our animated graphic. After a few of those spots aired, Shell Oil shelled out to put their logo on Election Watch.

Despite our international focus, I didn't travel much during this phase at CNNI, other than a few conventions and speaking engagements. Donna Mastrangelo took me to visit the CNN London bureau and to a new German-language partner channel, NTV, in Berlin. That led to a return visit to Munich in 1995. Beth met me there, and we stayed with personnel director Dick Wiest. At that time RFE/RL was planning a move to Prague and was going through the torturous process of choosing which employees would make the move and who would lose their jobs. Dick asked me to speak to the staff to discuss how CNN worked and what opportunities might exist. I agreed, although I knew that CNN had little to offer these poor folks, most of whom were academics or broadcasters with limited English skills.

I spent a morning of my vacation giving more than 50 attendees an overview of CNN and what skills were required for employment. Dick then added a twist. Some employees were asking for one-on-one sessions to plead their cases. I felt sorry for them and agreed. The two dozen individual meetings took up most of the next day, denying me another day of enjoying Munich with Beth. Nobody I talked to had a remote chance of landing a job at CNN. During a break I ran into Terry Willey, my former colleague from the night of the bombing and a current newsroom manager. It was not a pleasant reunion. She accused me of trying to poach staff members while management was deciding who should go to Prague. I told her I was only there as a favor to Dick Wiest, but she was having none of it. All I could do was shrug and walk away, thinking of that cliché: No good deed goes unpunished.

I had learned along the way that an organization inevitably reaches a point where originals have to move aside for new ways and new ideas. A few make the transition, but not many. Such was the case at CNNI. Less than a year after opening the new production center, the network was decapitated. Peter and Donna were moved to other duties, and International News Vice President Eason Jordan took control during the search for a new CNNI chief. In the interim, CNNI's daily operation would be overseen by three people with the new title of executive producer. On a Friday, word got out that two were Rena Golden and Sid Bedingfield. The third was a mystery. Over drinks that evening, Rena assured me it had to be me. By then I knew how to run the control room as a supervisor, but Jeff Ofgang seemed the logical third choice.

After I twisted in the wind all weekend, Eason called me into his office on Monday and told me I was the third executive producer, even though my role would primarily remain as chief editor. In the ensuing months, the three of us forged a remarkably smooth and symbiotic working relationship. Sid handled production; Rena was in charge of the anchors and programming, and I covered editorial issues, schedules, and hiring other than anchors. We knew our roles, stayed in our lanes, and meshed as a team. Eason, meanwhile, kept a benevolent eye on us as he dealt with his many other duties. One edict was most welcome: He ordered an end to shift rotation.

*1997: Vice President Al Gore visits CNNI. Rena Golden is in the background. (CNN photo)*

While the three of us kept CNNI running, something was missing. We were buried in day-to-day concerns but couldn't step back for a broader look at the network's future. We needed a vision. That came with the arrival of Chris Cramer, whom Eason stole from the BBC to be managing editor. Chris had the pedigree one would expect for a senior BBC executive, and his added claim to fame was having been held hostage briefly in Lebanon. He was self-effacing about that and just about every other facet of his life. But his lighter side did not mean he was frivolous; he could be a tough manager with an edge that sometimes was a bit too sharp. Nevertheless, he was just what the network needed.

Most of my time by now was taken by personnel matters—hiring, scheduling, and staff management. I spent little time in the newsroom and entered the control room only to fill in for a supervisor or to help manage breaking news. While still supervising the editorial product, finding and hiring writers, copy editors, and producers took a lion's share of my time.

By then, business was good enough to underwrite overseas recruiting. We brought in talent from England, Scotland, South Africa, Ireland, Sweden, Germany (including several Americans from RFE/RL), the Philippines, Liberia, Australia, and Argentina. At one time 22 nationalities were represented in the CNNI newsroom. Diversity gave us a larger and stronger editorial safety net with a greater chance to catch something wrong or inappropriate before it made air. We reached such a level of sophistication

*1998: With CNN President Tom Johnson and colleague Lorraine Bennett.*

that CNN/US started airing our coverage of international breaking news stories for American viewers.

Our set also hosted an impressive roster of international newsmakers. I could drop any number of names, but some were particularly memorable. Pakistan's Benazir Bhutto was as lovely and gracious in person as on camera. I have a photo of me shaking hands with Vice President Al Gore. Buzz Aldrin and I stood in a buffet line lamenting the lack of moon missions. Actor Peter Ustinov and I chatted about world affairs for 15 minutes—in German. I told the Dalai Lama that I had peeked into his apartment while touring the Potala Palace in Lhasa, Tibet. He smiled and asked in his rich, baritone voice, "Was it clean?" It was.

One encounter away from work was priceless. In 1996, the sailing portion of the Olympic Games was anchored in Savannah, and the opening ceremony was emceed by then-retired Walter Cronkite, an avid sailor. The organizers had asked local barbershoppers to sing the national anthem, and the chapter called for help from others in the region. As a member of Atlanta's Stone Mountain Chorus, I couldn't resist.

As we were gathering to start the ceremony, a fierce thunderstorm halted the proceedings. We were waiting for the weather to clear (it didn't, and the ceremony was cancelled) when I spotted my lifelong hero and idol standing alone under a canopy. I sidled up to Cronkite and asked, "I wonder how Maggie Richards would write this?"

Cronkite gave a perfunctory mm-hm and then snapped his head around to look at me. "How do you know that name?" he asked.

I explained, and we chatted briefly about our shared Kansas City and wire service roots. Sponsors pulled him away to meet VIPs, and I trotted through the rain to rejoin my singing pals. If lightning had hit me at that moment, I would have died a happy man.

Chris Cramer let us three executive producers run the network while he took his time learning all about his network. It was time well spent; when he started advocating changes, they were subtle and well-informed. Meanwhile we shared personnel management challenges that no training could ever prepare us for.

Mine involved a delicate newsroom problem with a copy editor. A gentle and charming anchor who never seemed flustered by anything walked into my office adjacent to the newsroom one afternoon and asked if she could have a word. When she asked me to close the window blinds, I got nervous, thinking I had done something wrong. She sat down, squirmed a bit, and revealed that her newscast team had drafted her to speak to me about a workplace distraction that the team could no longer tolerate. Looking at the floor, she revealed that a team member suffered from frequent gas attacks, and everyone around him suffered from the consequences. They wanted me to clear the air.

Struggling to maintain proper managerial stoicism, I promised to do my best. The next day, after rehearsing several ways to broach the subject, I called the offender into my office. He had been a colleague and friend for years, so the invitation seemed routine to him. I closed the door and the blinds as he sat down. I asked him how he was feeling. He said fine. I asked him if he was having any health issues. He said no as his suspicions grew. I told him I had received word from the newsroom that that there was a problem. He asked if it was his editing. I assured him that would never be an issue. With as much empathy as I could muster, I told him about the complaint. He was mortified and started blurting apologies. I tried to assure him that it really wasn't that big of a deal, and I suggested he change his diet while at work and maybe try pills made specifically to control his malady. He did, and that was the end of it.

Chris's challenge, however, was far more delicate. A CNNI director, we'll call him George, had taken an extended leave that drew little notice among the staff. Weeks later George returned—as Jane (another changed name). Within days, a delegation of female staff members marched into Chris's office and demanded to know which restroom Jane was authorized to use. Chris asked for time to study the matter and called human resources. With typical conflict avoidance, HR said Chris would have to find a way to determine whether Jane's evolution had progressed sufficiently to qualify her for the women's restroom. Chris was appalled and called me into his office to tell me what was happening. I think he hoped I might play the role of loyal subordinate and take the whole mess off his hands. That was way above my pay grade, so I wished him luck.

As it turned out, he did get lucky when the problem solved itself. Jane went back to directing newscasts but was prickly about her new identity. Everybody tiptoed around the issue, but the slightest perceived reference to her altered state would spark

*1997: Singing the National Anthem at a Braves game with the Stone Mountain Barbershop Chorus.*

*1998: With the Stone Mountain Chorus in London, dragging Albert the Dinosaur in the London Festival Parade on New Year's Day.*

a tantrum. Finally, a supervising producer in a moment of breaking news stress called her George. Jane stood up, reached inside her blouse, pulled out her bra, slammed it on the director's console, yelled, "That's it. I've had enough!" and stormed out the control room and out of the building. Another director took over, but Jane had sealed her fate at CNNI. Abandoning a newscast for any reason was a firing offense. Jane never returned to work.

In terms of news, Chris's first crisis was the 1996 Atlanta Olympics bombing in Centennial Olympic Park, across the street from CNN Center. He rushed to the scene, and he somehow ran into a tourist who had caught the blast on videotape. Chris coaxed him into CNN Center and alerted other executives. I heard that this guy was taken to a room at the center's Omni Hotel, where he was offered a priceless array of Olympic tickets for the rights to the video. He agreed, and CNN had exclusive images of a historic atrocity.

Another historic atrocity from that night was security guard Richard Jewell's false implication in the bombing. CNN was one of many news outlets who reported Jewell was a suspect even though he had not been arrested or charged. Ed Turner (no relation to Ted), the vice president for news gathering, assured me later that sources from both the FBI and the Georgia Bureau of Investigation had insisted to CNN that Jewell was the guy. He wasn't, and CNN was among several news organizations that settled with Jewell out of court. Nevertheless, his life was ruined.

I can't second-guess CNN for joining the Jewell pile-on, but it reinforced my preference to wait for formal charges before identifying a suspect. It was not the first time we had taken the bait. As we covered a series of college student murders in Gainesville, Florida, in1990, CNN fell victim to a law enforcement trick of naming suspects or even "persons of interest" to give the impression that authorities under intense public pressure were making progress. In this sordid case, four people were named before the real culprit was caught.

After the Jewell fiasco, I argued that CNN should never name a suspect until formal charges were filed. Media in other countries worked under such limitations, with some withholding names until after conviction. Tom Johnson challenged me on that one, asking how we would look if we were the only ones covering the story without the name. He had a point, so I countered that we should try to be the last to report a name. Nobody would remember or care who had it first, but they would definitely remember when a news outlet screwed it up. I still hate hearing a suspect's name before formal charges are filed. Too many reputations are ruined that way, and in almost all those cases, nobody is held accountable.

As Chris's control of the network solidified, I heard ominous rumblings even as we remained friends outside work. It was a series of hints and off-hand comments, a common tactic for presaging changes in a newsroom. He thought I was being too hard on some of the staff, which I took as something of a Munich reprise. I was getting along fine with everyone, but I accepted the critique and looked for ways to improve. He challenged several of my writing style edicts as being too American, but I shrugged that off as his understandable preference for British usage.

Then came my first performance evaluation. He listed all the criticisms I had heard and a few more that were new to me. My overall grade was "satisfactory," meaning average, in effect damning with faint praise. I studied it for a day and then insisted on a rebuttal. He had said nothing about the successful computerization of CNNI's entire production system that Sid and I had planned and managed, nothing about the quality of the outstanding writers and producers I had recruited and trained, nothing about my complete overhaul and simplification of the staff scheduling system. It was as if I had accomplished nothing in the past year. When I cited each of these points, he would nod and tell me to include them in a written response to my review. I did, but I never knew whether that went into my file attached to his one-sided and hurtful evaluation. I felt no further repercussions from Chris, and we went back to our usual good working relationship. But something had changed.

In September 1997 I took a week off at Hilton Head, South Carolina, ostensibly to experiment with a new staff scheduling concept (never used) but in reality, to consider my future. Was I doing a bad job? Was I going to be fired? What would I do if that happened?

Beth joined me for the weekend, and that added more issues to confront. Our relationship had been steadily cooling for years, but difficult conversations that weekend hardened my suspicion that our marriage was in trouble. We had no children (by mutual choice), separate careers, separate interests, and in effect separate lives in the same house. Three months later I moved out, hoping the separation would spur us to patch things up. It didn't, and in June 1999 we ended our 25-year marriage. We stayed in touch as friends until her death from cancer in 2016.

Even with my concerns about Chris, the Sid-Rena-Ted troika kept humming along until a merger blew the top off CNN. In 1996, Time Warner bought Turner Broadcasting, including all CNN properties. With the change in ownership came a new corporate culture.

The days of Turner's quaint, hands-on control of his historic creation were gone. His idea of a Christmas bonus had been a supermarket coupon for a turkey. He had mandated free Braves ticket coupons for employees each season. The annual holiday staff party had the feel of a singles mixer because spouses were not invited.

Through it all, the staff never lost its affection for its world-famous boss. Then, almost overnight, CNN was big business. It was changing, and not all for the good.

Bob Furnad had moved to Headline News. The leadership void was filled in 1997 with the hiring of Rick Kaplan, a larger-than-life graduate of CBS News, where he had been Walter Cronkite's producer. CNN had never seen anyone like Rick. He was the ultimate grand thinker, and his plans for the network matched the new owners' wish to raise CNN out of its comfortable news niche into to the broadcast major leagues. The emergence of two competitors—Fox News and MSNBC—added to the impetus for change. We didn't think much about Fox. We talked more about the combined threat of Microsoft's big pockets and NBC's network power.

The evening of August 31, 1997, I was at a car race with Bob when we heard something had happened to Princess Diana. I was supposed to be on call that night, so I raced to a track office phone and learned that she had died in a Paris car crash. Instead of calling me, Rick called Sid into work and watched him manage the coverage for all networks from the CNNI control room. Rick was impressed and later asked him to come back to CNN/US as general manager. That broke up the band. Sid took over daily operations of "the mothership" while Rick concentrated on bigger things like a complete production center redesign and new network-style prime time programming.

CNNI kept going fine without Sid, but it had a new, unsettled feel. I waded into 1998 separated from my wife, unsure of my job status, and wondering if I should be moving on. After all, I was past my three-year threshold.

Sid tossed me a lifeline with one brief conversation in April 1998. He needed help managing the network's editorial product. Senior editor Kim Engebretsen was gone, and he wanted me in that role. I had already reached my life's goal in Germany; now I was reaching the professional mountaintop I had hoped for since my college days. I snatched that golden ring, and he even gave me my preferred title of executive editor. That was important to me. Your salary tells you how much your employer values you; your title tells the world how much your employer values you.

Leaving CNNI was harder than I had expected. I was not responsible for its birth, but I was certainly a midwife. I had hired most of the staff and supervised all of it, and I liked everyone I worked with. A farewell party at a local pub featured a goodbye poem by Neil Curry, a crafty producer and overqualified writer. It summarized my tenure and even noted my divorce-induced weight loss.

Here it is:

**I LIVE, I LEAVE, I LIFF**

Divine hands wrote the Bible
And likewise the Koran
But the author of **our** wisdom
Was a somewhat different man.

Ted Iliff wrote a volume
Which was thick as it was wide
Comprehensive and Compendious
The CNN Style Guide

It's like the Ten Commandments
But in numbers Ninety-Four

And if you dare defy it
You will be shown the door

Where ignorance predominates
Vulgarity ensues
Avoid alliteration
And all akin abuse

No room for British slang words
In the prose we put on air
And don't you font the Queen as such
But make sure you name her heir.
Don't use flowery language
And call a spade a spade
Not a "bloody shovel with
an earth-removing blade."

Shorten all your sentences.
Keep them brief. OK?
Don't use abbreviations
And let metric rule the way.

The global face is changing
It's Ted's work, that's no lie
With a quick computer keystroke
Bombay becomes Mumbai.

The power of Almighty
Came to him from Heaven sent
Change "President of Uganda"
To "Ugandan President."

On the seventh day God rested
And I had planned that too
But Ted rewrote the schedule
So I worked from 4 till 2.

For his influence was manifold
You had to go through Ted
If you wanted leave or time to grieve
Or even to be wed.

With files and fonts and schedules
His armory was full
Then another challenge beckoned
From upstairs he felt the pull.

He was a man of stature
Persona large as life
But now he's half the man he was
Without the surgeon's knife.

His exit from the newsroom
Was stealthy, without sound
As Ted grew slim we spotted him
departing pound by pound.

Behind he left a vacuum
Not just his thermos flask
Replacing such a character
Will be a thankless task

Warm-hearted, now departed
Later lamented yet alive
And bound for resurrection
And another chance to thrive.

In the teachings of Ted Iliff
When time has come to go
We don't say "'Bye" at CNNI
We just tease the next show.

Stay tuned out there in Asia
And Europe, hold the dial
For just ahead, the mighty Ted
A man to make you smile.

Best wishes from Neil Curry

**CNN: Back to the Future**

The return to CNN was easy; I knew most of the 60 writers and copy editors from my previous stint in that newsroom. Several were still golf or poker buddies. When Sid was not happy with my early staff schedules, he didn't get mad. He got help, and in came Marty Hill as editorial director. The tall, athletic Michigander had been with

CNN as long as I had and was popular with the staff. He took over schedule preparations and other administrative duties.

One of Sid's chief reasons for drafting me was to help him direct the CNN newsroom's digital conversion as we had at CNNI. It was an arduous transformation requiring meticulous planning, but we got it to work. Paper scripts, videotape playback, and other vestiges of the 80s were gone. Scripts now went straight to the anchor's teleprompter, video was stored and played back in a digital server system, and on-screen fonts were coded in scripts to appear automatically on screen, eliminating the need for control room operators retyping every font. Robotics controlled studio cameras. Entire job categories were wiped out. I don't recall anyone losing their job from the modernization, and the savings and improved efficiency were undeniable.

I also helped to design the writing area of Rick's new production center. Comparing the old and new facilities would be like comparing a log cabin to a spacecraft. It was quite a project, befitting Rick's vision and style. The cramped control room was replaced with a more spacious and complex B-Control featuring a mosaic of monitors showing competing networks, incoming video feeds, and previews of a newscast's visual elements.

Rick had even grander ideas. He walked into the job on a mission to change CNN's prime time presence. Newscasts and *Larry King Live* were not good enough. He wanted a magazine show fashioned after successful programs at the major networks. Under an umbrella title of *NewsStand*, one-hour shows would air weeknights. Each would have a focus matching a Time Warner magazine—news, money, entertainment, and people.

Rick demanded a separate staff for the *NewsStand* shows, implying intentionally or inadvertently that the CNN staff was not up to the challenge. He cherry-picked a few CNN standouts but mostly hired outsiders with major network credentials. Understandably, this did not sit well with the rank and file. The unit was placed in separate offices in CNN Center, further fueling indignation. I was the network's executive editor, and I never met any of the unit's new staff members, including the top two producers. I had plenty to keep me busy, but the lack of even casual contact struck me as odd.

The first episode, heralded with intense promotion, aired on June 7, 1998. "Valley of Death" told of a Vietnam War operation called Tailwind. The report alleged that U.S. forces used poison gas in Laos against a group of American defectors. Peter Arnett, one of the "Boys of Baghdad," voiced the report.

It was an instant sensation for all the wrong reasons. A quick Pentagon investigation found no corroboration. Worse, key sources in the report retracted or denied their contributions. CNN launched its own investigation headed by noted media attorney Floyd Abrams, and the conclusion was damning: The report was journalistically flawed and was retracted—a first for CNN in 18 years of 24/7 news broadcasting.

Repercussions were swift and the staff's reaction harsh. Tom Johnson called a series of "town hall" meetings to let employees vent their rage. Standing with Johnson

***1999: With Mohammad Ali in the control room as the U.S. Senate prepares to vote on Bill Clinton's impeachment. (CNN photo)***

at the front of each session were Abrams and Rick. The staff was merciless. Speakers from all ranks ripped the "elitist" *NewsStand* staff of newcomers for soiling CNN's theretofore spotless reputation. It was brutal, particularly for Johnson, whom most employees viewed as collateral damage from the disaster.

Chris Cramer often used a great line, "Deputy heads will roll." That's what happened in this case. The two unit leaders, April Oliver and Jack Smith, were fired; a few others were reassigned. Peter Arnett was reprimanded and later resigned. The series hung on for a few years under different manifestations, but its fate had been sealed on that opening night.

The same could be said for Rick. My impression was that some of the fire went out of him after that debacle, even as he oversaw coverage for one of the century's biggest political dramas. In October, the House of Representatives started impeachment proceedings against President Bill Clinton. The hearings resulted in two articles of impeachment, and the Senate trial spilled over into early 1999. On February 12, the Senate scheduled a vote on both articles. Rick supervised network coverage, with Sid handling the details.

My job that day was to sit in the control room during the roll call and record each vote. My plan called for a control room staffer to type the running total into an on-screen graphic.

*1999: Rick Kaplan (center) produces CNN's millennium coverage, flanked by me and Director Tom Gaut. (CNN photo)*

Two days before the vote, a tech-savvy producer, Jon Orlin, had a better idea. I was compiling the vote on an Excel spreadsheet, which he said could be rigged to automatically display the tally on screen, eliminating the technical middleman. Behaving like a hidebound dinosaur, I said no, we were set up to do it my way and didn't have time to experiment. Fortunately, Sid told him to give it a try, and he had it working in 24 hours. That made my job easier.

However, minutes before the first Senate vote, I heard a commotion in the hallway outside the control room. I looked up, and here came Rick with a guest—Muhammad Ali. The champ was in the building for some reason, and Rick had invited him to watch the Senate vote from our control room. I shook his massive, calloused hand and then tried to concentrate on my job even though the world's most famous athlete was sitting two seats away. In his breathy, almost whispering voice, he asked a few questions about how things worked and then silently watched. I forced myself to focus, and I didn't notice when he left after the first vote. Clinton was acquitted, and our system and coverage were flawless.

As Rick's time at CNN headed toward its end, he managed a few more accomplishments, including completion of the new production center. He took personal control of CNN's global coverage of the millennium's arrival. Building on a feature I had devised at CNNI, we prepared brief spots showing places around the world where 2000 was arriving, starting, and ending in the Pacific Ocean. When possible, we aired live pictures of the celebrations. The Sydney bridge fireworks and the Eiffel Tower illumination in Paris were among the many spectacular images of that day and night.

Rick was massaging rundowns as we approached midnight in America. I think he was at his best in that arena, producing magnificent coverage. I mismanaged one top-of-the-hour spot during the evening, but he kept his notorious temper in check and kept on going to my everlasting gratitude. Maybe it was the tux I was wearing to mark the occasion. We and other news organizations had been covering all the dire warnings of apocalyptic Y2K chaos. From that perspective, the night was a dud. But CNN looked great.

His last hurrah was organizing the gala celebration of CNN's 20th anniversary on June 1, 2000. By then, many of the familiar CNN stalwarts were gone, unhappy with AOL's takeover in January of Time Warner and, in effect, CNN.

I was most sorry to see Tom Johnson go. He was always friendly and supportive. He even loaned me his Jeep one winter night when my car wouldn't start. One day in his office, Tom let me hold the pen that Mikhail Gorbachev used to sign the Soviet Union out of existence. Tom was in the room on December 25, 1991 as the last Soviet president received the official documents to sign. Gorbachev then realized he did not have a pen. He asked if anyone in the room had one he could use, stipulating that it could not be an American brand. Tom pulled out his Swiss Mont Blanc and handed it to Gorbachev.

Tom liked to show off his staff to visitors. He once stopped me outside the café and introduced me to a guest. "Ted," he asked, "what's the one word that you consider the most important characteristic of CNN's writing?" I had to think fast and came up with "clarity." He gave me an approving pat on the shoulder as he and his guest walked by. The finest example of a Southern gentleman, he shepherded CNN from its status as "chicken noodle news" to the most respected and recognized broadcast news service in the world.

Historian and *Time Magazine* editor Walter Issacson succeeded Tom but did not arrive until July 2001. He faced some of the same unfair criticisms Tom faced: no TV background and too political. We didn't interact much, and like Tom he left the details of CNN operations to his staff.

The CNN 20th anniversary gala showed Rick at his grandiose best. The event was scheduled for Philips Arena, the sports venue adjacent to CNN Center. It would be filled with invited VIP guests from all entities involved in the merged enterprise. Rick asked me to write a script summarizing CNN's 20 years to be read by an all-star cast of CNN personalities, including Larry King, Bernard Shaw, Bobbie Battista and Nick Charles, the charming sports anchor who characteristically strolled in less than a minute before he was to go on stage. Rick wanted to fire him and kill him all at once but resisted for the sake of the show.

The main attraction was supposed to be rocker Rod Stewart. A contract had been signed and accommodations arranged, but it all came undone three days before the event. Stewart had throat surgery and backed out. Rick didn't miss a beat. I was in his office as he started calling his showbiz friends. In a matter of hours he had secured Diana Ross. She was rehearsing for an upcoming tour in Los Angeles and agreed to come to Atlanta to bail Rick out. That was impressive.

Other than the Nick Charles episode, the evening went as planned. The script worked, Ted Turner, now sidelined from any involvement with CNN or Turner Broadcasting, gave a typically folksy Ted talk, and Diana Ross had the place rocking for over an hour. I slipped onto the front row a few seats down from Turner and AOL chief Steve Case and soaked up the moment. It was magical, but it also felt like a New Orleans-style funeral for the CNN we had known.

On September 2, 2000, I was walking off a plane in Odessa, Ukraine, to attend a regional economic development conference when a companion pulled me aside and told me she thought she had heard news about important changes at CNN. I got on the phone as soon as I could, and Sid confirmed that Rick was out and he had been put in charge of CNN.

Rick's tenure had been turbulent. Much of the staff never got over the *NewsStand* fiasco, and others complained that he had never tried to understand the CNN culture. But he treated me well and was generous with compliments. Weeks after he left, my ex-wife, a cousin, and I ran into him outside an Atlanta restaurant. After introductions, he pointed to me and said, "This guy got things done." I'll take that as an epitaph anytime. Years later, when Celia Wexler included a chapter about me in her award-winning book *Out of the News*, Rick called me "the word czar" of CNN.

The AOL deal turned out to be a step too far for CNN. It was a bad corporate fit, and tension between the two staffs was palpable in the few times we interacted. To us, the AOL folks were young, cocky, sneaker-wearing nerds. To them, we were haughty, hidebound dinosaurs who needed to make way for the future.

The deal also sparked the first major wave of layoffs in CNN history. Ted Turner always insisted that layoffs should be the last resort in budget cutting, but the new guys had other ideas. In January 2001, the company announced plans to shed about 400 jobs, or 10 percent of the CNN work force, to "sharpen its focus" and "capture synergies for growth."

Those making that call were not the ones like me who had to make the cuts. I was told to rank copy editors and writers from best to worst. Then the bean counters decided how many people to cut from the bottom up. My tally was two writers and two copy editors. We were taught a film noir method of how to speak to the unfortunates. We could only tell them they had done nothing wrong, there was no appeal, and goodbye. No good luck wishes or expressions of sympathy, not even "I'm sorry."

The victims were summoned from the newsroom one at a time while on duty. Each was directed to a small spare office, where the executioner delivered the verdict. My four were good at their jobs, just not quite as good as others. All were of an age that would make finding a new job difficult. I felt queasy, struggled to look them in the eye, and wanted to promise them something to ease the pain all of us felt. But the boffins who ordered the carnage didn't work at CNN, so it was easy for them to mandate stoicism.

As the day progressed, longtime colleagues walked with boxes full of personal effects through the newsroom and out of the building. A few were crying; none were allowed to say goodbye. Each was accompanied by a uniformed security guard, supposedly to discourage any disruptive behavior. I considered it another layer of cruelty. I'm not sure there is a good way to cut staff, but that wasn't one. It was AOL's most memorable legacy at CNN. Ultimately, the merger fell apart.

Sid's elevation as Rick's successor had little effect on my duties. He urged me in one performance evaluation to be more of a "protector and advocate" for the writers and copy editors. There it was again, another reminder to ease up. I tried to adjust, but I had inherent disadvantages. I was big and had a voice that could sound gravelly. When I talked to a writer or editor in the newsroom, they were usually sitting as I hovered over them like a bear on hind legs. I had purged obscenity from my at-work vocabulary, and my only yelling was directed at myself for something stupid I had done. I tried light, often self-deprecating humor when appropriate. During one meeting with writers and editors, I paid two massage therapists to move from person to person around the table giving brief chair massages.

About this time, I came up with a theory about manager behavior. Even if supervisors are scrupulous in the way they speak to their staffs, that's not enough. They should behave as if they are on stage. Employees don't judge words alone; they study facial expressions, posture, and even what the boss is wearing, looking for clues about the manager's mood at that moment. "That's just great" can have a variety of meanings when matched with expression, voice tone, and body language. It's the perception that matters, and a good manager shapes that perception.

Casual body contact—a pat on the back, a quick shoulder rub, even a hug—was still tolerated in those days, but I worried about the consequences of any misunderstanding. If I wanted to pat someone on the back while they were working, I tapped the back of their chair. If someone liked to hug (a few did), I let them make the first move. In keeping my distance, I may have appeared cold or aloof. Sid actually warned me about that, but I chose to stay on the side of caution.

I did go easy on the staff when it came to personal issues, particularly sick calls. Even if they wanted to work, writers and editors were told to stay home if they were ill, no matter what staffing complications they caused. I didn't want them infecting others, and they wouldn't be any use to us anyway. The rule extended to more than illness. When a distressed writer called in to say he couldn't work that day, I wished him a quick recovery. He said that wasn't the problem, hesitated, and then revealed his cherished cat had died. My answer was the same: stay home. He was too upset to work.

And then there was poor Pete Christiansen. During renovation, the anchor set and newsroom were moved to temporary quarters on the seventh floor. Writers had their backs to a door, and tour groups could look in through its small window.

Pete had been assigned a script about a couple who announced to the world they wanted to consummate their marriage online. We couldn't let that go, and the producers knew Pete would give it the delicate treatment it needed. As part of his due

*2001: With baseball legend Buck O'Neill and CNN anchor Leon Harris at Kansas City's Negro Leagues Baseball Museum.*

diligence, he went to the website where the happy couple planned to do the deed. It was a porn site. To his instant horror, he realized that a tour group was looking at his work station through the window. He lunged at his keyboard to close the offending website, finished the script, and then called me to offer his resignation. When he told me the sordid tale and how he was sure he had shamed the network, I stifled a laugh, calmed him down, and told him he had nothing to worry about. That was the end of the matter.

What I consider my finest hour as a manager involved a long-tenured copy editor who was fading. Age and a head injury had reduced his ability to do the job. There was no place to sideline him, and the staff loved the guy. What to do? His annual performance review was a well-documented indictment of his work. I asked him if he felt up to the job, and he insisted he did, so we were at an impasse. To fire him would have been inhumane, and he probably would have sued CNN.

A few days after the review session, he returned to my office and confessed that he wished he could retire, but personal finances ruled that out. I was not allowed to suggest retirement, but he had put that option on the table, opening the way to a new discussion. I visited with HR's Virginia Tanawong, an innovative problem solver—not a common commodity in the human resources departments I had worked with. She authorized me to explore the retirement idea with the editor, so I asked him why it was out of the question. He explained he had borrowed a large sum from his retirement account, and if he retired he'd have to pay that back, something he couldn't afford. I went back to Virginia, and wheels started turning. What would it cost the company, we wondered, if we fired the editor and then had to defend our decision in court? The choice for CNN was giant legal fees if we won or at least a six-figure settlement if we didn't.

Comparing the potential legal costs to the sum he owed his retirement fund, the solution was obvious. If he retired, the company would pay off his retirement fund, and the editor could retire with dignity. Done deal. The staff gave him a fitting farewell, and he strolled into a comfortable retirement. Before he left, he gave me a coffee table book with a thank-you note in it.

Sid's time at the helm, while brief, would span two agonizing historic events. The first was the interminable 2000 presidential election. CNN declared winners state by state based on information from an election service shared by networks and wire services. CNN's political director, Tom Hannon, sat in the control room on election night listening in on a conference call linking the service to its clients. Calling a state for George W. Bush or Albert Gore that night was in most cases by consensus.

I was in the control room that November 7, standing behind Hannon, managing the on-screen fonts that helped to tell the story of the election. Fairly early in the evening, Hannon and others agreed with the election service that Gore had won Florida. About that time, I turned sharply to tell a control room editor something and slammed hard into Ted Turner, who was showing a friend how we worked. I had not seen or heard him, and the shot he took from me should have put him on the floor. But he just absorbed it, graciously accepted my profuse apology, and moved on as if nothing had happened.

Almost as soon as the call was made, the vote totals started to tell a different story. Later that night, CNN and others had to retract their calls, making Florida undecided and denying the nation a clear winner. An exhausting, inconclusive drama of recounts and court hearings dragged on for the next 36 days. Each day I had to huddle with a news desk editor to update our tally of county recounts, hoping it was close to what our competitors had. Finally, the Supreme Court sided with Bush, and Gore conceded. Hannon suffered no adverse consequences, nor should he have. One star was born during the ordeal: Bill Hemmer, the "chad lad." He was more than that; the guy was a pro.

During a subsequent period of relative calm, a vice president promotion was announced. I started wondering, "Why not me?" When I asked Sid, his honest answer squelched that idea. There was no other rung for me to climb on the CNN ladder, so I decided to concentrate on what I enjoyed best: control room supervision.

I started every day by walking into the control room at 8:45 a.m. to monitor the scripting, fonting, and other editorial aspects of the morning newscasts. When Washington took over at noon, I would break for lunch and then spend the rest of the day handling whatever needed attention—style and writing, recruiting, hiring, staff performance reviews, and so on. I was comfortable. Too comfortable. I was crossing another metaphysical three-year threshold, so I started looking around.

*2001: Interviewed by Ukrainian TV crew outside IREX seminar in Kiev.*

I couldn't imagine finding a similar gig at another news organization. I had been active for years with the International Research and Exchanges Board (IREX) as an advisor for its international media development programs, so I wondered if I could find a more formal role with IREX. When they advertised for a new media development director in September, I raised my hand, and the response was encouraging. I was set for an interview at their Washington offices on September 14, and I was pretty sure I had the job.

That's as far as it went.

The morning of September 11 started as usual. I got to the office at 8:30 a.m., briefly checked messages in my office, and then walked into the control room, sitting down at my workstation at 8:45. A few minutes later, one of the screens on the huge monitor wall came to life with a baffling image. Against a clear New York City sky, smoke was spewing from the World Trade Center. It looked as if a plane could have hit a tower. I thought about the 1945 crash of a B-25 bomber into the Empire State Building, but that was in fog and in an age of primitive aviation technology. This was different.

We started mobilizing coverage as we showed those first images to our viewers. About 15 minutes later flames erupted from the second tower, and we found video of an airliner flying into it. We were reporting what we knew, but that wasn't much. Barely a half-hour later came the first images of another airliner's crash into the Pentagon. Another 20 minutes, and we could hardly believe new reports of a fourth airliner crashing in Pennsylvania. Sid poked his head into the control room, yelled,

"We're at war!" and raced away to take overall command of coverage. I thought that might be a bit of an exaggeration; that's why he got the big bucks.

Our incomparable control room copy editor, Nicole File, hammered out breaking news fonts as quickly as we had new developments. By 10:30 a.m., we were getting a news crawl operating at the bottom of the screen because on-air coverage couldn't keep up with everything. A separate team of writers and editors was set up just for the crawl, which became permanent fixture of the CNN screen. On the fly, I had to figure out extended staffing assignments and editorial details—headline, style present tense, no more than 40 words per item, all-capital text to spare us capitalization issues, configuration of the computer system generating the crawl—all the while keeping an eye on our coverage.

Not since John Kennedy's assassination had television news faced such a challenge. On that day and days afterward, there was no such thing as competition or partisanship. When the question of Emmys came up later, everyone involved in coverage for any network that day got an Emmy citation. It's my finest award.

As the coverage that day moved past the initial shock, we heard all kinds of rumors, but we were following the strict two-source rule, with the only exception being information from CNN sources. We made our only error of the day when our national desk reported an explosion at the State Department. No other news outlet had that, but it was from our people, so we went with it. It was wrong, and we quickly aired our only correction of the day. After that, we required verification of our own reporting as well.

The pictures, of course, spoke for themselves. We watched one tower and then the other collapse. We watched the rescue and recovery efforts at the Pentagon and later saw the stark black hole where the fourth plane had crashed. Our on-air talent wisely let the images do the reporting. There was no "crap gap" on 9/11 or in days afterward. Too much news was breaking hour after hour, day after day. Our global reach gave us instant access to international reaction and developments. As U.S. authorities pieced the clues together, we learned about Osama bin Laden and the Taliban and saw war in Afghanistan coming.

The national no-fly rule meant that my September 14 job hunting visit to Washington was off. I called IREX and withdrew from consideration. There was no way I could leave CNN. We didn't have long to wait for the other shoe to drop. On Saturday, October 6, I was in Chattanooga, Tennessee for a barbershop singing contest. I was rummaging through a hotel gift shop when my cellphone rang. It was Sid. The code signaling imminent hostilities in Afghanistan had arrived. I rushed back to Atlanta and worked the control room as the war started. Within eight weeks, the Taliban were out, and Osama bin Laden was on the run.

As 2002 arrived, things were simmering down a bit in Afghanistan. But not in Atlanta.

In late February, I got a call from a CNN buddy to warn me that we were getting a new boss. Walter Isaacson was making Sid his deputy. I never learned why, but by this time Fox News had climbed past CNN in the ratings. The caller also told me the name of Sid's successor, Teya Ryan. My reflex reaction was, "I'm outta here." I don't even know why I said that. I knew Teya as a respected executive at both the CNN financial network and Headline News. She was driven, focused, and confident. All good, but I sensed trouble.

Teya started her tenure with one-on-one meetings to ask executives to describe their duties. I explained my editorial and administrative work. Her response surprised me: "I would think someone with your title would be working on the vision and mission of CNN."

I lamely told her I did that too. I should have said that I was in effect the quality control agent for CNN writing, ensuring accuracy, balance, taste, background, and context. But I didn't.

Within a month, word circulated that more high-level changes were coming. On April 3, as I was leaving work for the day, Teya's assistant called and asked me to be in her office at 10 a.m. the following morning. That night I convened a small group of CNN friends and my ex-wife at a local pub to try to figure out what was up. I had my suspicions, and one colleague with good sources predicted trouble.

In her office, Teya didn't waste time or words; she was making changes and was eliminating my position. She believed my role could be filled by producers and editors as part of their normal routine. My deputy Marty Hill's position was also being cut.

I had steeled myself for bad news and expected the axe that morning. I was single, had pondered leaving for months, had a strong professional network, and was confident I'd find something else to do. My contract, while no golden parachute, guaranteed at least a gilded cushion in terms of money and benefits. Marty, on the other hand, had an artist wife and two razor sharp kids. His record was spotless, and he could have taken a newsroom editing role. Teya was unmoved, and I learned later he got the news while on vacation. That was an outrage. It was beneath Teya.

All this was done behind Sid's back, and he was livid. I still have some of his messages to me, and they leave no doubt about his assessment of my value to the network. I heard later he complained to Teya and railed at Isaacson, then assigned himself a trip to Israel to calm down.

Teya asked me to stay an extra month to continue my duties and help with the transition, whatever that was supposed to be. The following Monday morning I withdrew to my office and never set foot in the control room again, except for my last day to say goodbye. The few follow-up meetings with Teya were cordial; during one conversation she complimented my handling of the situation and added, "You are an elegant man." That was a first.

I filled my remaining days working on my resume, winning several severance skirmishes with human resources, reactivating my network, and printing out several hundred pages of my editorial directives to use as source material for a book on writing. That pile is still in my closet.

My last day was Friday, May 3, 2002. Cradling a small box of belongings, I wandered through the control room and newsroom saying goodbye, walked out of

CNN Center, just like those unfortunates in the 2001 layoffs. Sid arranged a farewell gathering that night with the following network-wide notice:

> *Please join me in bidding farewell to a fine friend and colleague—Ted Iliff. For the past decade, Ted has been my able partner in crime—first at CNNI, later at CNN/US. He'll be greatly missed here—but his departure does offer the opportunity for a first-class farewell party. A few hundred of Ted's closest friends will gather FRIDAY at PARK TAVERN, 10th and Monroe, to lift a glass in tribute.*

It was a gratifying and lively send-off, drawing all levels of CNN staff from newly hired writers to Eason Jordan. The party went well past closing time, and a few colleagues walked with me through Piedmont Park to my midtown condo for a final round of drinks on me.

Then I was alone, and for the first time since college, jobless. Dan Taylor, my Kansas City UPI bureau chief, once said you haven't had a real career until you've fired somebody and you've been fired. So now mine was complete, but far from over.

Teya left CNN in September 2003. I've often said that if I ever saw her again, I'd kiss her on the forehead. In the #metoo age, I'd make that a handshake. If a virus was going around, a nod would have to suffice. Nobody likes to get canned, but by kicking me out of the nest, Teya sent me on the way to my greatest adventures.

First epilogue: Some time after I left, with my position unfilled, CNN aired video with a font "Jerusalem, Israel." This violated an ironclad CNN rule against branding the holy city as a part of Israel. To do so ignored international law and Palestinian claims to the city as their capital. Walter Issacson was not pleased. At the daily senior staff meeting, he demanded to know who was in charge of preventing such a gaffe. After an awkward silence, someone said, "That used to be Ted Iliff." I heard this secondhand. I hope it's true.

Second epilogue: Many years after I was gone, I would once in a while visit CNN. Without fail, I would run into folks I had hired or worked with at CNN or CNNI. Their welcomes were always warm, their comments gratifying. In one case almost two decades after I had left, a couple I had recruited from England for CNNI, David and Julie Lindsay, introduced me to a new CNN employee: their daughter.

# CHAPTER 9

# Consulting

## *I Talk, Therefore I Am*

The only period of official unemployment in my life didn't last six weeks. In late May I received a call that put me on the path for a series of consulting jobs that were as instructive for me as I hope they were for my clients.

The call came from the International Research and Exchanges Board, a Washington-based non-governmental organization (NGO) that specialized in global media development. I had served on its media advisory board since my CNNI days and had participated in several IREX international workshops and seminars. This was where I thought I was headed when 9/11 shut that idea down, and it was one of the first places I called after leaving CNN.

My consulting assignments originated at the U.S. Agency for International Development (USAID). This State Department unit was the wellspring for media development projects throughout the world. When the Cold War ended, USAID decided that aiding new and evolving media in post-Communist countries would foster civil society, so it ramped up its media development efforts through IREX, Internews, and other NGOs.

USAID would solicit bids for a project, and IREX and its competitors would compete for the contract. I'm sure USAID kept an eye on my projects that it funded, but I never felt any attempt to influence or interfere with my work. The same goes for the host governments; I only heard of one official complaint from all my USAID-funded work, and it was rejected. More on that later.

The late May call concerned an annual gathering in Istanbul of IREX program heads from Eastern Europe and the former Soviet Union. The agenda included panel discussions on the role of media in civil society, and I was invited to moderate the sessions and write a summary. That was four days all expenses paid in Istanbul, plus a fee. If I had known what was coming, I would have paid them.

The program heads, called chiefs of party, served as resident supervisors for IREX media development programs. Istanbul brought together, among others, Joe Raffelberg from Montenegro, Tim Kenny (a former *USA Today* colleague) from Kosova, Shelly Markoff from Albania, and Bill Canter, who would later move on to Armenia for Internews. Over the next year, I would work with all of them.

Consulting was a comfortable escape hatch from the exhilarating grind of CNN. I was being paid for what I knew, not what I could do. It was a lot of talking, a little writing (memos and reports), and not much work. In addition, I felt I had already enjoyed a good career run, so now it was time for me to pay back the profession by helping it to develop in other countries. It was still international news, but at a different pace, in different cultures, with journalists whose standards and ethics were as diverse as their populations.

One limitation I had to work around involved language. Translation helped only to a point. The term "lost in translation" is more than a cliché. I've read Goethe and Shakespeare in both English and German. Trust me, the translations never match the originals.

With news organizations, I could teach production methods, studio technical skills, video shooting and editing, professional standards and ethics, staff and business management, and even marketing. Early on, I astonished myself with the broad range of expertise I brought to my consulting jobs. I had absorbed far more than I realized all those years at CNN. More than once after applying a dose of broadcast know-how, I thought to myself, "Where the hell did *that* come from?" But my expertise could not reach across the language threshold, so writing rarely factored into my consulting. Accuracy, fairness, balance, and clarity—the pillars of my journalism—could only be addressed if the translations closely matched the originals. Storytelling, however, did fit my brief. I knew a good story when I saw it, even if I didn't understand it.

I did have something to say about bias in news. Young journalists in developing countries, and even in some advanced ones, grew up reading and hearing journalists sprinkle opinion into their reporting. They assumed everyone did it, so they did too. Fighting through the language barrier, I spent a lot of time pointing out bias in their work and explaining why opinionated reporting would hurt their credibility and their employer's reputation as well as bottom line. Some got it; others couldn't resist the ego boost that came from folding their own point of view into a story. With partisan fissures emerging in American news media, it became an even tougher sell.

Anywhere I went, I could count on confronting two pressing needs, starting with management. The bosses didn't know how to organize things or people. The top dogs were either owners who couldn't stop themselves from micromanaging their creations or print journalists who had little or no interest or expertise in broadcast news. Their subordinate supervisors, having little formal journalism education and few professional role models, were either tyrants trying to assert their authority (remember me with Carol Brooks at CNN?) or weaklings afraid that giving orders would cause the staff to fear them or hate them or both. Even the universal broadcast concepts of time and timing were treated as optional. Newscasts would start late and end late, and workers' shifts matched bankers' hours with no relation to program schedules.

The other need involved infrastructure. Much of my consulting was spent urging owners to invest in the equipment and facilities needed for quality news programming. Even modern, well-equipped operations would lack such basics as clocks, adequate lighting, soundproof booths and studios, and internal communication systems. Sometimes the bosses would grudgingly buy the needed items; other times they would cower at the expense, and IREX (read U.S. taxpayers) would help out.

The first three contracts for WorldWise Media (my one-man consulting firm's name) were in three struggling Balkan states: Montenegro, Kosova, and Albania.

In 2002 the former Yugoslav republic of Montenegro, still tied to Serbia, was emerging from the hangover of the Balkan conflicts of the 90s. It was a poor country with a proud history and a blighted coastline and seemed to be biding its time until it gained full separation from Serbia. That was four years away.

Kosova, its population mostly ethnic Albanian, was a former Serbian province that had broken away with the help of NATO airpower in 1999 and was moving toward its declaration of nationhood in 2008, when it ditched the name Kosovo for its preferred Kosova.

Muslim Albania was struggling to find its way after decades of abuse under the Communist weirdo Enver Hoxha. Its economic and political development was hamstrung by endemic corruption.

In Istanbul, the IREX chief for Montenegro, Joe Raffelberg, asked me to help him with a TV project. Joe was a jovial, pipe-smoking German who had worked seemingly everywhere for Reuters. He had no TV expertise, so he recruited me.

## MONTENEGRO

Less than a month after Istanbul, I landed in Montenegro's sleepy, dusty capital, Podgorica. It looked like a typical capital city of a developing country—a shabby place trying hard to spruce up. It had a few green places, but the overall look was third-world utilitarian. Joe took me to my pleasant apartment that by local standards was posh, and the next day I took my first strides into the world of media consultancy.

I could not have started in a better spot. My "patient" was Montenegrin Broadcasting Company (MBC). This small operation with big ambitions had been on the air as Yugoslavia fell apart in the 90s. During the 1999 NATO bombings, MBC had tried to hold on to its audience with alternative programming—pornography. I never learned how that worked out, but by the time I got there, the owners had relaunched the channel. They wanted to make MBC a respected source of news and information, and IREX was trying to help.

MBC occupied two floors of an office building providing basic infrastructure (power, plumbing, heating and air conditioning) and little more. The station was showing mostly music videos interrupted by periodic, rudimentary news summaries called cut-ins. The newsroom had seven computers but only one Internet connection. The computers were used for researching and writing news, editing video, creating graphics, playing video during cut-ins, and recording reporter audio tracks. During recording, the entire newsroom went silent until the reporter was finished. Competition for the computers was fierce and sometimes got physical. The news set was in a corner of the newsroom with the presenter standing before a projected chromakey (green screen) image. My memo listing needed improvements filled five pages, and that was just the overview.

*2003: The refreshingly female-dominated staff of Montenegrin Broadcast Company in Podgorica.*

Management issues turned out to be at the top of the fix-it list. The station owner, Nino Radulovic, was a hands-on guy with a technical background. He enjoyed fiddling with the latest control room equipment but didn't like distractions such as administration or programming. For example, he didn't mind that nearly all his staff went home at 7:30 p.m., preventing any updating of prime-time newscasts.

I had three weeks, so we worked on the most glaring deficiencies. We improved the content and production of the two evening newscasts, rearranged the main work space into a more efficient newsroom and studio, persuaded everyone on camera to dress the part, and, perhaps the greatest accomplishment, got the newscasts to start on time. Ending on time would come later.

Perhaps the breakthrough drawing the most public attention involved live news coverage. One episode showed a roundtable discussion of media development in Montenegro. Not exactly stuff that brought folks in from the fields, but it showed viewers and the station staff what could be done.

I was learning, too. I asked a producer about her use of gory video showing victims of a West Bank tragedy, something a U.S. newscast would never air. When I suggested it might have been too bloody, she said, "No, it's okay for us. Our people have seen a lot worse."

As noted earlier, time in the MBC newsroom was elastic. Newscasts started late and never ended on time. My protestations were acknowledged and then ignored. At one point I discovered someone had turned back the on-air clock to make it look as if the show was starting on time.

One talent I admired was their ability to read newspapers in Roman or Cyrillic alphabets, moving easily from one to the other. I, meanwhile, barely managed to say "good morning." I did learn Serbian for two numbers, two and five. If I wanted to show off at a bar or restaurant, I would always try to order something in amounts of two or five. Two meat pies. Five sausages.

While learning about MBC, I learned about its competitors. They were either state-run stations with all the advantages of official status in a poorly regulated political and economic system, or newer private stations owned by tycoons with lots of money but less commitment to the expensive and cumbersome business of news. They saw a TV station as an unlocked ATM machine, and their idea of a news story was a recital of a government meeting's agenda with video of old men in chairs. That became my metaphor for lazy or incompetent TV news—stories showing old men in chairs.

Most summer evenings I walked a few blocks from my apartment to a bar on one of the main downtown streets. I'd sit outside sipping a Heineken and just watch. It didn't take long to see Montenegrin cultural norms in action. At 5 p.m., the street would be closed to traffic, and residents would take a leisurely stroll through the neighborhood. Most were attractive young Montenegrin women—tall, slim, and athletic—what you'd expect in a land that had supplied the best women volleyball players in the world to the Yugoslav national team. They were accompanied by what I assumed were mothers or other female friends and relatives. Something was missing—men. In other countries, these strollers would be stared at if not harassed by young men on the prowl.

One mild evening as the sun was setting, I asked my waiter why the ritual was an all-female affair. He looked up and nodded toward nearby buildings. That's when I noticed men watching the parade from rooftops and balconies and around corners. They were fathers, brothers, and cousins watching over their women. If any young man was foolish or rude enough to approach a young lady in the street, he could count on a visit from one of the watchmen for a stern lecture or worse.

With those rules, I asked, how do young people meet?

He said clubs served that purpose, where young women were allowed to mingle with young men. Not as much supervision, and plenty of music, dancing, drinking, and darkness.

Other discoveries in Podgorica included burek, a flaky roll with a variety of fillings, sausages called cevapcici, and new wines and beers. Several excursions out of town with Joe Raffelberg and his engaging wife Monica exposed me to the beauty of Montenegro's Adriatic coast, with Budva, Petrovac, Kotor, and the picture postcard island Sveti Stephan. This region had been a favorite spot for German tourists in the 70s and 80s because of its scenic beaches and reasonable prices. In 2002 it was trying to come back.

Having barely scratched the surface, I left MBC with a list of guidelines, procedures, and recommendations to keep the station busy until I returned in

November, when I found several pleasant surprises. Newscasts were telling local stories developed and reported by station staff, while competitors relied heavily on news agency material lacking a local angle or context.

The station had moved into more space, allowing for separation of the control room from the newsroom and creation of a small auxiliary set for news cut-ins. A server stored video, but it required a link to a newsroom PC, still complicating newscast playback. Reporters were writing better scripts (as much as I could tell from translations), and cameramen were learning how to shoot eye-catching video. On the business side, the staff had grown to 60 and was experiencing little turnover. Regular, reliable audience surveys put MBC sixth among the eight main channels in Montenegro, but viewers were noticing its focus on news and information programming, with specific praise for its coverage of October elections. Things were getting better, so it was time for me to push even harder.

MBC's next big splash was hourly news cut-ins during daytime programming. Ownership wanted them to start at 15 minutes before the hour instead of the top of the hour. That was unorthodox, but they argued that they knew best what the audience wanted. I let it go, encouraged at least that management had grown confident enough to make such calls. Managers also learned how to post schedules, pay the staff on time, and put all employees under contract, in part to prevent them from moving to another station. With revenue rising, the station hired a marketing director.

While the content and programming had improved, the set for the main evening newscast had not. A presenter stood in the newsroom with desks as a background, a futile attempt to copy a trendy design. It was ugly, especially compared to the slick sets of the competition. MBC had better news content but was hard to watch. The debut of a new prime time newscast on November 13 started 15 minutes late and suffered just about every snafu imaginable. People would walk behind the presenter during a newscast; new equipment would fail, and instructions would be misunderstood, miscommunicated, or forgotten. One newscast featured a presenter in shadows because a painter had walked off with a light needed for the set.

I ended my second Podgorica stint with a list of suggestions and challenges that urged more financial and sports news, better management practices, signal extension beyond Podgorica for better market share, more technical training for the staff, and creation of a newscast set that enhanced, rather than blighted, the main evening productions.

By the time I returned for my last consultancy in February, 2003, MBC was climbing in audience surveys. Its newscasts were growing in sophistication and production quality, and the station had started to dabble in talk shows, featuring its well-connected and popular program director, Momcilo Stoyanovic. By this time he was a friend, but we did have our issues. I wanted fonts identifying his guests; he said that was not necessary because everybody knew who they were. I suggested a set-up report to tell viewers about the show's guest or central issue; he said viewers knew all that already. I told him to wear a suit that fit properly after showing him a replay with his jacket straining to stay together at his belt line; he agreed. Plenty of details could be nitpicked, but MBC's reputation for news and information was growing in part thanks to Stoyanovic's influence.

I left Podgorica for the last time on March 3, 2003, with a pile of suggestions and instructions in my wake. I expected MBC to do fine if it improved its sets and production facilities, streamlined its management flow chart, and added popular programming, notably sports. Joe Raffelberg moved on to other IREX assignments, and I lost track of everyone at the station. I learned much later that it stayed on the air for 11 more years. I never found out why it closed.

**KOSOVA**

In September 2002, following my first Podgorica stay, I was in the emerging republic of Kosova. Driving into Pristina from the airport, any doubts about how I would be received were erased by a five-story poster with "Thank you, America" above the towering image of Bill Clinton.

My host was Tim Kenny, an IREX project manager who was also a friend and former *USA Today* colleague. Under a USAID contract, IREX had helped to launch a new regional news agency, KosovaLive. My assignment was to set up an affiliate service for broadcasters. It would offer web-based local and regional news to stations desperate for an alternative to Kosova's partisan newspapers. Written in broadcast-style Albanian, it was meant for the many mom-and-pop FM stations that had sprouted after Kosova won its separate status. Many operated with little more than a control board and microphone with a transmitter wired to a rooftop antenna.

It was a Wild West of broadcasting—little regulation and less advertising. They aired pirated music, and if they tried to do news, it was whatever newspaper stories piqued the DJ's interest.

The platform for this new service already existed. KosovaLive was a functioning online news service with paying clients among the three national newspapers and larger radio and television outlets. It had a small but enterprising staff of reporters managed by a respected newspaper editor and housed in the headquarters of a television station. A state-of-the-art van equipped for remote TV broadcasting was parked outside the building. As a metaphor of the state of broadcast news in Kosova at the time, the truck was festooned with cables holding drying laundry. Print was still king.

My first Pristina stint was devoted to learning the media landscape, including the main players and the extent of training for journalists. Overall, it was better than I expected. Technical sophistication was mixed, but that really wasn't my concern. I had to create a broadcast news service and find a way to fill it with content.

We found our writer/editor, a Kosovar who had worked for Radio Free Europe's Albanian service in Prague. He was the perfect choice and was paid well. He filled the web pages with ready-to-read news stories and devised a format and schedule. We publicized the launch and introduced it free of charge.

The service was an instant hit. Most of the roughly 30 radio stations in Kosova grabbed it from the start and became addicted to it. As the service attracted users, they started making demands even though they weren't paying for it. They didn't like that our lone editor insisted on working banker's hours. This meant the service's broadcast copy first showed up at midday, with another feed around 6 p.m. Users needed news copy at the start of their broadcast day around dawn, and they wanted fresh news as it developed, even on weekends. They praised the local (Pristina) coverage generated by KosovaLive's field reporters but wanted more news from other regions.

Despite the service's popularity, KosovaLive's management didn't show much interest. The boss was a newspaper guy and had no experience or much interest in broadcasting. He ignored statistics showing the market potential with so many radio stations. During my second stay around Thanksgiving 2002, Tim and I visited stations in seven towns outside Pristina to get their feedback on the service. They all said they liked it and would be willing to pay for it if they could afford it (imagine an outstretched hand).

One of our stops was at a ninth-floor station (in a building with no elevators) serving Mitrovica, a predominantly Serbian city straddling the Kosova-Serbia border. The place was creepy. Partitions separating Serb and Kosovar sections of town made me think of Belfast. As a nod to that minority, KosovaLive had hired translators to offer a Serbian-language broadcast page on the website. With plenty of fraternal stations broadcasting from Serbia, potential clients couldn't care less about the Kosovar perspective, and the service never took off.

At the end of my second visit in early December, the service was up and running with plenty of clients but needed a new editor and additional staffing. KosovaLive is still a thriving online news service.

**ALBANIA**

ALSAT TV should have been a cakewalk. The all-news channel was the first of its kind in post-communism Albania, and everything about it was state-of-the-art. Its founder was Albanian tycoon Vebi Velija, who made his fortune in cigarettes and food processing. He ached to have a say in his country's development and chose media instead of politics as his preferred megaphone.

The IREX chief in Tirana was Shelly Markoff, an acerbic and sharp-eyed manager who left me alone to do my job while always ready to help if needed. I didn't hold it against him that my hotel was a shabby if clean hostelry in a rundown part of the Albanian capital with dark streets, shattered sidewalks, and leg-breaking open manholes. At least the restaurants were decent, mostly Greek or Italian.

ALSAT occupied an imposing red marble-and-glass complex on the north edge of the capital. It was less than a year old and had everything an all-news station needed: contemporary studios, the latest equipment, antennas and dishes for satellite and terrestrial signal propagation, and a staff of 100, enough to accomplish all of the

*2003: Newsroom at ALSAT-TV in Tirana, Albania.*

station's news and programming goals. The format was simple: a half hour of news followed by a half hour of informational programming (documentaries, long-form journalism, etc.) for 12 hours a day. The bottom of the screen carried an English language ticker, signifying Velija's wish for Albanians to learn English. The station's reach, thanks to satellite, was far into Europe. Velija estimated the potential audience to be nine million. That seemed inflated, but the signal footprint was impressive.

ALSAT suffered from many of the managerial shortcomings I noticed in all my consulting jobs. In some ways, Velija was his own worst enemy. He repeatedly said that he wanted his general manager and director of information to take care of daily operations, but when he saw something he didn't like, he'd get on the phone. This micromanaging caused his lieutenants to try to preempt such calls by checking with him first. Then he would complain that the managers were too indecisive. I tried to counsel him on how to avoid this frustrating cycle, but he was the owner. It was tough to let go.

For the staff, early instruction emphasized that details matter. Viewers would not notice an odd choice of lead story or a decision to drop a report due to time constraints. They did notice misspelled graphics, video not matching the script, uneven audio levels, and, most of all, late newscasts. I set out to streamline and rationalize the management structure so that everybody understood their job. Then they could concentrate on getting things right.

I had to put all of that aside just a week into my consultancy. War in Iraq was imminent. Albania was the only European country to hold a pro-America demonstration before the war, and we knew Albanians would closely follow the war's progress. As a 24-hour news broadcaster, ALSAT was uniquely positioned to give viewers all they wanted with real-time coverage. ALSAT's staff included several amazing translators who could keep up with coverage from any foreign source in just about any of the major languages.

Fine, except we had no source for that coverage. ALSAT had been slow to secure rights to the leading international news networks; other channels already had BBC, CNN, Euronews, and others tied up with exclusive contracts. There was only one option—Fox News. We decided to take a chance and carry it live when the war started, and we'd let them stop us if they chose to do so.

On March 20, 2003, the first bombs dropped in Iraq, and we took Fox for as long as our translators could hold out. The first two days were almost wall-to-wall Fox with simultaneous translation, interrupted by cut-ins covering other news. I kept an eye on the programming, and by the third day I had seen enough. The Fox coverage was so jingoistic that I thought it was inappropriate even for the pro-American Albanian audience. I made my case to management, and they stopped carrying Fox. From then on, live coverage was reduced to a few hours each day, rotating among various international broadcasters in hopes of not getting sued. Nobody bothered, and the war was short enough to let us get back to our regularly scheduled programming in less than three weeks.

This forced me to realize I had to abandon advocacy of the journalism principles that had guided my career. Albanian media was heavily partisan, but I couldn't preach balance, fairness, and neutrality if I had just pulled the top-rated American news channel off ALSAT. Bias was creeping into other U.S. media outlets, and much of Europe's news media had a tradition of weaving opinion into news. So I focused my consulting on non-editorial subjects such as production methods, use of technology, and administration. I touched on story selection and reporting skills but avoided saying too much about news content. For this, the language barrier came in handy.

After the war, we standardized the program schedule and organized production teams to cover four-hour segments of the 12-hour broadcast day. This introduced consistency into station operations, and the teams (producers, presenters, writers, editors, technicians) performed with efficient cohesion.

By the time I returned for a second stay in June 2003, ALSAT offered viewers 12 hours of credible, watchable newscasts. Digging deeper, however, I found a number of vexing cultural and political obstacles blocking quality journalism.

ALSAT's 12 reporters were almost totally reactive, doing stories as news developed and never going out to look for enterprise or investigative pieces. When I urged reporters to be more proactive, I faced a torrent of excuses. Newsmakers wanted to talk to editors, not reporters. Sources wanted to talk face-to-face, eschewing phone interviews. Reporters said the best place to harvest news tips was at casual meetings with sources in bars and cafes, and they said they didn't have time for that kind of leg work.

More confusion arose from the concept of bias. The reporters knew bias was bad, but their understanding of it was skewed. When I asked the managing editor why an important politician's public statement was not covered live as other stations had done, he said airing the politician's comments could be viewed as bias in his favor. In another case, ALSAT had an exclusive report on a letter by the foreign minister criticizing the prime minister—big news anywhere. When the staff learned of a second letter, the editors decided not to report it. They said reporting on the second letter would give the appearance of ALSAT siding with the foreign minister.

Tirana was a tough town, and that could warp editorial decisions. ALSAT had exclusive video of a café shooting in the heart of the government quarter. It aired only once, a grievous error for an all-news station. Editors said the shooter was a Mafia thug, and showing the video more than once could invite mob retaliation against the station. Authorities released the gunman's name, but ALSAT withheld it, again fearing retaliation. It took hours for the authorities to clarify whether the shooting was a personal matter or road rage. (It was both). Editors thought the motive should be known before the tape aired again. It never did.

I could rebut all those points, but I was a foreigner. Aggressive journalism was not always appreciated by certain quarters of Albanian society. All I could do was offer counterpoints and let them figure out how to balance the tenets of good journalism with the realities of their society.

Managers also avoided softer topics in newscasts, arguing that only "important" news should be covered. That ruled out "people" stories, light features, human interest, and other common newscast fodder. ALSAT banished stories like these to the second "information" half hour. That left newscasts full of stories showing speeches, conferences, meetings, and news conferences, illustrated with the dreaded old-men-in-chairs video. Public reaction to a story was rarely covered, and when it was, it was relegated to the second half-hour as "social news." Man-in-the-street interviews were banned on the theory that interviewees would be biased or would say stupid things. The obvious fixes (find people who weren't biased or stupid) never took hold.

When urged to cover more business or economic news, the editors and reporters said officials would not talk about those issues because most didn't understand the subject matter and were afraid they would look ignorant on camera. Suggestions to cover stories about small businesses, successful ones or those shackled by bureaucracy or corruption, were rejected as free advertising. You can see why my efforts gravitated toward set design and staff scheduling.

It took me awhile to learn that another broadcast entity was operating in the ALSAT building. ALSAT Radio was a 24-hour FM station airing music and hourly news updates. To my annoyance (I was no longer surprised by anything), the radio and TV station had exactly zero interaction. I pointed out the potential for sharing news and cross promotion. It seemed so obvious, but I once again was reminded that nothing was obvious until it was explained, and sometimes not after that. They made moves to play nice but never bonded.

Want more? Punctuality was a production challenge because there were no clocks in the newsroom or video editing suites. Velija had spent millions on his broadcast palace but had forgotten clocks.

How about monitors? Every other TV newsroom in the world closely monitored the competition. The ALSAT newsroom had six monitors hanging on a wall that were part of the news set's background, but none showed local stations. Management didn't want the competition visible in the newscast, even if the images were out of focus. Furthermore, when managers from the executive director on down were in their offices, they could not see what ALSAT was broadcasting. They had no monitors. Unless they walked into the newsroom, they could only watch ALSAT at home.

Finally, ALSAT could communicate to all of Albania, but the control room and master control could not communicate with each other. An intercom system installed for that purpose was worse than nothing. Anyone trying to talk to the other room battled screeching feedback to be heard. The result was usually yelling, which sometimes rose to angry levels. Not conducive to smooth television production, particularly when viewers can listen in.

Marketing dominated the talks I had with Velija in his office or, more frequently, over dinner at an excellent rooftop restaurant in the leafy quarter of Tirana where all the bigwigs had lived during the Communist era. I figured that as a successful entrepreneur, Velija knew how to promote his station. He didn't have a clue. Marketing TV news required different skill sets than selling cigarettes or canned olives. I preached a litany of ideas, from audience outreach to brand reinforcement to celebrity endorsements to special events for advertisers to offering studio tours. Since my focus was on production and administration more than business, I had to leave marketing to him.

ALSAT survived in its original configuration for seven years, one year longer than Velija did. In 2010, another conglomerate took it over, converted it to an entertainment channel, changed the name to Albania Screen, and then presided over its demise in 2014.

**ARMENIA**

I had always wanted to try teaching, and Armenia is where I got my first chance.

This contract with Internews, another major U.S. media development NGO, called for a six-week seminar in a classroom setting plus workshop activities. Bill Canter, another acquaintance from the Istanbul conference, hired me to teach Western principles of television news reporting and production to eight reporters and four videographers, all top performers at their stations. I arrived to Bill's cheerful greeting and moved into a spacious downtown apartment within walking distance of the Internews offices. It all seemed so easy. It wasn't.

*2003: Students attending my TV news seminar in Yerevan, Armenia.*

Bill was mentoring an eager young Armenian journalist, David, in the skills of program management. As part of his training, David was given responsibility for overseeing my seminar. As it turned out, he had a lot to learn. I walked into the first day of class with no idea what I was supposed to teach, no syllabus, and no scope of work. David spoke in generalities when I needed specifics. So I drafted a schedule of lectures and exercises to cover news gathering, story production, and newscast production, including technical skills such as directing.

That covered about two weeks. I had no idea what else was expected. After several requests for clarifications from David and getting none, I called a come-to-Jesus meeting with Bill and David over dinner. We met in a touristy Yerevan restaurant and hashed out what David wanted, what I needed, and how to end the confusion. We reached a consensus just as a local band struck up a screechy tune complete with dancing girls. I was in no mood for a floor show.

I filled an Excel spreadsheet with lecture topics and exercises to cover the rest of the seminar. I prepared lectures with the help of a slim textbook I brought or from online sources. It was heavily classroom oriented, covering ten hours a day, and all presented through a remarkably patient translator. The students were motivated and engaged; they were earning a stipend and did not want inattention or absenteeism to jeopardize the extra income.

The Internews offices had all the facilities needed for seminar topics, including a small studio with control room, video editing bays, and voicing booths. The classroom was bright and well equipped, but the seminar's structure caused more trouble.

Lectures covered one topic at a time for all 12 students. Camera operators heard about reporting and production; journalists heard about shooting and editing. It's always good to know how others do their jobs, but students spent a lot of time hearing about concepts they would never use at work.

As lectures gave way to practical exercises, problems mounted. David was interested in the students' progress, so he would occasionally join in on their classroom discussions. When his comments contradicted mine, I had to step in. He advocated the European method of package production: write the script and then get video to match. The American method was just the opposite: shoot the video, and then write the script. That's what my students were told to practice.

He showed up one day with a lesson plan that he had given to the students the previous evening, without telling me. They had prepared for his lecture, not mine. It was out of control, and I went to Bill with a blunt him-or-me ultimatum. That settled the issue once and for all. David was welcome to attend sessions and to meet with the students collectively or individually, but that was all. It was my show.

As soon as we started practical exercises, further complications interfered. To produce a story, they were required to come up with ideas and arrange their own interviews, while also scheduling time with a student videographer. The ideas were good, but sources were reluctant to, in their view, waste time talking to students. The finished packages were reviewed for technical quality and content, as far as translation would allow. Scripts were never fact-checked, so we were alarmed when a few of the students used contacts at Yerevan stations to have their work aired in newscasts. One bad piece of work and Internews could have been expelled from Armenia.

The teaming of one videographer with two reporters meant one had to wait for the videographer to finish the other reporter's story. The facility did not have enough editing booths, so projects missed deadlines. When the class moved on to newscast production, the experience was restricted by limited access to the Internews studio. We somehow got through the six weeks. The students showed promise, had fun, and got along most of the time.

One cultural clash moment involved a story about sales of votive candles in churches. The reporter was critical of the Church, arguing the candles should be free. When it came up in class, I had a ruckus on my hands. One of the cameramen was outraged that the reporter would say anything critical of the Church. He looked like he was ready to physically attack her. I calmed everyone down enough to have rational discussion of the issue, but I learned about the Church's delicate status in a former Soviet republic that was also the world's first Christian country.

Despite the full class schedule, I had plenty of time to learn about Armenia's culture and history, with the generous help of Bill and his intrepid wife Diane. I was present for the national holiday marking the Turkish genocide of Armenians in World War I, getting a feel for how deeply that massacre scarred Armenia's collective soul. (With apologies to my Turkish friends, I call it genocide and have seen slam-dunk proof at the National World War I Museum in Kansas City.) I visited the well-preserved Roman temple of Garni. On the way, my translator-driver took me past a massive industrial complex that had made submarine sections in Soviet times. It was now a rusting hulk, with men huddling at the main entrance every day hoping employers would pick them up for day labor.

Yerevan was trying to modernize, and one sign of progress was the golf driving range with Mount Ararat as a distant aiming point. Bill and I went there one sunny day, and we had to share the facility's one bucket of balls. The club house in a trailer had nice looking hats and other souvenirs with the range's logo, but the young lady behind the counter refused to sell them to us. They were only for show. Capitalism still had room to grow in Yerevan.

The Saturday market, the Vernissage, offered a flea-market array of everything from cheap carpets and knickknacks to military souvenirs from the Soviet era. Shopping in Yerevan was fun, but a saddle blanket I found in an antique store proved almost more trouble than it was worth. Armenia was trying to curtail the export of its treasures, including antiques. I lost a half day at the Ministry of Culture while its experts assessed the blanket and gave me written permission to take it out of the country. Despite documented approval, officious airport customs officers tried to confiscate it. Fast talking and cool heads saved the blanket and the day.

Foreigners could eat well in Yerevan; my favorite was a Tex-Mex place run by a Peruvian. I didn't eat out much. My apartment's kitchen was well equipped, and the language barrier did not interfere with shopping for basics. Having most evenings and weekends free with a lousy selection of TV channels, I killed my free time writing the first five chapters of my novel. Sometimes I'd write late into the night after waking up to the sound of car alarms in the parking lot. A cat padding across a hood would be enough to set off an alarm. The cars were all hulks that didn't look worth the cost of an alarm.

In all four consulting jobs, a lot of journalists learned a lot of good habits, but I wondered how many were able to practice those new skills working for older editors and producers stuck in their antiquated or arrogant ways. I do know that some of the journalists I mentored kept their newly acquired professionalism hidden, waiting for the day when they would rise to a position of authority and dust off the concepts of accuracy, fairness, and professionalism to use and show to their staffs and their audiences. The greatest of ironies was that as I taught those concepts in the Balkans and Armenia, their erosion was already underway at home.

# CHAPTER 10

# Iraq

*"You better hire Ted Iliff or someone like him."*

It's not easy to write about the 14 weeks I spent working to develop the Iraqi Media Network in Baghdad. It's even harder to read about those times. If you Google Iraqi Media Network or its TV offspring, al Iraqiya, the search will turn up stories that are misguided, misinformed, or malicious. In its struggle to create a new national media in post-Saddam Iraq, the U.S. military through the Coalition Provisional Authority (CPA) did not exactly slather itself in glory. It had some success, but as with anything in history, the nuances fade with time, leaving stark conclusions portrayed as an ill-informed consensus: The programming was horrible, the message was muddled, it lacked credibility, nobody was watching. All those arguments could be defended in IMN's early days. All of them could be rebutted by the time I left.

Most IMN critics never saw or heard any of its programming because they weren't there and didn't understand Arabic; their opinions were based on outdated or secondhand information. Several who had brief roles in IMN's creation presented themselves as experts long after the network had matured from the admittedly sorry beginnings they had witnessed or even caused.

Don't get me wrong; some of the criticism was fair. The U.S. military was brilliant at war but lousy at media (with one exception coming in a later chapter). Military minds are trained for one thing—winning. America and its allies drove all the way to Baghdad to win the war and then started immediately to unwin the peace. Part of the unwinning began with early mismanagement and misunderstanding of media and how to use it. Mass media are tools to be forged by skilled communicators, not warriors or politicians. Persuasion requires subtlety and credibility. Limiting your message to the virtues of your cause is not persuasive; a credible media campaign sometimes requires uncomfortable balance and painful candor. Too many decision makers in the hierarchy of the American military administration in Iraq didn't know how to talk to the Iraqi people. Some knew and were ignored; others tried but were overruled by other well-intentioned but naïve overlords. It was a flawed effort that ultimately failed, but it also had good moments with laudable outcomes. Like a lot of things in history, reality was somewhere in the middle.

My involvement started in August 2003 as I was finishing my work in Albania. I got a call one day and heard a voice from the past—Gary Thatcher, whose hiring as

RFE/RL current affairs director in 1989 was one reason I left Munich. Now he had the daunting task of overseeing communications for the CPA. In terms of media, the CPA's goal was to create a credible public broadcasting entity along the lines of America's PBS. In less than three months, it had gotten nowhere near that goal.

As soon as Gary set up shop in Saddam's gaudy Republican Palace, he started leaning hard on the media contract holder SAIC, a respected defense contractor based in Arlington, Va. Despite having no experience in media, SAIC thought it could handle the job and won the contract. It was a pyrrhic victory. A series of managers had come and gone; a few later became widely quoted critics of the mess they had left behind. The national television network was barely watchable. Gary wanted a quick fix and told SAIC he had someone in mind to turn things around. He called to ask if I was interested in the challenge, and I instantly said yes. It sounded like a grand adventure. His next call was to SAIC with a firm suggestion to "find Ted Iliff or someone like him to fix this." They found me, brought me to Arlington for a few brainstorming sessions, and signed me up. During a welcoming dinner I met John Sandrock, the overworked IMN general manager who had been brought home for those programming meetings. John was a friendly but somewhat reserved former Air Force cargo plane pilot with no media experience. At one point during dinner he mentioned proudly that he had not taken a day off in three months. I didn't think that was much to brag about. I wondered how effective he could be in Baghdad under that kind of stress.

I don't have room to list all the firsts in my life from this assignment. It started with orientation classes in Kuwait explaining the security realities in Iraq, which I called "scary" in my diary. Then came my first ride in a C-130, strapped into a webbed seat as comfortable as cheap lawn chair. Alongside me were other civilians, a Humvee and its fumes, and a few dogs which I assumed were security assets. Our first stop was Mosul, and that's where I was introduced to the concept of tactical landings. To dodge any antiaircraft fire, the pilot jerked and bounced his plane and us for the last few minutes of final approach. It tested the stomachs of everyone on board, including the dogs. Even the Humvee looked pale.

After a quick stop, we were off on the short hop to Baghdad, thankfully with a normal landing this time. Down came the ramp, and in came my first blast of Iraqi heat. I strolled into a gaggle of slightly dazed newcomers trying to sort out their paperwork, rides, and luggage. Cots without blankets flanked the flight line, and we were told those would be our beds that night if we didn't get on the road to town before dark. That, along with the tactical landing in Mosul, made me wonder just how much winning we had done in this war. I found my SAIC transportation and loaded up for the half-hour drive to the CPA headquarters in the fortified enclave called the Green Zone. Before we could leave, I put on an armored vest and helmet, and I shared the back seat of a black SUV with two guys in khakis and body armor pointing weapons out each side window. Honestly, it was kind of exciting.

We got to the palace at sunset, and I announced my arrival by pulling the handle off my rolling bag as I dragged it up the front steps. I struggled to the SAIC desks crowded into one end of the "green room" (they couldn't find another color?) and met some of the SAIC team. Bonnie Corbin, the irreplaceable office manager, took me to my quarters—one third of a 20-foot container configured as a room with a bed, desk, and upright locker. The middle section was a refreshingly well-equipped bathroom, and another room like mine took up the other end. Lacking sheets and linens, I spent my first night in Iraq on a mattress wrapped in dusty plastic sheeting. I wasn't sure I had the authority to unwrap it. The long trip made sleep easy. After that, not much else in the Green Zone was easy.

There was so much to learn and so much to do. I slipped into autopilot mode and for the first few days tried to absorb as much as I could—where I would work, how to get there, who I'd work with, what my mission was. My mind didn't have room yet for all the TV news production issues I'd have to sort out. After a few nights in the trailer, they moved me across the Green Zone to the Al Rasheed Hotel, the repository for CPA personnel and the place where CNN's Boys of Baghdad did play-by-play at the start of Desert Storm 12 years earlier. It was like a nice Holiday Inn room back home. Most rooms had two occupants, but I was alone in my third-floor room; I never learned why, and I didn't ask.

I dumped my hastily repaired roller bag on the bed and dropped my new Army-issue green duffel bag on the floor by the window. A lovely welcome gift in Kuwait, it included a khaki shirt and pants, a matching helmet, desert hat, combat boots, and a gas mask. I never touched any of it again. Instead of begging a ride every morning from the palace, I could now walk out the well-appointed lobby into the blast furnace that was Baghdad in September and cross the street to the convention center, a glass and concrete building that housed the Iraqi Media Network production facilities.

The studio, control room, editing stations, and other offices were crammed into stuffy third-floor spaces never intended for a broadcast operation. IMN at that time was offering tired TV fare, including shows Saddam had pirated and shown to his people for years. I observed the production of a newscast, which my diary entry described as "rough." Secretary of State Colin Powell was in town; it was the fourth story. "So much for being a propaganda network," I wrote.

In the first week, I was in the drinking-from-a-firehose stage, meeting Iraqis and Americans with no hope of remembering their names, interviewing Iraqi staff candidates with no idea of our real needs, trying to figure out what various cohorts toiling away in various offices actually did for the network, and just trying to find the paper clips and toilets (they were modern and worked). My American colleagues were a competent and entertaining gang of veteran expats who felt right at home in a post-war zone.

Bob Teasdale was the de facto No. 2 under John Sandrock, and he was a living definition of rollicking. His expertise was technical, but he was equally valuable as a sideshow character. He drove around in a white Toyota pickup carrying a cooler stocked with ice-cold cans of soda. He'd race up to a tank crew or sentry station, skid to a halt, and shout an offer of refreshment for the poor guys in full gear stuck in the heat that could top 100 Fahrenheit all day. Some gratefully accepted; some needed coaxing, and some weren't sure who this big guy was, so they'd pass. As he repeated this stunt with me riding shotgun, I wondered what would happen if a spooked rookie squeezed off a few rounds just to be safe. Later in my stay, a nervous private new to Iraq did just that to an SAIC driver, thankfully causing no serious injury. By then, though, Bob had listened to reason and had ended his charity runs.

Bob also knew his way around downtown Baghdad. This was the golden age of the occupation before the insurgency got organized. We'd roll into the once fashionable Karada district for a quick visit to a liquor store—a vestige of Saddam's version of Islam, with its loose interpretation of the Koran similar to Turkey's. Folks on the street wore styles ranging from fundamental to functional. Shops hawked everything from ceramic dishes to satellite dishes, and the general mood was relaxed. We got stares, but I don't recall any overt hostility.

Our security briefings warned us of risks outside the Green Zone, so we had to be careful. One night the owners of an Iraqi business invited Bob, myself, and our Iraqi technical manager David Isaac to a fish fry along the Tigris. We met our hosts downtown and started following their BMWs out of town along the river. Vestiges of civilization faded as we drove farther from town until we told them by cellphone that we were out of bounds and had to go back. They understood and bought us a fish dinner at a restaurant. That was the first time in Iraq that the hairs on the back of my neck stood on end.

As security warnings grew more ominous, we had to settle for socializing at the Al Rasheed. This was not a hardship. The hotel had a restaurant and a café, three bars, and an outdoor pool with yet another bar. The pool was clean, beer was cold, bourbon was reasonable, and the hamburgers were tasty. There was plenty of swimming and diving. Everyone was expected to be on their best behavior, but a few forgot and suffered for it. Punishment could range from a reprimand to a ban from the premises to, for military personnel, career-crippling personal file entries.

I was tasked with improving IMN's TV broadcasts, so my focus narrowed to a few priorities: administration, facilities, and programming. We needed serious help making IMN watchable. For that, SAIC turned to the Dubai-based Mideast Broadcasting Company (another MBC) to buy a comprehensive package of entertainment programs (dramas, children's shows, cooking shows, comedies), reruns of shows that had fared well in other Mideast markets. We found out later that Iraqis had seen many of those offerings during the Saddam era, but at least it made IMN's output tolerable. Because we were approaching Ramadan, MBC added a schedule of programs suitable for family viewing, an important component of the rituals during the Muslim holy month.

Meanwhile, we had to phase out IMN's existing programs. John Sandrock pushed back, insisting on continuation of a weekly music and variety show he had a hand in creating. It was produced in a hotel conference room gussied up with decorations to look like a poor version of the old "American Bandstand" show. It featured local music acts performing in front of a live audience. It was well intentioned but cheesy. John insisted it was popular, at one point warning that if it were cancelled there would be "rioting in the streets." It was cancelled, and there was no rioting. The show's director, who provided his own lights and sound equipment, was relieved. He showed me a recorded episode and pointed out the composition of the audience. It was almost all young men. He said good Iraqi families were reluctant to let their daughters appear in such a setting on TV. When I pointed out that there were a few young women in the crowd, he made a face and said, "They're not good girls."

My days were filled with meeting after meeting, leaving me little time for training the TV news staff. While I worried about where to move the network for better facilities, how to rebrand it, what kind of in-house programming to introduce, the daily newscast staff drifted. That changed after SAIC found more American consultants. Cameraman Michael Kenney, technical specialist Lee Hilliard, and former CBS newsman Ed Rabel gathered Iraqi staffers matching their areas of expertise and got to work training them. A little later, Gordon Robison, an Arabic speaker who had worked with me at CNN International, arrived to take over newscast production. In that environment and under those conditions, everybody had strengths and weaknesses. But the team collectively moved the needle closer toward our goal of watchable, credible news.

When I got started, the staff was disorganized, dysfunctional, and bloated. Karen White, SAIC's administrator for IMN, was trying to sort everything out by herself. With my support, she finally got staff evaluations under way so we could learn who could do the job and who was just warming a seat. Staff schedules were standardized so that everyone worked six days per week and had consistent days off. We told some Iraqi employees they would have to work on Friday, their prayer day, and a supportive Iraqi manager corps headed off any protests. I did hit one snag when my proposal for a five-day work week drew the staff's unanimous opposition. David Isaac explained that workers were paid by the day, so a second day off would amount to a pay cut. Also, employers in that part of the world traditionally provided lunch for their employees. For some, it was the only decent meal they got each day, and they would squirrel away leftovers to take home to their families. A day with no work could mean a day of no food. We kept the six-day week.

Another culture clash involved ending IMN's role as a charity. A talk show host had nine people working for him to prepare his weekly one-hour show. We discovered that they were all his relatives. When I told him to cut his staff to four, he protested on humanitarian grounds. I sympathized, but the order stood.

In terms of news and information, we concentrated on two areas: a prime time evening newscast and live coverage. Prime time news presented a logistical challenge because the broadcast was not transmitted from the production center. Several miles to the north, a small estate called Salheya housed the transmitter and a remote broadcasting truck that was borrowed from a Turkish company. Together, the jury-rigged setup got the newscasts out to the audience. It was much better than an earlier method of rushing the newscast tape by car through Baghdad's notorious and sometimes dangerous traffic from the convention center to the transmitter site. No wonder newscasts in their first months had a poor on-time record.

The small and imaginative Iraqi and American staff at Salheya had designs on hosting the entire IMN production studios, arguing that the convention center was too small and inefficient for a serious broadcast operation. However, their proposals kept bumping up against one insurmountable obstacle—safety. With Salheya's location outside the Green Zone, security would be impossible to guarantee. Plus, the convention center-based staff liked working in the greater protection of the Green Zone.

We then set our gaze on a high-rise near the Al Rasheed Hotel. It had slight war damage and was abandoned, but it could have been reconditioned into a workable home for IMN. The building was known as the Scooby Palace because of the howling sound the wind made as it blew through the broken windows. We thought we had a deal with the CPA to get it, but at the last minute some military unit big-footed IMN, and we lost it. It was another case of the CPA insisting that IMN was a top priority until it wasn't.

As we sought other options, we wrestled almost daily with the petty obstructions of the convention center's manager, known only as May. She had managed the place since its construction during the Saddam era and had supervised repairs of the damage from two wars. She acted as if it was all she had in life, which was probably true. When we wanted to move furniture, she objected. When we wanted to rearrange the center's main control room for office space, she objected. We once moved desks from one office to another, only to find them stacked in the hallway the next morning. She had not authorized the move, so she had ordered the desks removed. This went on for months. I'm sad to say I was out of town the day she was escorted out of the building in handcuffs. I never learned why. Embezzlement or cooperating with the insurgency topped the staff's list of guesses.

It would be easy to let the narrative of these times get bogged down in a chronology of meetings, because that's what dominated the entries in my diaries. Meetings on marketing, logo design, TV network branding, program schedules, staff schedules, budgets, training. But we were actually making progress.

We stopped live coverage of the mind-numbing daily CPA military briefings and started to plan for brief public service ads, called interstitials, to give the CPA a regular and more palpable platform for its messaging. We didn't get involved in that content; that was for "psychological operations" to create.

We started acting like a real news operation. IMN cameramen covered an explosion in the Green Zone and a protest demonstration at a main gate near the convention center, stories that would have gone unreported a month earlier.

Around this time, my savior arrived. Shameem Rassam, an Iraqi Christian who had anchored for Saddam's television news before fleeing the country, returned to take over the radio network. With her cultural sensitivity and mother-tongue Arabic, Shameem could concentrate on content, keeping an ear to television news as well. The radio staff was more nimble and skilled than the TV side, so they often gathered news, such as VIP interviews, and shared them with TV.

*2003: Damaged room after rocket attack on Baghdad's Al Rasheed Hotel. (Courtesy Steve Marney)*

Now free to concentrate on TV when I wasn't mired in meetings, I saw I had to change attitudes before I could change the product. Newscast producers learned the rules of timing and deadlines. Show rundowns became standard and standardized. Newscast structure and flow were introduced as principles for improving the viewing quality.

Until Gordon Robison arrived to take over TV news production, I had to rely on translations by English-speaking Iraqis, most of all by my angelic assistant and interpreter Samar. She was not a trained journalist, but she was smart enough to recognize trouble. Always pleasant and smiling and wearing proper Western office attire, she navigated the informal ways of the American workplace to preserve her reputation as a proper Islamic woman. No hugs, no handshakes, no lunch breaks together. She was even more reserved in her first month at IMN. Every day she wore a black outfit as a sign of mourning for her father, who had been killed by carjackers. She did give me a watch for Christmas, nothing fancy but surely a strain on her personal budget. I wore it the rest of my time in Iraq and still have it. She met her future husband Marwan, another translator, in the convention center. They later married and had a son, Mohammad.

A few years after I left Iraq and not long after the baby was born, I received a chilling email from Samar begging for help to get out of Iraq.

Here's the exact text of her email:

*There was a horrible thing happened to me, Marwan and Mohammed when we transferred Mohammed to the doctor. When we came back from the doctor we went to buy the drugs to my son from the pharmacy, then 3 cars with armed people stopped us and they put the pistol in Marwan's face and said you are working as a translator. I was crying and begging them and said he is working with the Education Ministry and thank God Marwan was carrying the id of the education. he showed it to them. i swear to you i swear to you mr ted what happened to us is true. today just now. please try to help us pleeeeeeeeeeeeeeeeeeeeeeeeeeeeeeeeeeeeeeeese.*

I started a frantic search for help, even writing to Sen. Edward Kennedy after he made a moving floor speech calling for the United States to rescue the brave Iraqis in danger because of their work with Americans. The response from Kennedy's office was a form letter condemning the Bush administration's Iraq policy, and the salutation was blank. It symbolized the callous disregard the United States showed toward Iraqis who were being terrorized because they had helped us. I tried to call Samar after that, but one day Marwan answered and insisted that I never call again. I didn't, and I never heard what happened to Samar or her family.

By October, we started seeing evidence that we were actually turning IMN into a real news operation. One milestone was the September 27 rocket attack against the Al Rasheed. The small projectiles had barely scarred an upper corner of the building, but it was new evidence of an emerging insurgency. I awakened at sunrise to the sound of three quick explosions. After verifying no injuries or major damage, I went to the news center to check our coverage. We were not able to cover breaking news live yet,

***2003: IMN translator Samar Amar,***
***later terrorized by insurgents for working with Americans.***

but I expected to see it in the next news cut-in. The news director at the time, a cameraman by trade, announced there would be no coverage. "It might encourage the insurgents to do it again if we give it attention," he said. We covered it, and the next day we had another news director. Parenthetically, the attack did cause one outrage—the Al Rasheed swimming pool was off limits from that day on.

As the insurgency strengthened, we dispatched crews whenever possible to cover demonstrations and confrontations, not just in Baghdad but also Najaf, Karbala, and other cities close enough to send crews out and get them back in time for the evening news. As IMN crews, they faced extra risks. A crew was interviewing bystanders at a Baghdad demonstration when a reporter from the international network Al Jazeera interrupted and scolded the crowd for talking to IMN. We ordered the crew back to the station for its own safety.

A popular IMN offering was sports. On October 8 we pulled off a flawless live broadcast of an Iraqi national soccer team match in Malaysia. Strangely, airing a few recorded repeats of the game was harder for the staff to manage than the live broadcast. The repeats started late, mysteriously lost sound at times, and froze on screen. The staff's explanations: an Arabic version of stuff happens.

But the next night featured unprecedented breaking news drama. We set up live coverage at a Baghdad stadium for a "friendly" soccer match between Iraqi army and air force teams. This included play-by-play at field level by a skilled and energetic sports reporter named Suhad. She drew plenty of attention from men in the crowd because she was a blonde woman doing something only men usually did. Everything was fine until late in the second half, when the referee made a controversial call. One group of fans in the crowd howled in protest, and the other roared back in defiance. Then somebody started shooting. Suhad stayed at her post broadcasting while members of her crew rushed to interview people in the crowd. That ended abruptly when the SAIC security grabbed Suhad and whisked her and the crew away in their caravan of black SUVs. But Suhad wasn't done yet. She got to the convention center in time for the start of the evening newscast. As the tape rolled, she recapped what had happened without placing blame for fear of retaliation. It was a remarkable and encouraging breakthrough for IMN.

On October 12, the news team again showed it could cover breaking news and get on air after a downtown hotel was bombed. Within 20 minutes, news producers edited Associated Press video of that bombing, paired it with IMN video of another bombing that day, and wrote a script covering both. The network was showing another live soccer match between Iraq and Myanmar, so at halftime the TV team borrowed a radio anchor and broke in with the breaking news report, all less than an hour after the hotel bombing. Two hours later, the 4 p.m. news cut-in expanded the report and added a soundbite from a Governing Council member who had witnessed the hotel attack.

IMN's distant critics never saw any of this. IMN's journalists were risking their safety to give their countrymen breaking news coverage they had never seen on Iraqi TV. Their work still showed plenty of rough edges, but their improvement was undeniable.

A week later, October 19, was the day to try IMN's first live prime time newscast. The production staff solved several last-minute glitches and pulled off as good a show as could be expected under the circumstances. It even started and ended on time. We didn't know how many viewers we had, but we knew the audience included most of the CPA staff at the palace.

Here's the email reaction I received the next morning from Pete Sidle, the conscientious and sharp-eyed administrator overseeing SAIC's IMN contract:

> *We all went over to 'your side' of the Green Room to watch last night's newscast. It looked like a party there were so many people over there. And it turns out there was a lot to celebrate! The two words that come immediately to mind regarding last night's newscast are Impressive and Exciting!! As your anchor roared from one short-punchy-story-with-video-clip to the next, people actually began cheering—with Gary up front playing cheerleader...we both thought you and your team did a fantastic job. You left us incredibly encouraged about the future of the whole doggone network.*

We had momentum, so we tried to build on it. MBC had offered to train the television staff with a few days of workshops at their gleaming broadcast center in Dubai. We selected an all-star team covering the key job categories and flew the group to what for them was the Promised Land. What they learned could only be considered aspirational; maybe someday they would have the facilities and technology they had seen in Dubai. Before boarding a C-130 for the flight home, they managed a ferocious round of shopping. I have photos of the tired, happy faces on that flight home. A few more groups later shared the experience.

One eager trainee was an anchor, Lekha. She later married another Iraqi working for the Americans, and he was assassinated weeks after the birth of their first child. Not long after that, as she visited an office to fill out paperwork related to her husband's death, she also was assassinated. It still hurts to look at my photo of her in that C-130, beaming as she clutched her big white bag of treasures from Dubai.

The turning point for IMN and the occupation as a whole came at the Al Rasheed on Sunday, October 27, 2003, the first day of the Islamic holy month of Ramadan. Just after dawn, an explosion woke me up. Then a second, then a third. That's when I rolled onto the floor for protection between my bed and a wall.

More explosions followed in quick succession. I heard glass breaking and debris falling and felt the building shudder with each hit. I counted eight.

As the echoes of explosions faded, the silence was broken by screams. I threw on some clothes and hurried down the hall to the stairs. A few people, some in pajamas, went ahead of me, careful not to slip on the blood-smeared steps. As residents congregated in the lobby, I went to the café and asked the staff to put all the water bottles they had on the bar. Word spread, and the dozens of bottles were gone in minutes. First responders, mostly military, were shepherding everyone out into the parking lot and then on to the convention center across the street. The crowd parted near the hotel front doors to make way for stretcher bearers hurrying a wounded American woman to an ambulance. She had arrived the previous day and had agreed to another woman's request to switch rooms.

As I moved outside, I looked for my IMN team, all of whom were housed in the hotel. After I found all of them unharmed, we huddled to compare notes and plan coverage. As soon as we were allowed, we rushed to the convention center production floor, marshalled our IMN staff, and got to work.

We were on a reduced staffing schedule for Ramadan, but we aired breaking news updates throughout the day. We got no help from any CPA sources and had to rely on briefings and announcements issued to all media. So much for a special status.

As pieces of the puzzle started fitting together, we learned that the military authorities had opened a major thoroughfare the night before, saying the security situation had improved to allow this goodwill gesture at the start of Ramadan. Insurgents exploited the occasion by driving a white Chevy pickup with a flatbed trailer to a spot about 500 yards west of the hotel. As curious and unarmed Iraqi security guards approached the truck, the driver ran away. Seconds later, a remote signal launched the rockets mounted on the trailer. As we would learn repeatedly, goodwill had a short life span in occupied Iraq.

Visiting Deputy Defense Secretary Paul Wolfowitz had spent the night in the hotel; he appeared shaken but unharmed as he was spirited away. Others were not so fortunate. Fifteen people were wounded, and one died. That was Lt. Col. Chad Buehring, a man I had worked with in the Green Room just 12 hours earlier. He was an earnest Army lifer, eager and able to do anything asked of him. When the attack started, he ran to his window and fired a few shots at the distant trailer before one of the rockets found his room.

That was the only time I felt my safety threatened in Iraq. Rocket and mortar attacks into the Green Zone were intermittent and, as far as I was told, never did much harm or damage. I heard about a hostile fatwa (edict) or two directed at me by radical Islamic clerics, but I couldn't believe they would waste their time on anyone at IMN.

The hotel was declared off limits, but eventually I was given 15 minutes to clear out my room. That gave me a chance to look into the charred shambles where the rockets struck. My room faced west, where the rockets had come from, so I was lucky to have been on a lower floor. The nearest impact was two floors up. I packed quickly and left, abandoning the duffel bag and its khaki contents.

The hotel had offered excellent laundry services, and I had sent out a load of underwear the day before the attack. Three weeks later, I was summoned to the central laundry facility to pick up my things. More like pick out, though. All unclaimed items had been dumped in a waist-high pile on the laundry floor. I had to sift through the mound of unmentionables to find mine. I didn't get them all, but I did discover that some folks in the Green Zone had decidedly unmilitary preferences for lingerie.

With the Rasheed permanently closed, nearly all its residents were herded into a hastily arranged dormitory in the east wing of the Republican Palace. It was grotesque. Hundreds of staffers working for or with the CPA (including my IMN team) were crammed into a vast expanse of creaky, lumpy beds with communal bath and toilet facilities. The CPA was a 24/7 operation, so denizens were rising and retiring at all hours. Nobody slept well. For reasons I never knew, I was spared this ordeal when Gary Thatcher handed me a key to a trailer room, similar to the setup I had my first few nights, with one big difference.

The Green Zone's chronic housing shortage, exacerbated by the Al Rasheed closure, required two persons to share a room designed for one. My roommate was a sergeant working in the palace. He was amiable, tolerated my snoring, and split the sparse storage space down the middle. He even chuckled when, as I settled down for my first night in these new digs, an unholy bang over my head jerked me awake. Then another, and another. They didn't seem like explosions, but I wasn't sure. He solved the mystery for me; they were palm nuts falling onto the trailer's metal roof.

A few days after the attack, we Americans at IMN learned we weren't as tough as we thought. IMN video showed the rocket-launching trailer being towed from the scene—not Emmy stuff, but gold for us. We told newscast producer Thamir Ibrahim to open the newscast with it. For unknown reasons, he didn't. When Thamir emerged from the control room after the show, we laid into him. Four of us crowded around him in the narrow corridor taking turns yelling, forgetting our stated policy to treat the Iraqi staff gently. They had been through a lot and didn't deserve abuse from their foreign bosses. This collective tirade shocked and upset poor Thamir and his colleagues. More importantly, it shocked us. We looked at each other wondering where all that venom had come from and why. After a quick post-mortem in my office, we agreed that we had strayed way over the line. We realized that maybe we weren't dealing with the effects of the rocket attack as well as we had thought.

I arranged a session with a CPA mental health counselor the next day, and attendance for the American team was mandatory. He concluded that we were suffering from a form of PTSD. He gave us suggestions for dealing with it, and the advice helped. We had another huddle and decided to give the Iraqi staff a second shock. We called a staff meeting, and we apologized individually and as a group. In their entire lives, the Iraqis had never heard a superior apologize for anything. Nothing like that happened again on my watch. The work atmosphere was generally calm after that, although two Iraqis did get into a hallway fistfight arguing over who could cover a sports event.

Despite IMN's quantifiable improvements in its news product, the drum roll of criticism pounded on in American media. Sen. Richard Lugar, chairman of the Foreign Relations Committee, wondered why the State Department wasn't running IMN. (Not a bad idea, actually.) Internews chief David Hoffman, a respected authority on international media, called IMN "the worst mess I've ever seen" without ever seeing the results of our work. We were getting slammed for something that no longer existed.

Despite the progress, we knew IMN had a long way to go, and so did SAIC. A few days after the Al Rasheed attack, an SAIC executive called to tell me John Sandrock was out and I was the new IMN general manager, doubling my salary. (I had horribly undersold myself at the start.) A management shuffle included the long overdue elevation of Shameem Rassam to manager of TV and radio programming. While contributing to IMN's improvement, she was refreshingly realistic about the Iraqi public's skepticism toward the American-run media.

"I hate to be compared with Al Jazeera and Al Arabiya," she told an AP reporter. "We're working with people who had no chance to think for themselves for 30 years. And our audience, for 30 years, saw only one thing on television. In six months, you expect them to believe this institution?"

I learned a lot about those 30 years from Iraqi and American colleagues. One question that lingered from the Iraq War and its checkered aftermath was whether Iraqis were better off without Saddam. His regime had been secular, and women had not suffered the second-class status imposed in fundamental Muslim societies. Islam, while the national religion, was a moderate version, and other religions were tolerated. As is the case in many authoritarian systems, people who didn't cause trouble got by.

Personal recollections of the Saddam time painted a different picture. One young IMN employee told me he never dared to look at the government enclave while riding by on a bus to school. Anyone who showed too much interest would get a tap on the shoulder from a uniformed rider asking why they took so much interest in those buildings. Another said he had learned English listening to the Voice of America. In one class session, his high school English teacher demanded to know why he spoke English with an American accent.

As IMN general manager, I was supposed to oversee the CPA-run national newspaper, *al Sabah*. It seemed to be functioning fine on its own. I was later told that it was a favorite outlet for stories planted by military psychological operations, known as psyops. My lack of Arabic meant I couldn't do much about it if I wanted to. I visited the newspaper's offices once. The editor gave me a tour while lobbying for more support and more space. As he spoke, we walked past several empty rooms, and I asked why they were not being used. Nobody would work there, he said. Saddam's henchmen had used those rooms for hanging political prisoners on meat hooks.

In the Republican Palace, two halls decorated in what could be called Saddam baroque were converted into dining facilities for the CPA staff. They gave ornate a bad name, but their histories were even worse. We were told of a banquet Saddam staged in one hall, ostensibly to honor stars of his Baath Party. The meal progressed until a few participants passed out face down in their plates. As servants dragged the bodies away, Saddam announced to the remaining guests that those departed ones were disloyal Baathists. I don't know whether any other guests finished their meals.

The most chilling encounter with Saddam's brutal legacy came in the basement of the Republican Palace. Gary Thatcher persuaded a colonel to bend the rules and let me and another civilian see that part of the building. The officer used a combination of keys to open a thick armored door that was better suited for a vault. As we turned left, he showed us a modern movie theater with about 20 seats. That, he said, was where Saddam and his family watched films. His favorites were Bulgarian soap operas. The colonel then led us to the right and down the marble-lined corridor to a nondescript door that opened to reveal a dazzling chamber of treasures. The apartment-sized space was stacked high with goods that could stock a world-class duty-free store. Premium liquor like Johnny Walker Blue scotch, Remy Martin Louis VIII cognac, fine wines and liquors, plus jewelry, perfume, luxury ceramics, and crystal—whatever you would give a ruthless dictator if you wanted to get on his good side.

In an open space in the center of the room was a stack of four Hitachi stereo systems, all unopened in the original boxes. The contrast was as stark as it was puzzling, until the colonel explained. Those were the property of Saddam's depraved sons, Uday and Qusay. The boys were known to prey on attractive women, any age, married or not—in some cases brides snatched from their weddings. These pigs would haul their victims off to one of their villas along the Tigris and do whatever they could think of. If a woman resisted or acted as if she didn't enjoy the encounter, her body would be found the next morning in the middle of a Baghdad street. But if she acted as if she didn't mind being repeatedly raped throughout the night, she was tossed out at dawn with a lovely parting gift—a brand new bookshelf stereo. So much for life being better under Saddam.

As overall general manager, I had plenty on my plate: network development, facility improvements, programming strategy, and overall administration. John

Sandrock and Bob Teasdale were gone, the latter replaced by Loren Flossman, a scary good project manager dealing with the non-broadcast issues dogging IMN, such as signal propagation and tower construction.

My responsibilities even wandered into the field of diplomacy, requiring visits with coalition officials and trips to foreign missions. One visit to the Italian embassy showed me the deteriorating security situation in Baghdad. For a drive of just a few miles, we needed the standard two-SUV convoy bristling with weapons. As always on a road trip, I wore stifling body armor while squeezed into a back seat between two all-business security pros.

Soon after leaving the Green Zone, our entourage got bogged down in Baghdad afternoon traffic. I looked around, enjoying the opportunity to see Baghdad life I never saw from the Green Zone. To my escorts, the gridlock made us sitting ducks. The lead driver stomped on the gas, jerked the wheel to the right, and led a frantic charge along sidewalks, green spaces, and any other gap he could find until we reached a side street leading to the embassy. Nobody was there to greet us, but the trip was not a complete waste of time. It had allowed me to see how Baghdad had become a dangerous place for anyone involved with the occupation. I appreciated and even admired the extreme measures taken to protect me, but I also appreciated the popular resentment growing against Americans. For a few minutes on a busy Baghdad street, the occupiers had posed the greatest threat to public safety.

For IMN and SAIC, a new threat emerged, and it came from Washington. The Pentagon was tiring of recurring negative publicity, and CPA cheerleaders wanted more rah-rah content in IMN broadcasts. The result was a punishing left-right combination that staggered SAIC.

First, the Pentagon issued a "cure order" demanding to know why the SAIC contract should not be cancelled, even as we were finally giving the CPA plenty of evidence of progress. Then, around the same time, word circulated that the Pentagon would require SAIC to compete for the next phase of the IMN contract covering 2004. SAIC had won the first contract almost by default; now it had to stack its performance and future intentions up against competitors, some with broadcast pedigrees. SAIC, unhappy with the stain on its reputation, was wondering whether the whole thing was worth it.

In early November, I went to Washington for meetings with SAIC executives to plot the cure order response. After my return, my diary for November was full of one word—meetings. Meetings with staff, meetings with consultants, meetings about staff schedules, meetings in Amman, meetings in Dubai. Meanwhile, an ambitious cadre of CPA officials was realizing that the network, rebranded al Iraqiya (the Iraqis), had potential after all, so they started maneuvering to get their hooks into it. Al Iraqiya wasn't pro-American or pro-democracy enough, they said. Too soft, too subtle. They doubted that Iraqis could absorb Western ideals and principles at their own pace; Iraqis would only "get it" if the message was hammered into them.

The network hosted several talk shows because they were easy to produce. Then a new idea came up for a different kind of talk show, with CPA boss Paul Bremer submitting to a half-hour of impromptu questions from two Iraqi journalists. The set would resemble a café, with the three participants sitting around a small table conversing via simultaneous translations in their ears. The journalists would be invited on a rotating basis from a number of Iraqi media outlets, not just friends of the CPA. Bremer graciously and courageously agreed to do this live.

The first show went fine. The Iraqi journalists were respectful and polite while asking probing, relevant questions, mostly about security and the economy. Bremer was relaxed and was prepared for every topic tossed at him. But a few mid-level neo-conservatives and military officers in the palace were nervous. They yammered that such an uncontrolled forum could lead to embarrassment for Bremer and the CPA. They didn't seem to think Bremer was sharp enough to dodge any zingers tossed his way.

As the weeks went by, the nervous Nellies demanded tweaks in the format and a list for vetting participating journalists, gumming up the works to the point the show was cancelled. It was just one example of a few CPA minions refusing to accept the possibility that Iraqis could comprehend what IMN was trying to do and accept it for what it was. Their idea of public persuasion was to pummel the audience with pure ideology with no room for a contrary thought or idea. Any lack of control over the message, such as an unrehearsed interview show featuring independent journalists, could, in their way of thinking, jeopardize the mission.

That hardline approach ran counter to every manual on military psyops and propaganda. It took courage to let the people hear news or commentaries that might make the people in charge uneasy, but that candor bred credibility, and that in turn nurtured trust. Every time IMN, particularly al Iraqiya, took a few steps down that path, the hardliners jerked its leash. As conditions in Iraq deteriorated under the occupation, their resistance intensified.

Under such self-inflicted wounds, the hope that al Iraqiya would grow into an Iraqi PBS was doomed. Even so, it could have served a useful purpose if allowed. But it wasn't, so it didn't.

The whole Baghdad adventure took a climactic turn on November 22. The day before, I had received an email from the office of the Voice of America's director. I had seen a posting for a job titled associate director of central programming. The description fit my resume, and I was already thinking about work in the distant future after Iraq, so I applied. The email asked if I was interested in the position. I answered that I was committed to SAIC as IMN general manager, and leaving was out of the question. I got a quick, polite reply, and thought of it as case closed.

The following morning, I joined Loren Flossman for breakfast in the palace. We were heading to Amman, Jordan later that day to inspect a warehouse full of broadcast studio equipment Saddam's Ministry of Information had purchased but never received. I had barely said hi when Loren broke the news. SAIC would not be competing for the 2004 contract. The CPA had announced it was folding its tent on June 1, 2004, making way for the Governing Council comprising only Iraqis. SAIC was tired of the grief it was getting anyway and didn't see any reason to fight for a contract that would automatically expire in six months when the CPA shut down. So SAIC threw in the towel.

I almost sprinted to the nearest Green Room computer and sent another email to the VOA saying that circumstances had changed overnight and I was indeed interested in that job. Within a few days, they arranged to have me fly to Washington in mid-December for an interview.

When we returned from Amman and a bucket-list side trip to Petra, a new kind of IMN disaster ruined Thanksgiving weekend for the whole team. Gary Thatcher convened a meeting to ask Loren and me why broadcast towers weren't up as planned in several northern Iraq locations. Loren assured him that the engineers in charge of that project had confirmed they were up. Gary then lowered the boom; CPA inspectors had found only concrete pads where towers were supposed to be. The engineers had lied. SAIC fired the derelicts and scrambled to fend off the CPA's justified rage, but any lingering hope that SAIC could find a way to hang on to IMN died.

My last month in Baghdad is something of a blur, except for the still sporadic but increasing rocket and mortar attacks, usually at night. The Al Rasheed barrage had been in effect a launch party for the insurgency. Almost as unnerving as the explosions was the rocket alarm announcement that echoed through the Green Zone just after the first blast, never before. A pathetic siren would introduce a voice reminiscent of Carlton the Doorman in the *Rhoda* series. "Rocket attack, take cover. Rocket attack, take cover," it wheezed. Not very energizing or reassuring. Most of us stayed in our trailer rooms. We tried to shrug off the threat, but it ratcheted up the stress level for everybody.

The night before my flight to Washington, the residents of our trailer row threw a Christmas block party featuring lots of liquor and music. I retired early to be up at 4 a.m. for my airport ride, and the festivities ended around 11 p.m. The two guys in the room at the other end of the trailer weren't ready to call it a night, and they carried on while I tried to fall asleep. Finally, my roomy charged over to their side and told them to knock it off because I had an early flight in the morning. They got quiet, he got back in bed, and all was calm. For about a minute. Somewhere in the Green Zone, maybe a half mile away, a ground-shaking 105mm mortar shell exploded. Before the echoes could fade, a voice from the other room yelled, "That wasn't us!"

The VOA interview went well, and I spent a few extra days meeting with SAIC leaders about the still unresolved cure notice and other transition issues. I returned to Baghdad on December 19 and soon learned I had the VOA job. I gave notice and spent the rest of my days in transition meetings. My successor was an easy choice. Steve Marney had vast broadcast experience and had been MBC's chief liaison at IMN. He knew the place as well as I did.

The bad guys celebrated Christmas Eve with a heavier than usual dose of fireworks, adding to the security jitters in the Green Zone. On Christmas morning, as I walked the 100 yards from my trailer to breakfast at the palace, two Marines kept their weapons trained on me nearly the whole way. A lumbering old white guy didn't exactly match the profile of a terrorist, but that's how nervous everyone was.

I couldn't leave without one final disappointment. The CPA had always wanted satellite distribution of IMN, and we persuaded the top brass that the channel was ready. We had an uplink available, and we prepped for a New Year's Eve debut. A set of graphics designed for the satellite channel was prepared, and I left Baghdad on December 30 confident of its success. The signal never made it out of the dish. I later learned that a CPA control freak had unilaterally decided a satellite channel wasn't the right thing to do. He gave no reason (it wasn't his idea, maybe?), but it was a symptom of the political and professional cross currents that undermined IMN.

A partnership between Harris Corp. and a Lebanese broadcasting company won the IMN contract for the first half of 2004, and then the Governing Council took over. Less than two years later, al Iraqiya had morphed into a pro-regime outlet, exactly what the CPA had hoped to avoid.

My first return to Iraq was a brief but encouraging one. On October 30, 2005, while I was working in Istanbul (more on that later), my old benefactor Joe Raffelberg was IREX chief of party in Iraq. He was trying to help a young TV producer, Jano Rosbiani, start a station in Irbil, already the de facto capital of Kurdish Iraq. It was to be the area's first Kurdish-language station, offering mostly entertainment and documentary programming, some of it produced by Jano himself. Due to an airline scheduling snafu, I could only stay in Irbil two days, but it gave me a glimpse of what Iraq could be.

At the airport, it was clear who was in charge. The flags were mostly Kurdish, as were the shoulder patches on the uniforms of customs officers. Photos on buildings and billboards throughout town showed the paternal countenances of Kurdish leaders. Driving through one of the world's oldest cities was a breeze on freshly paved streets (a sign of an upcoming election). No concrete security barriers blocked our way; no checkpoints slowed us down. The Kurds had been waiting an eternity for their own homeland. This wasn't quite it, but they made it look close enough. I spent my limited time with Jano learning about his goals and the market he wanted to penetrate and then flew back to Istanbul. My report was sympathetic and encouraging, but he wasn't professionally ready or financially able to start that kind of station, so it never happened.

A month later, I was back in Baghdad again, this time to judge the network I had helped to create. By this time al Iraqiya was firmly in government hands, and Joe asked me to assess its political coverage in the final week leading up to national legislative elections. Arriving on December 9, 2005, I saw in no time that Baghdad was still a dangerous place, even if I could arrive on a commercial airliner. The ride into town from the airport was as harrowing as ever; my SUV caravan bristled with weapons as it sped to the Karada district where I had once patronized liquor stores with IMN buddies. It was even more disheveled now, grimy and listless under the cloud of a growing insurgency. Its ranks were filled with former soldiers left idle after Bremer had disbanded the Iraqi armed forces. They were jobless in a stagnant economy that offered little opportunity to feed their families. They wanted the old times back and were willing to fight for them against a confused occupation army that thought its job should have ended the day Baghdad fell.

After I spent a couple of nights in a sparse hotel room, IREX moved me to the al Mansour Hotel, similar to the al Rasheed and a popular place to stay for foreigners working in Baghdad. It was conveniently across the street from the al Iraqiya studios in the former Ministry of Information complex. However, I couldn't stroll across the street to work. Each morning, two armed security guys would come to my room and escort me through the lobby to my two-SUV caravan. Wearing body armor, I sat in the back seat of the first vehicle flanked by two escorts pointing weapons out both back seat windows. More armed guards were in the following SUV, which enjoyed the added protection of a 50-caliber machine gun pointing out the back. We pulled out into the street, turned right, drove 50 yards to a break in the median, u-turned, and returned the 50 yards to the studio entrance. All that to go 100 feet as the crow flies. The parade was repeated every evening when I returned to the hotel. That was Baghdad in 2005.

Al Iraqiya, however, had one thing going for it—nice digs. The CPA and SAIC had always coveted the Information Ministry site as a potential home for IMN. But it had been severely damaged in the war, and squatters had settled into apartments on the south side of the complex. One military operation to evict them was cancelled at the last minute, and the CPA decided the potential cost of taking over the ministry in terms of money, public relations, and most of all blood was not worth the effort. After SAIC gave up the IMN project, Harris Corp. found a better solution—cash. The squatters were paid handsomely to move out, a section of the smashed ministry was carved out for al Iraqiya, and a modern TV production facility rose from the ruins.

When I entered on the first morning, I was impressed, and jealous. Why couldn't we have done this? The al Iraqiya general director escorted me into the main newsroom, where the gathered staff, including IMN holdovers, welcomed me with a standing ovation. It was humbling, but it was misguided. A rumor had spread that I had come back to take over the network. When I quashed that idea, they still enjoyed the reunion. Later, individuals would take me aside to complain about a manager or a policy or some other perceived injustice. I thanked them for their trust in me but had to remind them I was just there to assess the network's political coverage.

Again, my lack of Arabic was limiting, but a team of translators made the job easier. Nearly a week of analysis was enough time to compile a 15-page report on the network's performance. I tried to be gentle, but I was paid for my assessment and had to be candid.

As we had feared, the CPA's departure had left al Iraqiya to the Iraqi government, and the channel's political coverage left no doubt who was paying the bills. Its campaign coverage was not heavy-handed propaganda. It was more subtle and effective. Newscasts didn't concentrate on the ruling Shia-dominated party while ignoring all others. It gave all parties an opportunity to present their cases, but al Iraqiya journalists avoided "examining and challenging the policies" of parties as called for in the network's own coverage guidelines. In one soundbite, a reporter allowed a military officer in Mosul to claim that in Iraq there were no differences between north and south. That patently absurd statement went unchallenged. Reporters asked citizens what they thought about the election, and they answered that it was great to be able to vote. Reporters focused on the public's enthusiasm for the election, but local, regional, or national issues almost never came up. If they did, respondents gave answers that they thought they were expected to give to the government's network.

On Election Day, Iraqis defied threats of insurgent violence and went to the polls, dipping their index finger in purple ink to show they had voted. I thought the middle finger would have been a better choice but kept that to myself. Al Iraqiya's coverage of Election Day portrayed a capital and country enjoying a tranquil exercise in democracy. The government's network did not mention false rumors that Baghdad's water supply had been poisoned, even though mosques used loudspeakers normally reserved for calls to prayer to spread the rumors throughout the night. Also missing from al Iraqiya newscasts was any mention of the three mortar rounds that landed in the city center as polls opened.

While reporters gave bland accounts of voting in various cities, they made no attempt to characterize turnout. As I said in my report, "To use a news cliché, al Iraqiya's journalism was a mile wide and an inch deep." I found no evidence of direct government interference in network news coverage even though dissident employees claimed it was a daily occurrence. Al Iraqiya's failures in covering the national campaign were more ones of omission than commission. Network management was not thrilled with my report. The chief executive even asked IREX to withdraw it, but Joe refused. That was the only time an official formally challenged one of my consultant reports.

My last, furtive glance at Al Iraqiya came in early 2013 when I visited Baghdad to assess the U.S.-funded television operation al Hurra for executive producer Shameem Rassam, my former IMN colleague. What little I saw of al Iraqiya did not change my assessment of what it had become: a typical government outlet in a developing country, slick looking but serving one master. Iraqis watched it, but they didn't trust it.

Al Hurra, in contrast, was faring well even with its known U.S. government connections. The staff deserved more training and better facilities, but it was holding its own in a crowded TV news market. Its status was confirmed for me on my last day there. Muqtada al Sadr, an influential Shia cleric who was formerly a vehement critic of the American occupation, had gone public to urge an end to protests sweeping An Bar Province. He wanted to reinforce his message by granting an interview to a national broadcaster. His choice: al Hurra. Al Sadr preferred a network run by the once-hated occupiers instead of the one controlled by government leaders from his own sect.

We tried at IMN, and we did some good things. Regrettably, it didn't end well. Later, in another war zone, lessons from IMN would be heeded, with better results.

# CHAPTER 11
# Voice of America

*Where Good Ideas Went to Die*

The day I arrived at the Cohen Building on February 8, 2004, I walked into the middle of a no-winners political donnybrook. One of VOA Director David Jackson's first directives to me was to concentrate on TV integration into the historically radio-oriented News Division and "let me worry about the politics." He tried to shield me from it, but he couldn't.

It should have been a perfect landing spot. The job, overseeing integration of the State Department's WorldNet TV news broadcasting service into VOA, meshed perfectly with my experience and expertise. As a Senior Executive Service position, it provided an excellent salary and sterling benefits, including free parking. I had an efficient office in the third-floor executive wing of the Cohen Building, a dour gray structure on the southeast edge of the Washington Mall a few blocks from Capitol Hill. My commute was an easy 15-minute drive across the Potomac from Old Town Alexandria, where I had a small but adequate condo. What could be wrong with that?

Well, a lot, actually. It's a saga of good intentions drowned by savage reality at the confluence of politics and bureaucracy. It was the only "bad" job I ever had.

The workplace culture in the News Division was entrenched and formidable. As at RFE/RL, the English-language division generated most of the material the 44 language services translated for their programming. From senior executives to the newest writer, the division, especially the Central News unit, considered itself the defender of VOA editorial purity. Its news product was impeccable. The standards for accuracy and clarity matched those at RFE/RL. The two-source rule was more than a slogan, and editors massaged copy without the gotcha-game zeal of their Munich counterparts.

On the other side, David Jackson was a Bush administration appointee labeled by his critics as a neo-con true believer. That was unfair and simplistic; what little I knew about his political beliefs nevertheless led me to think he wasn't the hardline conservative the News Division perceived him to be. Yet he didn't do himself any favors. He would routinely sift through the news files searching for something objectionable. More often than not he found it. Typically, it was a story's failure to include the American government's policy or position. He would relay his complaint to the newsroom directly, adding how he thought the flaw could be corrected.

To Central News, this was Jackson trying to politicize VOA news. Some even tarred his critiques with the most despised word in the building, propaganda. By any definition, that was nonsense.

In Central News and other News Division units, David was not trusted. He in turn perceived the newsroom's editorial imperfections and its resistance to his editorial opinions as evidence of bias against the Bush administration and conservatism in general. In David's defense, many of his suggestions could be construed as seeking compliance with the VOA Charter's requirement for presenting U.S. policies "clearly and effectively." Newsroom journalists would argue that such context was unnecessary or gratuitous.

I had another theory that lingered from my RFE/RL experience. By neglecting an American angle, at least some felt they were protecting newsroom independence and integrity. I always suspected a few Central News journalists felt tainted or professionally diminished by working for a government-funded news agency. Remember H.L. Stevenson's reaction when I quit UPI in Detroit to join RFE/RL: "Well, if he wants to go write propaganda, I guess that's his choice." Proud, talented journalists at VOA and all taxpayer-funded newsrooms had to shake off such condescension.

Writing an accurate story that was not favorable to the U.S. government could be a feel-good affirmation of journalistic neutrality. Central News writers and editors were quick, and justified, to cite the charter's mandate for "consistently reliable and authoritative" news, but they chafed at any attempt to enforce another charter requirement to "present the policies of the United States clearly and effectively." By the time I got there, the impasse was unbreakable.

As associate director for central programming, I spent my initial weeks saying or doing little while concentrating on learning all the facets of "central programming." I worked as a writer in Central News, sat with TV reporters and editors, web desk editors, and the tenured writers in "pod land"—a reference to the configuration of their work area—producing long-form reports and analysis. I introduced myself to other sections outside my responsibilities but kept my distance so I would not appear to be encroaching on the realms of other associate directors responsible for language programming and technical operations.

The lack of amenities for the newsroom staff bothered me from my first day. The basement cafeteria closed at 3 p.m., forcing evening and overnight staffs to bring food or leave the building for meals. I asked VOA administration to bring vending machines into the newsroom's lounge to give employees another choice. The laid-back union, the American Federation of Government Employees (AFGE) Local 1812, scoffed at the idea, probably because it didn't think of it. The food vending machine lasted a few months but was removed due to lack of sales. The beverage machine stayed. Management and staff chalked it up as a nice try.

By the time I was ready to focus on my primary task—integrating WorldNet TV news into the VOA News Division—I knew my first move. The News Division leadership loathed David and loathed TV as an abomination. My repeated attempts to engage top managers in transition discussions met with patronizing promises of cooperation or condescending indifference. David and I were left with no choice. We shuffled the News Division leadership, reassigning the director to the feature desk. Nobody was fired, but nobody could interfere with the introduction of TV news either.

In reorganizing the News Division management, I made a strategic mistake. I agreed at Jackson's suggestion to function as acting news director. As long as I focused on TV integration, I was out of the direct line of fire in the Jackson-News Division skirmishes. Now I was in no-man's land, exposed to salvos from both sides.

Any directive or suggestion I made to the News Division now passed through the political prism held up to Jackson's actions. While assessing the Central News interaction with language services, I noticed the need for a slight adjustment in newsroom staff schedules. When I introduced the new schedules at a staff meeting, one editor hung her head and mumbled "more Bush bullshit." How could scheduling be political? When I invited her into my office for an explanation, she apologized, but the storm warnings were up.

David didn't help things. A few of his complaints never got farther than me. I don't know if he was using me as a sounding board or filter. I triaged his complaints, relaying some unchanged, taking the sting out of others, and letting some die undelivered. We didn't always agree, and once we descended into a ding-dong shouting match in the executive suite lobby. He did not like how Central News had quoted Vice President Dick Cheney. The quote was not flattering to Cheney, but the copy had reproduced it word for word. David's complaint was that Central News should have paraphrased Cheney to give a better sense of what he meant to say. I defended the story as written. David got more agitated, and my rebuttal got more heated. When we both realized everyone could hear us, we agreed to disagree and shut it down. Central News never heard the complaint (from me, anyway), and David and I carried on as if nothing happened. He could have turned vindictive but never did, making my job easier.

As his micro-editing continued, he raised the tension level by objecting to two Central News reporters asking questions at a news conference by members of the Broadcasting Board of Governors, VOA's overseer. The veteran, respected staffers were attending on their own time, and their questions were reasonable requests for explanations of board policies. David alleged that their questions were confrontational and that the writers had no right to be there. He ordered me to reprimand both and wouldn't consider my alternative suggestions for handling the matter. I believe in managerial solidarity except in extreme situations, and this didn't rise to that level.

I called them to my office with a supervisor as a witness and informed them of David's displeasure. They were flummoxed, and I said I understood their point of view. Their standing with VOA was not harmed by this incident, so the only result was an even wider gulf between David and the News Division, with my legs stretched that much farther as I tried to straddle the gap. I needed help and found it by persuading Alex Belida, a golf buddy and former Munich colleague, to leave his VOA Pentagon correspondent post and return to the News Division as its de facto director. That restored some of the administrative separation between me and the division.

I was still adjusting to the internecine cold war when I was sucker punched by a debilitating flaw in the culture of VOA. A few individuals reveled in taking the News Division's causes outside agency walls. News organizations typically banned or tightly controlled employee comments to outsiders, including other media, special interest groups, and government officials. Speaking without authorization could be a firing offense, but not at VOA. A tiny number of rogue employees got their jollies embarrassing the agency without first seeking an internal remedy for their perceived or real grievance. Some went to former VOA officials who spread the news far and wide, including Capitol Hill. Others went directly to friendly journalists. The results were a mash-up of wrong conclusions or willful misrepresentations that took on a bastardized life of their own.

I suffered two bites from this tiny but irritating swarm of pests. One caused an annoying itch, the other a painful wound.

The itch came from a video journalist of limited ability who was fond of feeding her ego as unappointed defender of the VOA Charter. She claimed to be speaking for "many producers," but we heard otherwise from plenty of producers. Nevertheless, she caught the ear of one Washington freelance writer by accusing me of banning VOA coverage of U.S. anti-terrorism forces working in Africa. Somehow, the writer swallowed all of this as evidence of political interference in VOA news but did the right thing by calling me for my side of the story. I spent 45 minutes refuting every element of the story, giving him website addresses to see the very stories that I had allegedly blocked.

When the story appeared in a Washington political magazine, it recited the allegations chapter and verse and ignored my rebuttal. In professional slang, it was a hatchet job. I went to the VOA's public relations office demanding a response, and I was told to forget it because nobody paid much attention to that magazine anyway. The video journalist, by the way, later asked for a transfer to the New York bureau, and I arranged it as quickly as I could. She thought she had earned the move, but I approved it to get her out of town. Besides, she would be filing fewer stories from New York, curtailing her opportunities to foul the VOA TV news product. By now you no doubt understand why I'm not identifying her or the magazine.

A mightier blow from the VOA dysfunction forge fell as I entered my second year at VOA.

During routine analysis of domestic and international bureaus, the Hong Kong bureau caught my eye. After crunching budget numbers and considering other factors, I came up with an idea to shift primary news writing duties from the Central News overnight staff to Hong Kong. The savings were substantial ($340,000 per year), and the change would align the bureau's working hours with Asia's news day and reduce the onerous overnight shift in Washington, except for a supervisor with final editorial authority. David liked the idea, and the Broadcasting Board of Governors approved the plan in two separate votes.

As soon as the plan was announced, it got clobbered. The main complaints were that Americans in Washington would lose their jobs to "foreigners" writing VOA news or lose lucrative salary differentials against their will.

In fact, the plan cut no Washington positions, and the "foreigners" were two Americans, a New Zealander and an Australian already working at the bureau as staff or freelancers. As for moving staffers off the overnight shift against their will, the three supervising editors had family reasons for staying on overnights, and they would keep their shifts. A half dozen staff writers were losing differentials but not jobs. Furthermore, research had shown that overnight work could harm a worker's health. There were plenty of other justifications, like moving employees hiding on the overnight to avoid accountability. When I had time to explain the plan face-to-face, I could defuse the objections. My friend and former Munich buddy Evans Hayes, also a VOA veteran, told me he thought the idea was "stupid." After 20 minutes of explanation and rebuttal, he said, "Well, that's not so bad after all."

Resistance from Central News was expected, and some mainstream media coverage was skeptical. *The Washington Post*'s Al Kamen wrote a critical but measured column, extensively quoting David's defense of the idea. *A Baltimore Sun* editorial, again balanced with David's comments, called for Congress to block the change. Reuters reported the plan with its usual neutrality.

However, other reaction bordered on hysterical. Communist Chinese writing VOA news, they said. "Agency to outsource American jobs to China," bleated (inaccurately) the VOA local for AFGE, whose leader scurried up to Capitol Hill to orchestrate congressional opposition to the idea. One result was a bipartisan protest letter from 14 senators, including John Kerry, Edward Kennedy, and Barak Obama. In fairness, it raised valid regulatory concerns that needed attention. The National Writers Union called the move "appalling" in a letter to David and demanded its cancellation. In listing its objections, it quoted me as saying: "Any change is denounced by a core of VOA diaspora without them knowing the details of what's being planned and without them understanding contemporary media and business circumstances." I stood by every word. I also coined a slogan: "The Voice of America is where good ideas go to die."

Once again, as in Iraq and as far back as my time at *USA Today*, journalists prejudged the story and then went looking for evidence supporting their conclusion. In this case, the plan's critics decided or were persuaded it was a bad idea and set out to find reasons why, valid or not.

The final absurdity in the Hong Kong brouhaha came when I was summoned to Capitol Hill to explain my plan to a group of congressional aides. In an imposing Russell Senate Office Building conference room, I sat at a table for more than an hour with about a dozen minions from congressional and committee offices as I tried to explain concepts such as the value of proximity in news coverage, the way modern technology allowed Washington oversight of a bureau in Hong Kong, the backgrounds of the prospective bureau staff, budgetary and personnel advantages, and other justifications. My listeners all looked fresh out of college; I doubted any had ever managed anything of consequence or run a business. They listened without expression and then asked irrelevant questions or mouthed platitudes about workers' rights, outsourcing jobs and foreigners writing for the VOA. They never drilled down to any core issues, including the ones that were fair game. They didn't have a clue, and it was a pathetic waste of time.

In the intervening months, as the uproar faded, the plan hit unanticipated but legitimate administrative delays. When I left the agency, the plan somehow overcame all the flak, and the remarkable Hong Kong bureau chief, Jennifer Janin, kept it going for several years before another spasm of budget cutting forced the bureau to close. So much for saving American jobs or covering the world.

One last distraction—more ludicrous than serious—involved an unsolicited encounter with a woman calling herself an ombudsperson. I thought that title required diplomacy and tact in the resolution of internal disputes. But this woman walked into my office uninvited and started listing all the people that deserved to be fired and others who could never be fired. She followed that with an email eviscerating a VOA administrator I considered invaluable. I didn't respond but forwarded the tirade to the woman's supervisor, asking if this sort of institutional character assassination was accepted practice at VOA. He said it was not and promised to follow up.

Months later, without warning, I received a detailed discrimination complaint against me submitted by the ombudsperson after she had been suspended for several infractions. She accused me of discrimination based on gender and national origin. I underwent an inspector general interrogation to present my defense. I said I didn't know her national origin or anything else about her. I never heard any more about the complaint, but I did hear years later that she was imprisoned for cashing her dead mother's social security checks.

To be fair, it wasn't all ugliness at the VOA. The news staff as a group was cordial and cooperative as we merged TV into the service. Editorial guidance from me was rarely necessary. Besides, David often jumped on any perceived or actual issue before I saw it. The newly arrived TV staff was supportive and readily accepted their new environment, including an up-to-date studio David had ordered in anticipation of their arrival. For example, they helped me to find more than $300,000 in end-of-year unused funding to build a badly needed auxiliary news studio in the Cohen Building basement.

Another reassuring wave of support came from the language services. In the past, they had felt like second string members of the team, facing such News Division condescension that they avoided entering what they perceived as an inner sanctum. My schedule changes that aligned newsroom shifts with language service broadcast times signaled a change in attitude. I ordered an editor from Central News regional desks to attend the daily meetings of the corresponding regional broadcasters, amplifying my mantra that the language desks were the News Division's clients and deserved to be treated as such. Long after I had gone, a young man stopped me on a sidewalk near the Cohen Building and, after confirming who I was, identified himself as a broadcaster in the Cambodian service. "I just want to thank you for what you did for us," he said.

Despite VOA's global reach, I didn't travel much in this job. I flew to Karachi, Pakistan with Gary Thatcher (back from Iraq to his permanent executive position for

*2005: Aboard the carrier U.S.S. George Washington.*

the board) to discuss an affiliate agreement with emerging Pakistani TV channel GEO. It felt like Baghdad all over again; the U.S. Embassy provided SUV security caravans wherever we went, and we were required to dine in a hotel restaurant away from the front lobby windows. We stayed only two days, and that was enough for me in Pakistan's most turbulent city.

The only trip I took with David was to MacDill Air Force Base in Florida for a Pentagon-sponsored conference on counter-terrorism. The most memorable event (other than dinner with my former Iraq partner Bob Teasdale) was a psychologist's revealing presentation that deconstructed the prevailing profile of an Islamic terrorist. Rather than an angry youth fleeing Mideast poverty, he was just as likely to be the radicalized son of a middle-class family in a Western democracy.

In December 2004, I checked off a bucket list item. A VOA correspondent, Alysha Rhu, had worked with me at CNN. She had superb military contacts, and one day I mentioned that I had always dreamed of visiting an aircraft carrier. Alysha worked her magic, and I was invited to Norfolk Naval Air Station, Virginia, where a Navy transport plane flew me and eight other civilian guests to the deck of the U.S.S. George Washington, CVN 73. The next two days would be a blur had I not taken dozens of photos. We were shown almost every square foot of the ship, except for the nuclear reactor area. We watched flight operations while standing on the deck and from the command positions on the "island." We ate with the crew and slept in officers' quarters. Every taxpayer should get a chance to see that payoff of their investment.

Even with some good times, they couldn't override the tough ones. The phony African story and the Hong Kong brawl, plus other smaller blow-ups, chipped away my enthusiasm for the job. I was learning that I had no stomach for the hurly-burly inside the Washington beltway. Much of the criticism directed at me and the agency was unfair, unbalanced, or just plain wrong. It was the first time I had experienced the other side of the media-government divide, and I didn't understand how careerists in government and politics put up with the small faction of incompetent, lazy, or intellectually corrupt journalists who hid behind the First Amendment to craft news stories to their personal taste, not caring about facts or fairness. I respect and defend the media's watchdog role, but I can understand why so many talented and capable people stay clear of the public sector because it's just not worth the aggravation. David and others in the VOA executive wing rolled with the punches and kept on doing their job.

In June, 2005 I had had enough, so I served notice to David, agreeing to stay on eight weeks or so to allow time for filling the void I was creating. As a lame duck, I focused on finishing what initiatives I had started and preparing transition materials for my eventual successor. I didn't tell David what I would do next, because I didn't know. But karma and networking took care of everything.

# CHAPTER 12

# Istanbul

*Leisurely Lecturing on the Bosporus*

This gets a little complicated, so work with me here. To explain my life after VOA, I have to go way back to a Bavarian mountain-top resort in 1988. RFE/RL leadership decided it was time for supervisors to get formal training on how to manage people. Among those selected for this training were Central News supervising editors, so off I went to a week of daytime workshops and nighttime feasting and drinking billed as team-building. We were confined to the resort the entire time, except for one evening in Garmish-Partenkirchen. Tough week.

Dr. Tom Clawson led some of the sessions. He taught us about Type-A personalities, how perception is reality, and other basics that were new to us but that competent managers now take for granted. Tom and I started sharing a table during the evening booze-ups. It didn't rise to the level of a friendship yet, but we enjoyed great conversations covering everything from world affairs to mental health to fine wines.

Fast forward a decade. Tom had risen to a position of prominence in the mental health counseling profession by taking over the National Board for Certified Counselors. In that role he had earned the rotating presidency of another certification group with a mind-bending title, the National Organization of Competency Assurance. That role made him responsible for planning NOCA's 1999 national convention at Doral Resort in Florida. We had barely stayed in touch, but when he heard I was CNN's executive editor, he asked me to lead a writing workshop at the convention and also speak to a plenary session about CNN. That was an all-expenses paid trip to Doral for less than five hours of work. He even tossed in a round of golf. How could I say no? We had time to socialize during convention off hours, and after that we were pals.

Skip ahead another two years. Tom's NBCC was the Greensboro, North Carolina nonprofit overseeing certification of mental health counselors in the United States, and it was ready to grow. Tom was not only a gifted counselor and educator; he was also a restless entrepreneur. For Tom the next logical step was going global. He needed someone to fill the public member spot on his board to help him guide the organization into its international phase. He invited me to a board meeting outside Atlanta in November 1999. I passed muster and joined the board.

Over the next five years, NBCC's board learned the intricacies of international business and mental health by reaching out to potential partner firms and organizations around the world. Taking time from wherever I was working at the time, I attended board meetings in France, England, Romania, Italy, Malaysia, Turkey, India, China—anywhere counseling as a service and a profession was welcome. As we piled up business deals, the administrative burden on the NBCC offices in Greensboro grew. By 2005, it was clear the company would soon need a separate international division.

At the same time, I was tiring of the turbulence at VOA. One summer day, I sat down with Tom and popped the question: If NBCC created an international division, why not let me get it started? Tom smiled and revealed he had been discussing the same idea with his staff. Done deal. I would become international vice president, but with one condition. The NBCC budget couldn't support a new executive until early in 2006. Accepting that caveat, I set my departure date at VOA, knowing I had enough in the bank to survive financially even if I didn't find any work for the rest of 2005.

Then things got weird. One of our potential international partners at that time was Bahcesehir University in Istanbul. This private university, a gleaming white campus complex on the banks of the Bosporus, was the pet project of Enver Yucel. This imposing Turkish tycoon had the beefy look of a longshoreman, but he was passionate about higher education as a key to Turkey's future.

Bahcesehir was interested in buying an NBCC curriculum for career counseling certification, and Tom saw so much financial potential in the deal that he took the entire board to Istanbul in July, combining a regular board meeting with a meet-and-greet session with Yucel. The deal was struck, and Yucel hosted a lavish dinner on the roof-top terrace of his apartment overlooking the Bosporus.

Tom was at the head table with Yucel and throughout the meal was pointing to board members at other tables as a manner of introduction. When he gestured my way, Yucel perked up. An intense conversation between them led to an invitation for me to sit at the head table. Through a translator, Yucel asked me questions about my background and, satisfied with the answers, popped a crazy question: Would I come to Istanbul to teach journalism at his university for a semester? I could hardly believe it; I was being offered a delicious way to fill the gap between VOA and NBCC. I didn't worry about the details and said yes. More clinking of glasses, another toast to the "great journalist Ted Iliff" (his words) and to his acceptance of a teaching position at Bahcesehir University. Smiles, handshakes, and congratulations all around.

As we waited outside for a ride to a nearby bar for a celebratory night cap, I turned to Tom, and all I could say was, "What the hell just happened in there?" The answer would come soon enough, and it was a Turkish delight.

David Jackson hosted a farewell luncheon for me at Washington's Capital Grille, and at a small ceremony in his office he gave me a certificate of achievement for the successful integration of TV into the agency. I thanked my colleagues, attended a few more farewell gatherings, and wrapped up my mixed-bag VOA adventure. Within days I was flying Lufthansa business class to Istanbul for a stress-free, three-month immersion in one of the world's most fascinating cities.

*2008: The author sitting at Agatha Christie's desk in Istanbul's Pera Palace Hotel, where she wrote* **Murder on the Orient Express.**

I stayed at the Hotel la Maison, a friendly three-star establishment on a hill overlooking Istanbul's Besiktas district. From my balcony, I could see the Golden Horn and beyond into the Sea of Marmara. One floor above my room was one of Istanbul's finest French restaurants. Every morning at breakfast I had a rooftop view of the shipping traffic on the Bosporus and the skyline of the city's European side. The campus was down a steep hill from the hotel; the walk was 10 minutes going down and 25 going up; that's all the daily exercise I needed.

My arrival unhinged the office in charge of journalism classes. The department leadership had changed just before I arrived. The resulting turmoil caused my class to be left off the fall semester roster. Already two weeks into the semester, it was hastily posted as course FTV3939: "Reporting for Electronic Media," meeting for three hours every Wednesday. The inaugural session of my first college teaching job convened in a large lecture hall with just three bemused students on the front row. They all spoke passable English, so they grasped my first edict: all lectures would be held at a café on the banks of the Bosporus, with refreshments on me. That got the semester off to a collegial start.

For 13 weeks, we covered the basics of radio and TV journalism, with periodic reading assignments but no textbook. The conversations, facilitated by my assistant Ozge when translation was needed, were two-way and instructive for both sides. These two young women and a lad on the school's handball team explained Turkish culture and society within the context of the journalism skills I was discussing. They invited friends to listen, just for fun and free espresso.

A big issue of that time was Turkey's new application for membership in the European Union. Within the context of the class, I asked why Turkey would bother. Europe had not always been kind to Turkey or Turkish immigrants, and Turkey already had a special customs agreement with the European Union. I argued that Turkey was well placed to profit from its historic role as an influential and independent hub linking Europe, Asia, and the Mideast. My students ended the conversation with one rebuttal: Turkey's EU membership would give them immediate access to jobs in Western Europe. Their future was their sole focus on that issue.

Three hours of class and one more for preparation per week left plenty of time for other pursuits. I sat in on other communications courses on campus, many in English. I explored every corner of Istanbul and its environs. I had time for trips to Ephesus, Pamukkale, Bursa, Pergamum, Kusadasi, Princes' Island, and other tourist spots—always with an eye out for fine art souvenirs, especially carpets. They were my weakness; a fair portion of Yucel's generosity paid for a half dozen, early pieces on my way to a collection exceeding 40 from around the world. As mentioned earlier, I also found time for two consulting forays to Iraq.

In mid-November, as the weather cooled, I had exhausted my list of diversions, so I buckled down to work on my novel. I had written five chapters while in Armenia. I picked up where I had left off and every night wrote in my room for several hours. *The Golden Times* had been churning in my mind for decades; it was a historical novel based loosely on the ordeal of my mother and her family in Germany at the end of World War II and her relationship with and eventual marriage to my American father. The narrative seemed to fly onto the screen night after night, and on December 31, 2005, I typed "The End" and went upstairs to the restaurant, drinking on the house and dancing with waitresses and barmaids until after 4 a.m. Best. New. Year's. Eve. Ever.

The book never interested an agent or publisher, so I made a print-on-demand deal with Rose Dog Books in Pittsburgh, who got it listed on Amazon. My mother grumbled about family skeletons being dragged out of the closet for the story line, but she got over it. I hired a friend in Los Angeles, Taylor van Arsdale, to write a screenplay version, but that never went anywhere either. I didn't care. I had always wanted to tell the story, and it was finally done.

In January 2006, I wrapped up my course with a lame final exam, gave the three students high marks (mostly for good attendance and class participation), and shut down FTV3939—but not before enjoying one of those magical moments a world traveler lives for. As a thank you gift to my translator and assistant Ozge, who was a film studies major, I bought tickets for a concert by director Woody Allen and his jazz group. Toward the end, the group struck up "The Old Rugged Cross." Here was a Jewish musician playing a Christian hymn for a Muslim audience. The tickets weren't cheap, but the moment was priceless.

My Baghdad buddy Pete Sidle joined me for my final days in Istanbul, and then off I went, Lufthansa first class this time, to my next stop.

After putting my Old Town Alexandria condo on the market and packing up, I headed to Greensboro, N.C. and started on March 1, 2006 as NBCC's executive vice president in charge of the international division. It marked the first time Tom had ever hired a member of his board. In one day, I went from his boss to his subordinate. And I, for the first time in my career, was out of journalism.

# CHAPTER 13
# NBCC International

*Promoting Mental Health While Improving Mine*

It all seemed so logical. There I was, slipping seamlessly from board to staff with a mandate to create and supervise an office overseeing NBCC's burgeoning international activities. We had agreements on five continents to promote and facilitate professional certification of mental health counselors and career advisors. In several countries, we were asked to help schools and institutions introduce counselor training. NBCC charged for some of this, and the revenue stream paid for our expeditions to new endeavors and potential markets.

Unlike in some of my previous jobs where I started from scratch, I knew the procedures and issues when I walked into this job. After all, I had helped guide the organization into its international phase. As we assessed the business at hand, two categories commanded most of our attention: economics and culture. Many of our potential partners were cash-strapped educational institutions in developing countries that were living on handouts from governments and NGOs. Universities in Mexico, Romania, Botswana, Malaysia, Turkey, Nigeria, and Argentina found the means to pay for NBCC's help. Programs in Malawi and Zambia looked to the African Union for funding. Companies in Japan, China, Germany, Bulgaria, and Greece found their own way to pay for NBCC programs. A queen of Bhutan, Ashi Sangay Choden Wangchuck, welcomed NBCC to help her make counseling a national priority.

Other countries, including India, Singapore, South Korea, Switzerland, and Kuwait, turned out to be dry holes. But for every opportunity lost, another one emerged, and that kept Tom, me, my priceless deputy Wendi Schweiger, and Tom's Romanian protégé Andrea Silagyi hopping, not to mention the conferences, workshops, conventions, and other events requiring our attendance as a business necessity or marketing opportunity. We were a UNESCO member and a World Health Organization (WHO) collaborator, taking us often to Paris and Geneva. A UNESCO request for help took me to Kabul, Afghanistan for a few days of meetings with the Education Ministry and my first foray into the carpet shops of Chicken Street.

I scripted and emceed the program for a mental health congress in New Delhi where we introduced a new, WHO-endorsed global mental health certification. I spoke at conferences in Singapore, China, Germany, and Malaysia. On a return visit to Istanbul, Yucel tried to pry me away from NBCC for another semester of teaching, but that fell through when Tom used me as bait for a complicated business proposition that Yucel rejected.

In 2008 we donated a mental health training program to the education office for a region of China's Sichuan province in southwest China shattered by a major earthquake a few months earlier. I had never visited an earthquake zone. I walked through an entire town with buildings split down the middle or crumbled to their foundations; one brown mound was an obliterated school with scores of children's bodies still buried in the rubble.

Add all this to our domestic U.S. activities related to counseling, and the frequent flier miles stacked up. In nine years at NBCC, as a board member or executive, I counted visits to 32 countries, more than once in many cases. I was single, healthy, and comfortable in just about any setting, so the fun and excitement of world travel offset the stress and strain of days or weeks abroad navigating the complicated shoals of business in foreign economies and cultures.

I had learned the ways of Western Europe and parts of the Mideast in past endeavors, but Asia and Africa were for the most part new worlds. Even as a board member, I knew that mental health counseling faced cultural hurdles in developing societies unlike anything we encountered in the developed world.

The function of counseling was often handled by societal figures with no professional training—clergy, shamans, teachers, tribal elders, doctors, and so on. How could we introduce the concept of counseling for issues traditionally considered private affairs to be handled by family or respected community members? The challenge was to wrap the idea of counseling around local customs, much as missionaries to foreign lands found ways to mesh their teachings with the beliefs and practices of their flocks. Our entrée was often career counseling. Regardless of race, religion, or ethnicity, people sometimes needed help finding a job or a career.

Exposure to new cultures also offered new ways to embarrass myself. In Zambia, the Education Ministry invited us to explain how counseling could be taught to teachers. Our visit to a school featured heartbreaking tales of teachers needing skills far beyond reading and math instruction. Children would come to class showing clear signs of abuse or malnutrition, or both. Teachers tried to intervene but needed training to know how to get a child to talk about their troubles or how to talk to parents without invading family privacy and worsening the child's situation. All NBCC could do was offer consulting services and support the ministry's search for funding.

Tom and I hosted a buffet dinner with an open bar at our Lusaka hotel, one of Zambia's finest. After welcoming remarks from all sides, the two dozen guests followed the education minister to the buffet. They filled their plates and returned to their seats and then just sat there. Nobody ate. When I gently urged everyone to start, the minister leaned over to me and said, "They are waiting for a prayer. We always do that before a meal." Pointing to a gentleman at the far table, she said, "He is very good at it." I invited him to offer the prayer; he graciously complied, and then everyone dug in. The main buffet was emptied, and then the dessert buffet was ravaged. After tables

*2008: The author representing NBCC International at a counseling seminar in Shanghai.*

were cleared, a few guests milled around the dining room, some eying the bar that had closed. The minister explained that the bar had offered liquor that most Zambians could not afford, and our guests were hoping to take a bottle home with them. We agreed, and the bar was cleaned out in minutes. Tom and I each got a Zambia-shaped clock with our name on it. With all I had learned, I considered it a fair deal.

In an unexpected bonus, I learned more about myself. Surrounded by counselors, I soaked up principles of counseling. A Myers-Briggs personality assessment branded me a gregarious introvert, and I thought that worked. The past warnings about sometimes being too harsh on subordinates were clarified when I learned about non-verbal forms of communication and empathetic questioning. They didn't turn me into an angel, but they helped unwrap more recognition of myself and improvements I could make.

As business grew, so did the travel, and so did my foreign education. I learned that showing your feet in Thailand was an atrocity (I never did that anywhere anyway). Some societies preferred hugs to handshakes. Negotiating business deals in China took patience and vigilance; the Chinese were clever negotiators, but sometimes they would seek new, more favorable terms after the contract had been signed. In Seoul, a government employment office staff invited me to dinner after a presentation. We were joined by the department head, a great honor. I sat down on the floor at the dinner table directly across from the chief. As the first course was served, he didn't move and just stared at me. As others started, I picked up my chopsticks and served myself. He then smiled and joined in. Later I was told he wanted to see whether I knew how to use chopsticks. I wondered what would have happened if I had asked for a fork.

All these good times, of course, couldn't last forever. By now I had realized that I had an attraction to and knack for start-ups. From *USA Today* through CNN International and my Balkan consultancies to IMN and VOA TV, I liked starting things. Sticking with them, however, was another matter. I was approaching that weird three-year mark.

The beginning of the end was my fault, and I should have known better. As NBCC grew, it needed a communications operation and strategy fitting its maturing needs. In mid-2008, Tom saw the need for a communications manager, and he naturally turned to me. We both thought that as a media guy, I should have been the perfect choice. It never crossed my mind that I was making the same mistake I had made at VOA. I was taking on a new, full-time job without any easing of my international duties.

In no time, the division of labor and focus took its toll. My two communications concerns were the corporation newsletter and the new website. I had worked in print journalism and had overseen website development elsewhere, so these should have been like riding a bike. They weren't.

Corporate communications for a nonprofit require skill sets unlike those needed for mainstream news media. Newsletters should read like letters from home, not like a newspaper. A nonprofit's website goes beyond information; it has to serve customer needs and offer professional services. Furthermore, Tom had a habit of micromanaging a publication or document after it was printed, leading to prickly exchanges between us. He was right because he was the boss. He lost confidence in me as communications director about as fast as I lost confidence in my ability to do the job right.

As 2008 staggered into 2009, the Great Recession further eroded my enthusiasm. Although NBCC was in good financial shape, Tom prudently ordered a cutback in travel. That left me trying to manage existing international business and find new opportunities while tied to my Greensboro desk. The natural consequence was to push me deeper into my communications duties, where I increasingly realized I was a hopelessly bad fit. I had a nasty tiff with a staff member over the design of a mental health handbook. The details are not important, but it was just one more shove in my back toward the door.

I started looking around late in 2008, but the economy had put the brakes on just about any employment activity. In spring 2009, I came up with an idea that I thought could work for all sides. Sensing that Tom was thinking about a change in international operations, I offered him a deal. I would relinquish my titles and move to Washington, D.C. to work as his agent. He already had someone there focusing on domestic issues, but I could explore new opportunities on the international side, extending my efforts to the United Nations in New York as well. My international traveling would be curtailed so I could concentrate on overseas issues from my

Washington base. I offered to void my contract and give NBCC a break in terms of salary and benefits; I even said I'd pay my moving expenses. In case he wanted me out, I added that while in DC I'd look for other work.

Tom showed interest in the idea, and a few days later he invited me to dinner to talk things over. While we sipped our first glass of wine, he pulled out notes and started reading. It was a counter offer, and it was a whopper. He wanted to eliminate my position, cancel my contract, and send me on my way. Here's your hat; what's your hurry?

The offer was not as punitive as you might think. My contract had a generous severance clause—another gilded cushion like CNN's. Either Tom was giving me a lovely parting gift for my years of service, or he wanted me out the door at any cost. We both knew it was time for me to leave.

# CHAPTER 14

# *UPIU*

## *Teaching Writers Among the Ruins*

Returning to the Washington area in the summer of 2009 felt liberating. I was ensconced in a small, pricey high-rise apartment in the Crystal City district of Arlington, Virginia, my favorite neighborhood. I was poised to get back into journalism or consulting. Tom's deal kept me solvent and technically employed as a consultant, so I had plenty of time for golf, poker, and other pursuits with my many friends. Meanwhile, I kept an eye on job postings.

Not long after I settled down, I ran across a notice for a part-time editing position at—if you can believe this—United Press International. The Washington-based web operation was a shadow of the global news agency I had left 30 years earlier. A series of ownership changes, each causing more damage than the one before, had gutted the service. It had fallen into the clutches of the Rev. Sun Myung Moon's News World Communications but tried to keep its distance from the parent organization's conservative world view. The part-time hourly editing position was for a noble experiment in journalism training called UPIU. Writers were urged to submit stories to be critiqued and edited. If good enough, their work would appear on the UPI news website with a byline. This looked like fun, so I hired on for $25 an hour, three days a week. For me, it was a new method of teaching.

The head of the program, Harumi Gondo, was devoted to the project but was not a journalist. She had created a remarkable foundation for the program, with entire classes participating from the United States as well as Japan and Kenya. With other interests pressing, she soon handed day-to-day supervision to me, and I made some changes. I discovered that professional freelance journalists were using UPIU as a marketing tool, so I limited submissions to stories from university-level journalism students. A few freelancers were grandfathered until we caught one submitting clever and elaborate features that he made up. Then the ban on non-students became ironclad.

It is fashionable for old timers like me to gripe about the poor writing skills of today's youngsters. This program offered a strong rebuttal to that bias. Under the guidance of their instructors, UPIU writers submitted quality writing and compelling stories. The only reward was a UPI byline, but that was priceless enhancement for their early-career resumes.

*2009: The author turning 60 on St. Andrew's Old Course in Scotland.*

I also supervised an intern on spring break from a Tennessee college. She was bright and well schooled in the principles of journalism, but she had much to learn about working in a professional setting. She also schooled me on how her generation approached news gathering. One morning I assigned her a story seeking information from the FBI and set a late afternoon deadline. As the hours passed, I noticed she was not working on the story. I asked her how it was going, and she said she had nothing to write because the FBI had not responded to her email. I pointed to the gray contraption on her desk with numbered buttons and asked her if she had tried using the telephone. She hadn't considered it. The phone, I guess, was too 20th century.

I critiqued more than 200 pieces in the next two months, hosted several online lectures, and made personal appearances at Michigan State and Louisiana Tech, where I also advised the journalism faculty on their plan for revising the curriculum. I was getting paid for all this, but, of course, I couldn't let well enough alone.

I don't recall who reached out first, but in mid-November I got a call from Internews concerning a consulting job in Kabul, something to do with an Afghan media development institute. I was intrigued, but Internews wanted the consultant to work in Kabul for an entire year. I knew from previous experience in the Balkans that a permanent presence for a job like that was a waste of time and money. I countered that I would prefer three separate visits of up to 10 weeks each. Even if they had to pay for three round-trips instead of one, the savings in terms of my fee and expenses would still be to Internews' advantage. They agreed, and UPI let me go with the understanding I would still critique student submissions from Kabul when I could. On December 8, I arrived at Kabul's ramshackle airport, found my driver, and started my next adventure that was almost my last.

# CHAPTER 15

# *Kabul*

## *A Media Institute to (Almost) Die For*

The Kabul job was unlike my other consulting gigs involving media organizations or training. This was an exercise in institution building. The object of my endeavors was a five-year-old Afghan NGO called Nai (Dari for *spring*) Supporting Open Media in Afghanistan. Squeezed into a rustic house in central Kabul, it was mostly a training center for journalists, but it also operated a small FM radio station and affiliated radio news agency and hosted a journalism advocacy program called Media Watch. It had established itself in the Afghan media industry as a known commodity, but Internews won a USAID contract to find a way to make it sustainable. My task was to come up with a plan.

My first surprise was the robust Afghan broadcast industry. Print was not strong because of the high illiteracy rate, so radio and TV were thriving. Private and public universities were catering to the growing demand for journalism training from students who idealistically were seeking a way to make a difference and in practical terms wanted a profession with jobs available. In terms of standards and ethics, however, Afghanistan was a media hodgepodge. The industry offered few role models for aspiring professionals. The government owned RAI, and an Afghan-Australian magnate ran the leading privately owned broadcaster, Tolo. Most of the other stations answered to oligarchs or former warlords with political agendas to advance. Public universities offered outdated courses taught by teachers with little experience in modern journalism. All state-supported journalism programs followed a curriculum set every year by a government-run committee. Private schools faced no regulation or oversight; some far outperformed the state schools, while others were scams.

Afghanistan was one of the most dangerous countries in the world for journalists. About a dozen would die in assassinations or crossfire each year, and many more faced beatings—often from officials or security forces. In one case, a police chief severely beat a reporter for asking an unwelcome question. When higher authorities ordered the chief to apologize, he did so with a traditional local gesture of remorse: He gave his victim a goat.

My challenge was to come up with a way for a journalism institute to find a professional and financial niche to raise the standards of an underdeveloped news industry in a poor country still wracked by war. The Internews chief of party, a courageous Australian named Charmaine Anderson, sat me at a dusty desk next to the wood-burning, pot-belly stove in Nai headquarters and got out of my way. My first six weeks were spent getting acquainted with Nai, Afghan journalism and the news industry, and touring stations and schools in Kabul. I visited Mazar-i-Sharif, a tranquil oasis in the north, and the not-so-tranquil Jalalabad in the east, where an anti-American demonstration delayed my departure by two days. I learned quickly that an early task was to train Nai staff how to train Afghan journalists. Nai needed massive upgrades in personnel, curriculum, and facilities if it had any hope of sustainability.

When Nai moved to new offices on the outskirts of Kabul, the facilities improved a bit, but the commute did not. The journey from my walled Cedar House guesthouse to the office could last up to an hour, depending on how many security detours, police checkpoints, and traffic-stopping goat herds we met on the way. Our drivers were ordered to vary our route every day and to stay clear of any military convoys, particularly American ones. Our route kept us on the opposite side of town from the U.S. embassy and International Security Assistance Force (ISAF) military headquarters, favorite Taliban targets.

We could not avoid cruising through the Afghan government quarter in the afternoon, a place not immune to its own excitement from time to time. We wore bulletproof vests for every trip, and I learned to keep my head on a swivel, even when Charmaine would lead entertaining shopping or dining forays throughout town.

The Taliban were both a threat and an enigma. A brazen and ultimately suicidal attack on the presidential offices offered a telling insight into the reason for their support among some Afghans. A half dozen Taliban stormed a five-story shopping mall to stage their attack from the rooftop. On their way up, there was no shooting. The fighters ordered out all civilians and store clerks, saving their firepower for the main target. This was an example of how the Taliban scored propaganda points, presenting themselves as protectors of the innocent in their battle against the government and its foreign sponsors. Some Afghans bought it, but the litany of Taliban outrages overshadowed that argument.

Bombings and suicide attacks were just frequent enough to keep us on our toes. One blast near Charmaine's apartment blew her front door off its hinges. Terrorism took other forms as well. An Afghan employee of Internews sprinted out of the office one morning as news broke about an attack on a girls' school. The building's water supply had been poisoned, making a few students ill. The employee's daughter attended the school but was unharmed. Wondering how the Taliban could do such a thing, I heard later in the day that the students were minority Hazaras, targets of sectarian strife dating back centuries. Any number of groups could have been responsible.

Some Afghans even looked back on the years of Taliban rule with a puzzling nostalgia, similar to how some Iraqis felt about the Saddam era and some Russians about Stalin. A Nai manager, Fawad, was no fan of the Taliban but recalled that under their rule a person could "walk down the street with dollar bills sticking out of every pocket without any worries."

Plenty of other Afghans told less flattering stories about the Taliban years, but Fawad was living verification of the lowest two levels of Maslow's hierarchy of needs: physical well-being and safety. People who are guaranteed those two levels of needs will tolerate just about anything else. It's a concept that the United States got right in Germany and Japan after World War II but failed to apply in Iraq and Afghanistan. It's also important to remember that the Taliban, unlike al Qaeda and ISIS, did not export their cause. They focused on their homeland. Don't get me wrong; the Taliban were evil. But they were ruthless and clever—two traits of other successful causes in history.

My diary from that first six weeks in Kabul features two keywords: meeting and research. I followed my practice in earlier jobs of saying little while listening and reading a lot. While I assessed Nai's programs and the Kabul media industry, I also watched Nai employees to learn how and how well they did their jobs. The 30 or so staffers were at least good enough to keep on the payroll, although from the executive director on down, they all needed mentoring. After six weeks, I had compiled a to-do list of the most pressing needs at Nai, all focusing on either internal organization or training for media professionals.

For the next five-week session from March 29 to May 9, 2010, my attention was on Nai internal issues—staffing, program development, internal communication, and budgeting. Not very exciting stuff, but I laid the foundation for building Nai into the media institute everyone seemed to want. (Spoiler alert: they got it two years later.)

With the weather improving, this segment of the Kabul job was the most fun. Charmaine guided me to the best carpet shops on Chicken Street. The city offered a tasty array of restaurants and cafés. I lived at the International Club, a downtown mini-fortress with a restaurant and bar cleverly doubling as a safe room, a rose garden, tennis court, and small gym. They never got the swimming pool filled, but no matter. My comfortable and spacious room featured a view of the rose garden and tennis court. A block away the ambitiously named Finest Super Market sold a laudable selection of foreign goods, notably Oreos, the expatriate's Eucharist.

The best outing came on a gorgeous Friday when fellow consultant Michael Alexander and I found our way to the west edge of town for a nine-hole round at the Kabul Golf Club. Established by an Afghan king in 1967, it had seen better days. We walked fairways rougher than any rough we had seen, putted on brown greens of oiled sand, and played with a limited, rustic set of clubs. Each player had two assistants, a caddy carrying the club bag and a ball boy, who would chase after a shot, find the ball, and then place it on a small patch of artificial turf for the perfect lie. These were my two favorite hours in Kabul, and I still wear the golf shirt I bought in the concrete blockhouse that served as a gift shop.

With internal issues sorted out, Nai could focus on the ultimate challenge of developing training and other programs that news organizations and individual journalists might want to pay for. Already looking forward to my next visit in August, I headed for Kabul airport and home.

***2010: The author at Kabul Golf Club in 2010, with colleague Michael Anderson and course staff.***

But it didn't quite work out that way. I got through the two bag inspections and check-in with no problem, but as I reached a passport control booth, the uniformed officer took an unusually long look at my passport, never a good sign. I knew my visa had expired a few days earlier, but Charmaine and others assured me that such oversights were common and were always sorted out on the spot. The officer told me my visa was expired, but he was in no mood to let it go. He directed me to a general standing nearby, who in cordial English told me I could not leave without a valid visa. The airline recovered my bag; I summoned the driver back to the airport and checked back in at the International Club for an unanticipated extra weekend in Kabul.

On Monday, an Internews Afghan employee escorted me to the Interior Ministry to manage procurement of my visa. At the visa office, a line of Afghan citizens stretched 100 yards into the street. I only had a few hours before my new flight, so I gave my escort a nervous look. He waved it off and led me past the entire line right to the visa office door. I got my visa in five minutes and walked out past the curious or resentful glances of the poor souls still in line. As we walked to our car, I asked my escort how that had happened. The visa officer, he said, was his uncle. That's how business was done in Afghanistan.

When I returned to the airport, I coincidentally drew the passport control booth with the same officer who had blocked my departure. He looked at me, leafed through my passport, and slowly shook his head. "This is not right," he said. As the blood rushed to my cheeks, he looked up and grinned. He had recognized me, and he was just jerking my chain.

The third visit took a turn I never expected and wouldn't wish on anyone. Arriving on August 3, 2010, I discovered that Nai had been busy while I was gone. The staff was implementing my recommendations for training course standardization, curriculum design, and other media-related programs. Nai was showing signs of maturing into a modern media institute. I spent my office hours mostly mentoring staff on how to fulfill the Institute's mission. The key unanswered question was whether Nai could find the financial resources to sustain itself. Years later a look at Nai's website showed that it had, with the help of USAID and Internews.

Before I could put my final touches on the project, I almost died.

My third Kabul residence was an adequate midtown guesthouse with small bedrooms, a shared second-floor bath, and no restaurant. If my housemates and I wanted something to eat, we went to a neighborhood grocery and cooked our own meals in the shared kitchen. The TV in the basement showed little soccer and lots of cricket. The Islamic holy month of Ramazan (the Afghan way to say it) started in early August, meaning that after a day of fasting our drivers would rush at sunset to the traditional iftar feast. They didn't want to be interrupted.

On the evening of August 30, I settled for a dinner of peanut butter sandwiches and Pringles and got ready for bed around 11 p.m. As I sat down on the bed, a searing pain in my stomach doubled me over. I tried everything I could think of to ease the pain, but nothing worked. After lying in a fetal position in bed for a half-hour, I knew I needed help. I called the Internews driver on duty and asked for a ride to an international clinic I knew across town. He tried every argument he could think of to talk me out of it, but I insisted. When he saw me, he knew it was serious and raced to the clinic.

I was examined by a wonderful Italian doctor who had removed a couple of stitches from my nose during a previous stay in Kabul. Tests showed nothing, so she sent me back home with a number to call if the pain persisted. Did it ever. Less than an hour later the poor driver returned me to the clinic, but that was the last he would see of me. The clinic staff checked me over again and concluded that I needed a higher level of care.

I was loaded into an Afghan ambulance for a long, painful ride to the French military clinic adjacent to Kabul's airport. Stuck at the gate, I made quite a spectacle of myself, writhing and groaning as passersby looked in to see what was causing all the commotion. After being carted into the emergency room for a quick exam, a technician gave me a CT scan. Back in ER, pain medication was starting to help when a French doctor strolled in with a catheter draped around his neck. He suggested that his ominous looking device might help to ease the pain if inserted in the appropriate entrance. He said I could think about it and he'd return shortly. I was desperate to try almost anything, but as he came back, I spotted an orderly standing behind him slowly shaking his head. His message was clear: don't let him do that. I didn't.

As I was wheeled into a 12-bed ward, I finally heard the diagnosis—acute pancreatitis, serious enough to require medical evacuation to Dubai. No air ambulance was available until the following day. I spent 24 long, sleepless hours under inadequate sedation in a room with men who had an assortment of maladies from battle wounds to blood poisoning. At night I left the hot room several times for the cooler air in the hallway. This angered the French duty nurse who shooed me back to bed each time.

Early on Sept. 2, an air ambulance arrived just after dawn. My dose of painkillers was wearing off as they wheeled my stretcher to the executive jet, but the angelic nurse/attendant gave me a fresh dose as I settled into my seat. For the first time in this ordeal, I was allowed to sit up, easing the pain even more. I woke up as the plane landed at Dubai's airport, and another ambulance rushed me to the ultra-modern Dubai Hospital. When the orderlies rolled me into intensive care, that got my attention. My concern spiked even more when a matronly lady poked her head into my room and ordered the four nurses out, leaving me alone. Within a minute or so they all walked back into my room, surrounded my bed, and sang happy birthday. The lady had seen the September 2 date in my passport. That was a powerful dose of kindness.

I don't remember much about the next two days in the ICU, but my condition improved enough to have me moved to a private room, complete with its own shower and huge flat-screen TV. For the next few days, I slept, read my Kindle, and tried to eat. Meal orders were taken by young women in waitress outfits and served by young men dressed like head waiters. What food I could force myself to eat was first class.

A week later I was on my way home, with a gauze belt to hold up my pants that no longer fit me after losing 40 pounds. Getting to the airport on time was yet another adventure. The evening I left was the end of Ramazan, one of the world's busiest travel days. Traffic into Dubai airport bogged down in gridlock, but my ambulance dodged the lines. A comfortable wheelchair ride through the terminal and past the gate ended in business class, although my condition prevented me from enjoying all the goodies offered in that section. Another medical van met me at Dulles and drove me home, where my friends Scott and Gale Herron brought what provisions I was allowed to eat during my convalescence.

Here I have to give a shout out to Internews. When I went to the French military hospital, the Internews security director in Kabul, Des Low, collected my belongings at the guesthouse and brought them to my bedside. All I lost during the entire ordeal was a belt. Meanwhile, Charmaine alerted Internews headquarters in California, and the human resources office updated my mother on my condition each day until I was home. Through it all, Internews covered every cent of the cost. When I delivered my final report on Nai three weeks later, they paid me in full for the consultancy with nothing deducted. That's how I define class.

# CHAPTER 16
# Kandahar Air Field

*The Army Gets It Right*

I took two months to fully recover from the acute pancreatitis (a cause was never confirmed). I gave myself time off through the holidays, fully intending to return to work in the new year. But for the first time, I had nothing on tap. My long-time, long-distance girlfriend, Linda Sher, was to fly from Kansas City to Washington for New Year's Eve, but an airline screw-up forced her to stay home. That desolate evening, I greeted 2011 alone and with no work in sight.

It didn't take long for something to turn up. A defense contractor called Strategic Social had a Defense Department contract to stand up an FM radio station at Kandahar Air Field in Afghanistan. The station would broadcast in Pashto to most of southern Afghanistan. They needed an American to run it. I liked the job description and the compensation package, but the contract was for one year—no other option. I worked the math and flew to Kansas City to talk it over with my mother and Linda, and with their approval I took the deal. Why not? I had nothing else going, and this windfall could springboard me financially into retirement.

On February 5, I arrived in Kabul for introductory briefings from the local Strategic Social staff and the International Security Assistance Force (ISAF). Four days later, I flew to Kandahar Air Field (KAF), a sprawling military complex on the high desert plains of southern Afghanistan 10 miles south of Kandahar, the Taliban's birthplace. KAF had earlier served as a Soviet air base during that ill-fated occupation. After stumbling around the civilian air terminal, I found an arrival hall where an Army delegation had arranged a small welcoming reception. Good start, for about 30 minutes.

After a short drive to the billeting office, I learned that my paperwork had not arrived, making my presence on base in effect illegal. A merciful clerk put me in a spare barracks bed that night, and the next morning I received another 24-hour grace period, during which I got my first close look at the world's busiest single-runway air base. My chauffeur was the radio station's technical manager, Eric Frazier. A tall, lanky redhead from Wyoming, Eric had a slight but constant aura of bewilderment, as if he wasn't quite sure why he was there. He showed me where I'd work and live for the next 12 months. We drove past the flight line with parked A-10s and AC-130s. We swung past all five of the dining halls, called defacs, and the "boardwalk" shopping and recreation square, looking like a discarded Western movie set. It surrounded a dirt sports field and a roller hockey rink.

Then came my first look at the radio station—three white 20-foot containers. The barely furnished office occupied one container that was stacked on another housing a simple but efficient newsroom. Adjacent to the stack, the third container held a surprisingly modern radio broadcast booth and a well-equipped control room. Canadians had done a fine job building and equipping the station. No plumbing, though, so we had to walk 100 yards to portable toilets. Weeks later the Army placed two in front of the station outside the surrounding chain link fence.

Nearby was the French PX, with a seductive bakery downstairs and a useful selection of personal care items upstairs. A later remodeling added a café. Walking west, past a major intersection, if you could call it that, came the rows and rows of "mods," modular barracks housing most of the 30,000 military and civilian men and women living on KAF. Each khaki mod had eight rooms designed to house four people each; nearly all had six. At one end of each mod was a bathroom with toilets, sinks, and shower stalls. Temperature control was spotty, but the hot water was reliable. Scores of mods were lined up in long east-west rows looking like an Army-issue ghetto. A solitary two-story brick apartment building at the east end of the mods housed allied officers and featured a clean, well-quipped fitness center dubbed the NATO gym. Farther west past the "American" dining hall was a nastier alternative rudely dubbed the ghetto gym.

Another few hundred yards west lay KAF's most inescapable feature—the cesspool known as the poo pond. This open lake of filth the size of two football fields stored the base's sewage. Decorated with a pathetic fountain in its center, it was always full but never overflowed. In winter it was an eyesore; in summer it could stink up vast stretches of the base, depending on the wind direction. I could not imagine how residents in mods across the road from the poo pond put up with the aroma. A sign was posted that read, "Biohazard. Do not enter." At least one Marine did. That jarhead, the story went, took a dare from his comrades one night and swam across the poo pond. It didn't take long for the poor lad to look like a body-shaped petri dish. He left KAF for home in critical condition and was never heard from again. According to *The New York Times*, the pond's only redeeming moment of glory came when it caught a Taliban rocket and swallowed it whole. One shudders to imagine the scene had it exploded.

My second day brought a KAF badge that made me legal but still no billeting. Three days later, the housing office said I'd have to accept an Army-issue cot in a flimsy transient tent until further notice. After being told how important the radio project was and how important I was, I balked. The third member of our civilian team at the station, Ace, talked me into bedding down in our office while our Army supervisors arranged acceptable quarters. We crammed two cots into the office, bought a PX microwave that sat on an existing fridge, and hunkered down. I learned that while the Army had jurisdiction over Regional Command South on KAF, the Air Force had overall command of the base. The two branches sometimes forgot they were on the same team, and our housing case had to leap up two chains of command to get resolved.

Meanwhile, days were full of work, and nights were full of fitful sleeping on pathetic cots, interrupted only by the need to go outside in the winter cold, through the gate, and 100 yards down the road to use the portable toilet. That torture ended when I learned to hoard Gatorade bottles for nighttime deposits. For showers, I had to sneak into a mod full of sympathetic soldiers. I surprised myself by taking it all in stride.

The inter-service standoff ended a week later when I got a key to a six-man room. I took a lower bunk, a nightstand, and a locker as my home for the next 11 months. I needed 15 minutes to walk to or from work, passing by the dining facility, the boardwalk, and the French PX. I soon had access to the station's SUV, making trips between the mod and the office weatherproof. A month after arrival, I felt right at home.

By then another problem had started to fester—Ace. I wish I could give his real name, but I don't want to cause trouble. This 30-something fireplug was the most outrageous person I ever worked with. Think of a cross between Hawkeye Pierce from *M.A.S.H.* and Dennis the Menace. He never met a rule he didn't hate, and he treated his time on KAF as a well-paid summer camp adventure. It took just four days for me to see that I had a problem on my hands.

Our supervising unit was part of the 10th Mountain Division, which held the rotating command for all of RC South. The unit held daily meetings, and my first was a doozy. As soon as Sgt. Maj. Jody Hall convened the meeting in the crowded Army-issue office, he announced he wanted to clear the air between Ace and another sergeant. That sergeant stood up and launched a vicious tirade at Ace, calling him a liar, a fraud, and a lot worse. When the sergeant ran out of steam, Hall calmly introduced me to the group as the new radio editor-in-chief. No sooner had I acknowledged the introduction than the re-energized sergeant resumed his rant, capping it off by threatening to kill Ace. Coming from a soldier with a weapon at his side, the threat had some hair on it. The storm passed when the sergeant stomped out, vowing never to speak to Ace again. The entire time, Hall never interrupted the sergeant, and Ace took it all in stoic silence.

The two had been butting heads for weeks, but apparently the spark that set off the sergeant was the acidic ridicule Ace had heaped on the sergeant for driving the station's van into a mud patch, bending its axle. Ace found the sergeant's button and pushed it mercilessly at every opportunity. The two were able to keep their distance after that, but I wondered whether this was just an isolated case of war zone stress boiling over. It wasn't.

A few days later, I stood by as Ace roasted our direct supervisor, Capt. Thomas Wood, an easy-going pipe smoker who didn't appear capable of riling anyone. For reasons Ace never explained to me, he pulled Wood aside one morning and ripped him up and down for five minutes, telling Wood how he was incompetent, lazy, and a liability to the project he was supposed to supervise. This time, it was Wood who took it without a word. I was so shocked I didn't know what to say to Wood until later, when I apologized and promised that sort of abuse would never happen again.

While Ace's people skills bothered me, other antics morphed from comic relief to serious concerns. When I moved into my barracks room, Ace refused to move to his and stayed in the office for nearly a month, until he went on home leave. He conned his buddies into finding an abandoned bunk bed and set it up in the office after I moved out. For a mattress, he organized a nighttime raid at a storage facility. The office became Ace's personal man cave and dumpster, even though we were supposed to be running a radio station in it. He ignored an order from our Army clients to remove the bunk, but I had it carried off the day after he left for leave.

As I settled into the daily routine, Ace decided he could adlib his hours. He took two naps a day in the office and vanished at least twice a day to work out or run. He refused to carry his cellphone away from the office until I reminded him that broadcast news managers were always on duty. He had found a little roadside snack shop he called the kebob house just outside the base perimeter on the main road to Kandahar. He was fond of taking the station's SUV out for a drive (against regulations) to grab a bite.

And to visit his goat. Ace had found it wandering near the kebob house and adopted it as his pet. He kept smelly goat fodder in the office, and he asked the Afghan staff to time their arrival so he could feed the goat at the base's perimeter fence before picking them up at the entry gate. One day he felt bold enough to bring the goat to work and tied it to the fence outside the newsroom. When its nonstop bleating drew complaints from our journalists, he brought it upstairs into the office, where it pooped—twice. Ace cleaned it up, but I had to remove the trash bag holding the offending deposits.

Some of Ace's worst transgressions stemmed from his penchant for scavenging. If he perceived a use for items lying in a trash pile, he retrieved them and stored them in the office or in one of the station's two vehicles. He would take discarded uniforms awaiting incineration at a burn pit hoping to sell them. If it wasn't theft, it was definitely a security violation. Imagine what the Taliban could do with a pile of American uniforms. One night Ace stashed a few discarded uniforms in the back of our SUV and then let our translator and administrative assistant Mohammed Tariq drive it home. The next morning, Tariq needed a high-level rescue when guards at the gate discovered American uniforms in the back of a vehicle driven by an Afghan.

In another caper, Ace found a pile of pre-treated lumber. He hauled it back to the station, lugged it to the roof over our office, and built himself a covered tree house, where he would survey his realm at the end of the day and sometimes spend the night.

At the American commissary, Ace befriended a female employee who would drop by the office, walking in uninvited during working hours. He would use a station vehicle to drive her "outside the wire" to the kebob house for dinner, against regulations covering both of them. If something else was going on, I never saw or heard any direct proof. But there was talk.

The final straw was Ace's scheme for easy passage in and out of KAF. Ace would create forms he called Major Pence memos, named after a soldier's toy monkey of the same name. They looked like genuine passes for leaving or entering the base. They made his junkets off KAF easier, but they were in fact forged military documents.

When Ace went on leave in mid-March, I sent a memo to my Strategic Social superiors documenting those issues and more. I vowed to snap him into acceptable behavior when he returned, but I never got that opportunity. Alarmed by my memo and other evidence, the company barred Ace from returning to KAF and fired him. We shipped his belongings home, and the Ace show was over.

For all his transgressions, Ace left one positive legacy. He had a central role in hiring the station's Afghan staff. The mission was to provide credible news and information to listeners throughout southern Afghanistan. The station's 88.5 FM signal originated on KAF, but repeaters reinforced by signal so it could reach nearly all Pashto-speaking areas of Afghanistan. Independent research had shown that Afghans only had ears for radio programming in their own dialect and respecting their local culture. With the help of a recruiter, Ace found eight broadcast journalists, four studio technicians, and four field reporters, including a woman, who came from local radio news outlets and were well known in the region. This gave the station a headstart on credibility.

Ace had also worked with the station's Army clients to fight off the provincial communications minister, known to us as Dr. Najeeb, who had designs on the new station as a loudspeaker for his own agenda. He tried to nudge and then bully the Army into hiring his puppets, saying he would consider it a gesture of reconstruction solidarity. He never stopped trying, and he never succeeded. Instead, we attracted an all-star team. Their unprecedented salaries eased any concerns they had about working for the Americans. As things turned out, they were a bargain.

Getting them to understand the job was easy. They produced a series of newscasts throughout the day, broke into programming for breaking news, and worked on special programs that fit the Army's messaging goals while sounding credible and local. The bulk of the programming was Afghan music the staff selected for its regional popularity. It was pirated, but so was just about everything else broadcast in Afghanistan in those days. News content came from our own reporters, remote radio stations run by forward operating bases (FOBs), and online news outlets.

The 10th Mountain Division had its own MISO unit (military information support operations, a sanitized replacement for psyops) to produce messages meant to persuade Afghan listeners to cooperate with the government, oppose the Taliban, and adopt principles of Western democracy and economics. Without my going into too much detail, this part of the operation was a mess. We persuaded the Army side to broadcast the brief messages four times an hour in public service-style breaks. The Army had its own team of Afghan-Americans to voice those spots.

The messaging itself was written by well-meaning but poorly trained reservists and translated into Pashto. They would urge farmers not to grow heroin-producing poppies, the Taliban's cash crop. They encouraged families to send their children to school, or women to assert their place in Afghan society. They espoused Western values, and they made sense to Americans. Not so much to Afghans. Farmers grew poppies because corrupt officials were stealing and selling seeds they had been promised for legal crops. Fathers were reluctant to send their sons to school if they helped to keep their farms or businesses going. Girls were to help in the house until they could be married off. Some Afghan women courageously tried to carve their niche in the economy, but at their own peril. American idealism often missed those counterpoints.

The Afghan-Americans further undermined the messaging efforts with their heavily accented, grammatically flawed Pashto known to repel Afghan listeners. We found out that as our news and music gained listeners, they would treat the messaging like Americans did bad radio commercials. They turned the sound off for a few minutes, switched stations, or just endured the distraction while waiting for more music.

These shortcomings should not overshadow the 10th Mountain Division's deft stewardship of the station that took the name Radio Yowali, meaning *together* or *unity* in Pashto. The division's information operations unit headed by Col. John Sims and our overseer, Lt. Col. Chuck Poole, figured out the key to the station's credibility. Unlike the military elements in Iraq's Coalition Provisional Authority, these officers let the Afghan journalists do their job. If they found a case of corruption, they reported it. Same for a bombing or assassination or anything else that might put the Kandahar provincial government or any element of RC South in a bad light. Occasionally we would alert the Army side about a story that might cause their superiors heartburn, but they gritted their teeth and let us report it without guidance. Of course, we knew who was paying for the station, so we looked for legitimate ways to further the ISAF mission, emulating the VOA Charter's mandate for responsible coverage of U.S. policy.

Furthermore, the Army and the provincial government sent us newsmakers and experts for interviews. The mayor of Kandahar was a guest in our studio a week before he was assassinated. Clerics were always a welcome source of religious instruction and commentary to counter the Taliban's vicious ideology. They also offset the teachings of some imams who took advantage of their illiterate congregations to warp the tenets of the Koran.

One rule was inviolate: Pashto was the language of Radio Yowali. If a foreign guest was too compelling to turn away, one of our journalists voiced over a Pashto translation of the interview before it was aired. An Indian officer showed up unannounced with an Islamic cleric, insisting that we interview him. The imam would have been welcome, except he only spoke Arabic. The officer insisted that we put him on the air, saying that all Muslims understood Arabic because it was the language of the Koran. I stood my ground, citing my days in Catholic school. Every morning I attended a Latin mass and followed along with a Latin missal. If I had listened to someone speaking Latin on the radio, I wouldn't have understood a word. The officer and his imam looked to an Army escort for help but got none, so they left.

Our field reporters never came on base except for rare staff meetings. We equipped them with the latest digital recorders, and they edited their reports on laptops before filing them from Internet cafes, where the bandwidth assured a quality transmission. Our female reporter, Samera Hella, required and deserved special care. Her coverage of stories about and for women was popular and courageous. She drew attention wherever she went, and she feared that someone overhearing her work at a

*2011: Comedian Jon Stewart, Lt. Col. Charles Poole and the author at Kandahar Air Field during a USO visit. (U.S. Army photo)*

café would cause trouble for her. For her protection, we paid for an Internet connection at her home, where she could safely prepare and send her reports.

The reporters all were exposed to the periodic wrath of the evil Dr. Najeeb. He accused them of not doing enough "good stories" about the provincial government. A quick look at our newscast logs knocked down that argument. He conveniently forgot to tell our reporters about scheduled announcements or briefings. If that caused our guys to miss something, reporters from other news outlets told them what they missed.

On one point Dr. Najeeb almost won. When he complained that Radio Yowali's enviable salaries might lure all his best employees away from his RTA radio station, Col. Sims promised that the station would not hire any of Dr. Najeeb's journalists. I countered that we should have the right to hire the best candidates, no matter where they worked. Sims compromised, saying we could only hire one RTA staffer a year. Sims's benevolent oversight of Yowali had, in our opinion, earned him some cover from us, so we agreed.

In our newsroom, the void left by Ace's departure was filled by John Davis, a military broadcast veteran who fit right in. With skills Ace could only dream of, John supervised the daily newsroom production and coordinated breaking news coverage when I wasn't there. Our studio technician changed as well. Eric Frazier's status became clouded by a long-ignored paperwork snafu, and he was homesick. After a couple of

***2011: Radio Yowali newsroom at Kandahar Air Field.***

false starts, we put the studio side of the operation in the hands of technical whiz Steve Densmore. With this dream team and the RC South unit in sync, Radio Yowali found its wings.

RC South wanted to find a way to collect feedback from listeners. Our answer was the most basic of radio tools—listener call-ins. Every day during our prime time newscasts we would ask a question related to the day's news and invite listeners to call in their comments, which were recorded on an answering machine. The next day Tariq would translate the calls and we'd pick a half dozen or so to air during the evening newscasts, followed by the next day's question. Each Friday, we chose the two best responses and gave the winners calling cards for cellphones; they could fill up their phone accounts with credits without divulging their identity or coming to the station. Callers loved to sound off, and the Army got a sense of what people were thinking. The thousands of calls recorded in Yowali's first year tended to complain about poor government services or corruption, and some weren't happy with the American military in Afghanistan. Only a few were threatening or hostile.

Even more astonishing and gratifying was the outcome of an SMS texting system devised by an Afghan telecommunications company in Kabul. This enterprise worked a deal with all five major mobile phone service providers in Afghanistan. We could write text messages on a website, and they would go out automatically to subscribing mobile phone users. The sender paid for the service on a per-message basis, while the

*2011: The author squeezed into an armored vehicle at Kandahar Air Field.*

subscriber could enroll for free. It was designed as an advertising tool for businesses, but the U.S. embassy saw its potential and covered the cost for Yowali to use it. Our newsroom staff would log on four times per day and send a news headline plus a brief promo for upcoming newscasts. Later we added breaking news. The Army side tried to add its messaging to the service but could never get its headlines ready on time, so it stopped trying, which was just as well.

It was an instant hit. Mobile phone users throughout southern Afghanistan exploited the free service to get the day's news from a convenient source. The Army hoped for 1,200 subscribers in the first month. In late August, after four weeks, it had nearly 30,000. We suspected the penetration was even greater. Anecdotal evidence told us that when subscribers received a text headline, particularly breaking news, they showed it to others at home, a café, a workplace and so on. The Army extrapolated the data to estimate up to 300,000 Afghans in Yowali's broadcast territory had seen the texts. That might have been high, but the effect was undeniable. By September, RC South had a fully functioning FM radio station reaching most of southern Afghanistan with news, information (talk shows, special reports, etc.), call-in feedback, and SMS text headlines. The clients were pleased.

Their satisfaction grew as Yowali generated favorable coverage. Stories mentioned the station's ownership and goals, but they also talked about Yowali's efforts to court listeners and build credibility with regionally sensitive programs and balanced news that did not always favor the military or the government. Yowali showed what Iraq's al Iraqiya could have been if someone like the 10th Mountain Division had been in charge in Baghdad.

Life on KAF was getting as good as Yowali's broadcasts. The dry summer heat could be brutal, and air conditioning failures in our mods on Easter and the Fourth of July made for tough nights sleeping. But summer evenings after work could be delightful. Sometimes I sat on the landing outside the office drinking Lowenbrau alcohol-free beer and munching on snacks while watching a brilliant sunset filtered through the desert dust. Walking to work each morning included a leisurely stop at a dining hall for a breakfast of eggs and bacon, or at a Green Bean coffee shop or at the French PX for a continental breakfast of coffee and croissants.

After work, I'd pass the rustic boardwalk, where I could get a taste of home at Nathan's hot dog stand, TGI Fridays, Pizza Hut, a Tex-Mex place, or an ice cream stand. Shopping opportunities included two carpet shops, a jewelry store, and the German PX, where in the back one could find pink fur-covered handcuffs for sale. I didn't ask. Two barbershops, a tailor, and a small bank with two cantankerous ATMs rounded out the retail offerings. Benches provided views of the sports field (at first dirt, later covered in synthetic turf) and a hockey rink. Roller hockey games featured national teams from the various military contingents at KAF. The Czechs and Slovaks could get mighty feisty in their games. If I wanted something different for dinner, another dining hall close to my mod offered Asian cuisine. A few hundred yards to the west of the mod was the American commissary that resembled a convenience store. It was good for snacks and microwavable meals to cook in the office. The aforementioned ghetto gym and two Morale and Welfare Support facilities rounded out the main attractions in my neighborhood.

East of the station, the Canadians boasted a Tim Horton's (donuts!). Once a month the base opened its gates to Afghan merchants for an open-air market. Goods included pirated CDs and DVDs, jewelry, carpets, clothing, and small electronics. The quality was diverse, but the diversion was welcome.

I arranged for each of us Americans to have one day off. Mine was Friday, when I'd read, do laundry, or shop at the boardwalk or commissaries. Another ritual was on Saturday nights, when I'd listen to English Premier League games on the radio.

At night, my five roomies and I tried our best to sleep in a space designed for four. I had the lower bed next to the door. My full-length locker stood with four others in the middle of the room. John Davis and Steve Densmore were there, plus two engineering contractors with other companies. The room was cooled or warmed by a wall unit over the only window. Every workday started around 7 a.m. with a stroll to the shower room. Getting dressed was easy; the dress code could be called shabby business casual. Then it was off to breakfast and work, which started at 8:30. In the evening, it was a simple visit to the shower room, change into bed clothes, and hit the rack for some Kindle reading before nodding off.

A good night meant you slept through uninterrupted, but there were bad nights. AC-130 gunships broke the night quiet with booming and rattling sweeps close to the base, and A-10 Thunderbolts, V-22 Osprey, and planes and helicopters would operate at any hour.

And, lest I forget, we heard the rockets land. The Taliban would set up eight-inch Iranian rockets in the mountains north of KAF and use cellphone signals to launch them at the base, with little control of or interest in where they landed. At night an explosion somewhere on the base would be followed (never preceded) by a warning siren. Military personnel and newly arrived civilians would follow instructions and lie on the floor until the all clear sounded.

After a few attacks, I learned from my seasoned roommates to just lie in bed and wait. If a rocket hit our room, lying on the floor wouldn't help. Reinforced concrete bunkers were scattered throughout the base, but at night they were too far away for a dash to safety. During the day, attacks would send everyone diving to the floor or sprinting to the bunkers. Again, civilians weren't bound by military regulations that required uniformed personnel to stay on the floor or in a bunker until all-clear.

I was in a dining hall for my first rocket attack, and I hit the floor like everyone else. A single blast far away was followed by a few minutes of silence, so civilians got up. But uniformed diners were still on the floor, creating a weird scene of civilians stepping over prone servicemen to get to their tables.

Rocket attacks never followed a pattern—a cluster could hit day or night, then none would come for several days. The one that came closest to me landed about 300 yards away in the billeting office, killing an American woman as she spoke to her family on Skype. Everyone showed various shades of bravado, but the rockets were scary and, apparently, unstoppable.

Speaking of unstoppable, that's one way to describe Yowali's Afghan staffers. I can also add courageous, resourceful, competent, loyal, and determined. That may sound like a Boy Scout oath, but this was no summer camp.

The staffers lived in Kandahar, and when the station went fully online with news and music in mid-March, they carpooled with their own vehicles up to 20 miles every day to and from the base. Their first obstacle in the morning was an Afghan military checkpoint, where overbearing officers loved to show off their authority by harassing the guys before letting them pass. Arriving at the main security gate, they had to leave their vehicles and stand in long, open-air lines to retrieve their entry passes deposited the night before in a security shack. The wait was never less than 45 minutes, and on busy days could take an hour in any weather. A Yowali supervisor or Army escort was waiting and drove them to the station in our van. Sometimes gate delays made them too late for the day's first live newscast, so we had to replay reports from the previous evening to fill the void. I tried repeatedly to take advantage of our supposed special status to circumvent the line, but the security administrators didn't see why the staff of a high priority radio station with a full broadcast schedule to fill deserved priority over cooks, trash collectors, and ditch diggers.

As was the custom in Afghanistan, the employer provided lunch. Every day around noon, we walked the group across a parking lot to a dining hall. After a half-hour, we walked them back. No straggling was allowed. Early on, the guys got a lot of looks—some curious, some hostile. After repeating the routine for a few days, someone demanded an explanation. With a crowd listening, I said these guys were broadcasting news and information to southern Afghanistan, hoping in part to persuade listeners to not shoot at Americans. That seemed to work; our team was never a distraction after that.

After a work day of up to 12 hours, the staff was driven back to the gate for another wait in line to surrender their badges before returning to their vehicles for another nervous drive home, often in the dark. The Taliban knew these men, who they worked for, where they and their families lived, and the route they drove to and from work every day. Thankfully, they were never threatened, or at least I didn't hear about it.

After a few months of refining the station's programming and staff schedule, we decided that we had enough employees to split them into two teams and stagger their shifts. When we previewed our ideas, they made an amazing counterproposal. Their goal was to meet the station's needs while reducing their commutes, thus cutting their exposure to any trouble. Each team would come to work at 11 a.m., cover the evening newscasts, the entire next day, and the following morning, going home at 11 a.m. as the other team arrived. Instead of going home for the two evenings on shift, all six team members would pack into a tiny guest room in a protected cluster of trailers just outside the main gate. We could never get permission to house the staff on base, so this was the closest they could get. At least the Army agreed to pay for the room. Their accommodations were pitiable, but it was their preference. It also meant they got a day and a half at home between shifts. With all the scheduling I had done in my career, I could have never dreamed up that system. It made everyone happy, and it worked.

At the office, the staff's work habits were a work in progress. Access to the Internet offered enticing temptations. One was pornography; we had to issue stern written warnings to discourage peeking. Sports and entertainment were other distractions, but the Afghans learned to police themselves to protect their lucrative jobs. As Muslims, the staff needed water for far more than drinking. With no running water available, their ritual hand and feet washing consumed staggering amounts of bottled water. The most vexing challenge involved toilets. Afghans were used to porcelain toilets on the floor, and some never could adjust to the seated versions in our American portable toilets. They stood on the seats, leaving sandal prints as proof of their preferences. It was a habit some of them could never break.

As October approached, the station was meeting the Army's goals while enjoying a niche acceptance in the southern Afghanistan broadcast market. The 10th Mountain Division was letting the journalists do their jobs. The staff knew it had wide latitude, but not carte blanche, for what it reported.

Then it all changed.

On Oct. 1, the 10th Mountain Division rotated out of RC South, to be replaced by the storied 82nd Airborne Division. The carefully crafted working relationships between client and station were gone, and the new client had other ideas. Our new supervisor was Lt. Col. Jonathan Keiser, and he was not happy to be there. I was told that airborne troops were happiest jumping out of planes, and Keiser confided to me that this assignment was doing nothing for his career. The 82nd was a buttoned-down outfit, and it had a more traditional view of military-sponsored broadcasting—lots of good news, no bad news, and tight control.

Within days, the meddling started. We covered a peace conference in Kandahar, a legitimate news story. The following day Keiser asked if we had stressed the importance of the meeting. As gently as I could, I said that was a matter for military messaging, not news, to address. A few days later, Yowali reported on a land dispute between a provincial official and a local police chief. I alerted Keiser because we knew there might be political fallout. After the story ran once, Keiser ordered it killed in later newscasts. Our direct overseer, Maj. Joel Millan, lifted the ban, but Keiser renewed it the next morning because it caused "too much controversy." Keiser said his superiors worried about such stories making somebody look bad or "not being complimentary" to the provisional government. An American colonel attached to that government even accused Yowali of inaccuracy and other misdeeds. A detailed review of the story proved his allegations baseless, but it was clear a new sheriff was in town.

More trouble followed. Yowali reported a district governor's complaint that his area was full of Taliban fighters. Keiser said the station should not have reported the story because the governor was repeating information from a military briefing. I replied, again diplomatically, that Yowali could not control what Afghan officials said but was obligated to report the comments to maintain the trust of our listeners. I also reminded him that he had a radio station available at any time to interview prominent Afghans to rebut or clarify anything in the news.

There was more. A bad guy in an Afghan army uniform killed three Australian service members at a base in Uruzgan province. The news was everywhere, but Keiser ordered Yowali to hold the story, arguing the victims' nationalities had not been confirmed. For our audience, the nationalities were irrelevant. The lid stayed on even after ISAF in Kabul issued a statement about the attack. It was not mentioned in our 5 p.m. newscast, but we ran it an hour later when our reporter in Uruzgan got a statement from a local commander. Still, we were late for no good reason.

Last example. An Afghan army trainer visiting the station agreed to an interview, during which he said the Taliban were infiltrating the ranks of army recruits because of lax security. This startling revelation prompted the staff to prepare a news story and a full airing of the interview. I gave the Army side a heads-up as I always did for sensitive stories. Keiser clamped a hold on the story, demanding to see an English translation. After sitting on the story for three days, Keiser said, "We ran the script up our chain and have decided we're not going to air it." All I could do was note that a credibility moment had been lost.

In fairness, such conflicts petered out in subsequent months as the 82nd Airborne adjusted its handling of the station. I never knew if anyone intervened or if the client's approach evolved on its own.

In anticipation of my scheduled January departure, we started looking for my replacement. That was easy: Brock Whaley, the ex-husband of a woman I had hired at CNN International, had just lost his job at a radio station in Hawaii. Offering him the job was a no-brainer, and he snapped at it. We were already working on transition in December when a couple of clueless nitpickers found a way to screw up a good thing.

A disbarred American attorney who had found employment on KAF decided on his own to review expenditures that the 10th Mountain Division had authorized for Yowali—digital recorders, office supplies, the one-room trailer housing for the Afghan staff, and so on. The attorney decided that the contract the Army wrote and Strategic Social signed did not authorize that kind of spending. The money was there, but our Army finance overseer had misread a poorly worded contract clause.

No problem, we said. Rewrite the section that the Army had improperly worded, and Strategic Social would sign the new version.

Nope, said the attorney and his Air Force officer boss. The entire contract had to be rewritten and posted for new bids.

Strategic Social had done nothing wrong, winning the original contract with a fair bid. A year later, Radio Yowali was a thriving, popular, and credible FM station with an extensive, quantifiable audience, fulfilling its mission to the well-documented satisfaction of its client. No amount of protest from Strategic Social, the Yowali team, or its Army overseers could overturn that ridiculous decision.

In the bare-knuckles arena of military contracting, the two officious paper-pushers exposed the Yowali project to a low-ball bid from a less qualified competitor who could knock Strategic Social out of the competition. That's exactly what happened after I left.

I had a good last month on KAF, despite the contract travesty. Brock slipped easily into my spot after overcoming a rough bout of flu. A question arose about how much Yowali owed for the SMS text system, but that was for the U.S. Embassy to sort out. Yowali's news staff was cranking out so much content each day that good stories had to be held or spiked because the newscasts were stuffed with better ones. Dr. Najeeb had given up his meddling, and Maj. Millan had learned how to work as a buffer between the station and his superiors.

The round of goodbyes started. Keiser hosted a farewell dinner, handing me a division coin and a certificate citing my work in "creating one of the top-rated radio stations in the region." Even higher praise for the entire staff came from Maj. Gen. James Terry, commander of Regional Command South, for "providing the Commander with the most effective means of communicating with Target Audiences of any ISAF Commander over the last 10 years." The American team gave me a Kindle Fire, and the Afghan guys came up with an engraved plate that expressed appreciation for my leadership and added in Pashto and English: "Don't forget me. I like your true friendship. I give you my heart. It's up to you to accept it." I always will.

The U.S. military left KAF in 2014. I'm told the station's three containers and all they contained were loaded onto trailers and carted off to parts unknown. The Afghan staff mostly re-entered the Kandahar broadcast market with no professional tarnish as former American-paid journalists. The Taliban were another matter. Harassment was steady and not so subtle, forcing many of the Yowali veterans to flee the country with visas in a program our abandoned Iraqi friends deserved. At least a half dozen relocated in the United States, most settling in Atlanta, Buffalo, or Louisville.

On February 7, 2012, I boarded a commercial Afghan airline flight to Dubai and then flew home to Washington, where I started my slow slide into retirement.

# CHAPTER 17

# University of Missouri-Kansas City

*Students Teach Me How to Teach*

The beginning of the end came in the spring of 2012 when I moved back home. It was time; my aging mother and disabled sister Helen had lived together for years in a convenient symbiotic relationship—when one needed help, the other was always there. As my Kandahar adventure wound down, letters and Skype conversations convinced me that they both needed help simultaneously. Family duties called. Another factor was my longtime, off-and-on, long-distance relationship with Linda Sher. It was time to find out how we would handle proximity (not so well; it ended amicably). In April I packed up and moved to Overland Park, Kansas, renting an apartment close to where my mom and sister lived. Looking at the calendar and my bank account, simple math told me I had just enough to make it to retirement at age 65. All I had to do was find a hobby and reconnect with old friends for an effortless slide into my golden years.

Well, that didn't work.

Almost as soon as I got settled, I found Peter Morello, a friend I had met in my CNN days. He was a journalism professor at University of Missouri-Kansas City and suggested I might want to think about teaching. I had always wanted to try, but the lack of a master's degree had stood in the way. Not for an adjunct lecturer position, he said. The pay was not great, but that wasn't a concern for me anymore. In August, I launched a new phase of my career as an American college instructor.

The course was called Writing for the Media. I knew about that, I reckoned, but I should have taken more notice of the subtitle: "Writing Intensive." Thirteen bright undergraduate faces showed up the first day. When the weekly writing exercises started, I realized the implications of "Writing Intensive." Every week I had a baker's dozen of writing exercises to grade. They were due on Friday and were discussed in class the following Monday, tying up way too much of my weekends grading papers. Nevertheless, I plowed ahead, guided mostly by instinct, and finished the semester without any dropouts.

Then came the anonymous student evaluations, and they made me wonder if the University should give the students a refund. The scores on each sheet ranged from average to excellent, but the comments told the tale. They liked my real-world approach to writing and respected my experience. On the other hand, my grading system was incomprehensible. Some considered my early emphasis on English principles a waste of time, and they wanted more in-class exercises. Those students in effect had beta-tested my class and my teaching methods; they taught me.

For the spring 2013 semester I made adjustments, resulting in uniformly positive evaluations from those 12 students and a dozen more in the fall of 2013. On one issue I wouldn't budge. I spent the first two weeks of every semester going over the basics of English—grammar, punctuation, spelling, figures of speech, and so on. I believe no writer can succeed without a solid linguistic foundation. As the writing exercises progressed, I could confront some students with evidence of their inadequate literacy using their own words. A few others needed only reminders of what they had learned earlier in life. Two could diagram a sentence; I wanted to pay their way through school.

I made two key points for each writing class. First, English basics were essential for preservation of the language. If anyone thought linguistic precision was not important, they could try to speak Latin in Italy or Spain. And as I mentioned earlier in this book, translated language never matches the precision of the original.

My other point was that writing was more than an academic exercise. I argued that a good writer would have an advantage when competing for employment or seeking promotion. Writing skills were bankable; that caught their attention.

Writing was not all I taught at UMKC. For the spring 2013 semester, Peter Morello needed a stand-in for his class "Cross Cultural Mass Media." He thought my background fit the topic, and I agreed. This twice-a-week class was a jury-rigged effort linking the 20-student Kansas City class by video to a lecture-hall sized class at the Columbia campus.

It was a valiant but flawed attempt at efficiency. The video hook-up was erratic, and the hoped-for synergy between the two groups of students never developed. The format interfered with the student-instructor interaction so important for such a sensitive topic. I would hold the class for a few extra minutes to cover issues that I thought needed more exploration. The evaluations proved my point; the students appreciated my real-world amplifications of the course's theoretical content. Many said they wished I had been the main lecturer. The class's intent was noble, but it was undermined by a misplaced faith in technology.

The third class I taught came in the fall of 2013. The scheduled lecturer for a class covering radio station management had to bow out at the last minute. The communications department asked me to pick up the three-hour class that met one night a week. I agreed so long as I could expand the focus to media management.

By then I had learned a few tricks of the academia trade, which came in handy for this one. Nearly half of the class sessions featured guest speakers. I broke the ten students into groups and gave them weekly tasks simulating media management issues for print, radio, and television. I guided the discussions, but they did a lot of the work. Again, the evaluations were gratifying.

# CHAPTER 18

# 435 Magazine

## *Something New Before I Go*

I would have been happy to continue teaching until retirement, but another opportunity paid better for less time on the job. It also introduced me to one of the few media platforms I had never experienced. A common acquaintance introduced me to Kathy Boos, the publisher of a city magazine called *435 South*. Interstate 435 circles metro Kansas City. Kathy had bought the magazine from Gannett several years earlier and had solidified its popularity through free circulation in wealthy areas of the Kansas City's southern suburbs. Now she had ambitions of raising the profile of her "fun-food-fashion" magazine to a more serious publication rivaling successful city mags such as those in Philadelphia, Boston, Denver, and Chicago. She brought me on board for a few weeks as a consultant to explore new editorial directions. As my third semester at UMKC was winding down, we started talking about a more formal arrangement. That led to my move from teaching to the magazine as editorial director in December 2013.

Kathy was steeped in the city magazine genre but had the courage to admit that editorial content was not her strength. She wasn't sure how she wanted the magazine to change but was open to experimenting so long as the core principles of a city magazine were honored. We hired two writers, padded the freelance writing corps, and added a web editor (a former student of mine). We dropped the "South" from the magazine's title and expanded its content and circulation to cover the entire metro area. Stories with a harder edge—business, schools, community issues—shared space with restaurant lists, fashion features, and lifestyle spotlights. We stayed away from politics, religion, and other divisive issues that would serve no purpose other than driving readers away.

Kathy was a hands-on publisher, but her instincts did not always match her intentions. A topic she had approved before deadline could become a source of discomfort when she saw it in print. A feature on flea markets included photos that struck Kathy as ugly and unworthy of *435 Magazine* (now *Kansas City*). Freelance pieces on the area's darker side also made her nervous. She would admire other city magazines but flinched when we tried to emulate their edgy editorial content. Adding to her frustration was the fact that she didn't have the budget to fill *435 Magazine* with the diverse range of content found in bigger city magazines.

However, none of this spoiled the working environment. I never saw her get mad; she laughed often, and the office atmosphere was light. She could be mercurial, which was her right as publisher, but she was never mean or abusive. The young employees in their first or second jobs had no idea how fortunate they were.

I stayed about a year at *435 Magazine*. As the months passed, I sensed that Kathy still preferred the soft content of traditional city magazines to the harder stuff we had tried. That wasn't my forte, so we agreed that she needed a different kind of editorial director. As soon as she found one, I scheduled my exit. After the December 2014 edition was at the printer and my replacement was on board, I left the last job I would ever hold. Except for three years at NBCC, I had been working in journalism in one form or another for 45 years. At 65, from one day to the next, I was living on social security and retirement savings. I didn't regret anything then, and I still don't.

# Epilogue

Retired is not the same as idle. There was no way retirement would consign me to endless days sitting on the couch watching sports and snarfing Cheez-Its. Golf was always an option, of course, but only when the precocious, infuriating Kansas weather allowed. Almost before all the moving boxes were unpacked in 2012, I signed up to volunteer at the National World War I Museum in downtown Kansas City. I was always a military history buff, but I knew little about the Great War, even though my two grandfathers—one American, one German—had fought in opposing trenches. As soon as I could qualify, I started leading tours. It's more fun than should be legally allowed.

I also was drawn into organizations advocating writing as a form of therapy for veterans. After working with several groups, I settled on the Veterans Voices Writing Project, publishers of *Veterans' Voices* magazine. This thrice-yearly publication printed prose and poetry (and later graphic arts) by veterans from any branch with any service record. It had started after World War II for patients in Veterans Administration hospitals but eventually opened its pages to all veterans.

Not only was writing a proven method of therapy for PTSD and other service-related afflictions, it also served as a journal for veterans to give their families and posterity an idea of what they experienced in military service. Many of the stories were touching, some funny, and not a few heartbreaking or disturbing, particularly stories by women veterans. After attending meetings of the organization's marketing committee, I joined the board and waded into the constant struggle to keep the financially strapped operation afloat while editing prose submissions to the magazine.

Then there was the miracle in my personal life. In the fall of 2016, having lost Beth to cancer that summer and then ending another long-distance relationship with the vivacious and captivating Kay Rogers in North Carolina, I let curiosity get the better of me and started poking around a dating site called ourtime.com. That brought Julia Kurguzkina into my life. She was visiting her mother and sister in the area, both naturalized U.S. citizens. Julia's story, from growing up in the Soviet Union to owning pharmacies while raising two boys in Syria, deserves its own book. Similar to my courtship with Beth, my first intention was to help Julia find work. One meeting for coffee led to others, and the topics of the conversations changed. On March 2, 2017, her 49th birthday, a retired judge married us in a simple ceremony in my apartment complex's theater. By the time of our first anniversary, she had a green card and was working as a pharmacist technician. Every day I marvel at my luck.

But luck has always been with me. I could have studied economics at Georgetown. I could have been drafted. I could have fallen into a marriage taking me in who-knows-what personal and professional directions. I could have bounced around little newspapers all my life. Beth could have vetoed our moves to Detroit, Munich, or Atlanta. I could have been buried in the obscurity of a crowded newsroom. I could have been killed in Munich. Or in Baghdad. Or in Kabul. Or in Kandahar.

Everyone has a mission in life. If they're lucky, they succeed in fulfilling that mission, however they define it. If they're really lucky, they have fun along the way.

I'm one of those.

After I wandered into journalism with just a vague clue as to why, I soaked up its rules, demands, traditions, benefits, and liabilities while happily letting it consume me. I learned about people and the world in ways few others could.

And in ways few others ever will.

Young journalists have relatively few prospects for ever building a career on the dream of covering or managing national or international news like I did. Healthy bottom lines keep news organizations afloat at the cost of closed bureaus, depopulated newsrooms, and the economically defensible but professionally cynical reliance on underpaid, disposable freelancers. Journalism can still be exciting and rewarding, but opportunities for full-time journalism work with decent wages, benefits, and working conditions are becoming as scarce as typewriters and tape recorders.

That's particularly the case for copy editors, my favorite role in the profession. When the axes are out in newsrooms, copy editors are often the first on the chopping block. Managers, be they journalists or not, order those cuts without understanding the vital function of copy editing. This is not just a theory. At CNN, remember, my new boss asked me to explain my role as executive editor. I botched the response, and soon afterward I was out.

Editing is quality control. So much of my mission in life was guided, nurtured, and sometimes protected by editors. On the other hand, excellent journalists—Christiane Amanpour and Helen Thomas to name just two—expressed appreciation for my editing of their copy, which rarely required more than a touch-up. As good as they were, they knew a capable editor would protect them from inadvertent errors while either preserving their fine work or making it just a little bit better.

A competent copy editor's mind houses an extensive and diverse array of alarm bells that go off at the discovery of any flaw in text, be it of language, fact, fairness, clarity, or ethics. The copy editor can try to improve the writer's work but must avoid excessive rewriting and, worst of all, inserting errors. The copy editor also must ensure that the final written product fulfills an editor's or producer's orders for word count (length) in print or time in broadcast. Often, headline writing is added to the copy editor's job description. Finally, the copy editor must manage, mentor, encourage, correct, and judge writers, avoiding all the hazards that those workplace interactions can create while assuring that a writer's good work is noticed and appreciated by superiors and peers. Some of the praise for a writer will reflect on the editor. Even if it is not expressed openly, the copy editor will know. Anyone who covets attention or craves compliments should stay away from copy editing. There are no Pulitzers for editing.

At one time, keeping bias and opinion out of news was at the top of a copy editor's job description. It took finely tuned eyes and ears to detect an imbalance in tone or perspective. Ensuring balance sat at the top of the editor's commandments alongside accuracy and clarity.

Now, those tenets that guided my life's mission seem quaint, and I'm a certifiable dinosaur. I still revere journalism and admire most journalists. I'm not so fond of the opinion-laced industry that employs them. Worst of all, I see no remedy for the profit-driven plague of disfigured news. The First Amendment protects charlatans and bad actors in the news media, but to rephrase or remove that protection would unleash unintended consequences we don't want or can't even imagine.

I hope somebody is on a mission to unravel that Gordian knot, but it won't be me. I'm at the end of my Mission Road.

I tell friends my life has mostly been an out-of-body experience. It seems like I floated along with somewhat detached fascination at everything that was going on. Once in a while, a personal loss or crisis would pull me down into reality, but in time I'd drift back up and watch new episodes of my privileged, adventurous life unfold.

There was no way that little boy in the Black Forest could see all the way to the end of his Mission Road. Turns out he had nothing to worry about. The view looking back is magnificent.

*The author*